COMING BACK ALIVE

Coming Back Alive

The Case for Reincarnation

Joe Fisher

Preface by
His Holiness The Dalai Lama

SOUVENIR PRESS

For Rodger Holmes

(1955 – 1997)

In Special Memory

Acknowledgements

The author wishes to express his gratitude to: David Kendall, vintage pal and shadow boxer, for his feral perusal of the manuscript.

Linda Pellowe, for acting so forthrightly on this book's behalf. Brother Malcolm "Laird" Fisher, for his diligence in Sydney, Australia.

Thanks also to Zasep Rinpoche, Tempa Tsering, Tendzin Choegyal, Ian Currie, Peter Commins, Ed Moran, Libby Sellwood, Helen Baltais, Ken Robertson, Kathy Brooks, Larry Kopman, Bill Lanning, Pascal Kaplan, Jim Wheatley, Yuzo Hatano, Cody Poulton, Karl Kamper, Gina Cerminara, Doug Cass, Uwe Ackerman, David Kopman, Faith Brown, Kevin Scanlon, Terri Degler, Al Wainio, Lena McEvenue, Steve Waring, Brian Postnikoff, Alexander Duncan, and Patrick Crean for germinating the seed of an idea most timely.

For help in preparing the new edition, special thanks to: Roy Stemman, Caroline Keenan, and Alexander Blair-Ewart.

ক্সুন্দ্রিম্যার্ম্ভার্শ্রীঁঃ

Office Of His Holiness, The Dalai Lama

Reincarnation is not exclusively a Buddhist or Hindu concept, but is a part of the history of human origin. It stands as a proof of the mindstream's capacity to retain knowledge of physical, vocal, and mental activities.

The theory of reincarnation is integral to Tibetan Buddhist lifestyle and applies equally to the good and bad mind. It is related to the theory of interdependent origination and to the law of cause and effect. It is, therefore, a major factor in the development of that wisdom and compassion ultimately leading to the attainment of the fully enlightened state of a Buddha.

There are incidents where people, in childhood, recollect and recognize past life experiences and environments. Furthermore, a considerable number of scientists are taking keen interest in the field. Buddhist philosophy can definitely contribute in the study of mind and its continuum, providing logical modes of inquiry into the controversial topic of reincarnation.

It is hoped that intensive and sincere comparative study of the various beliefs regarding reincarnation be carried further in order that a deeper and more scientific understanding can be conceived.

I am, therefore, happy to introduce this book by Mr. Joe Fisher and I am sure it will contribute substantially to explain and interest the average westerner in the subject of rebirth.

October 13, 1983 | *The Dalai Lama*

"As long as you are not aware of the continual law of Die and Be Again, you are merely a vague guest on a dark Earth."

– Goethe

CONTENTS

FOREWORD TO

THE NEW EDITION

Reincarnation Is Making a Comeback

FOR THIRTY YEARS, reincarnation meant nothing to me. Raised in a Christian fundamentalist household (my father was a Baptist minister; my mother hailed from devout Methodist stock and is now a Jehovah's Witness) I was oblivious to the idea that, for the sake of our spiritual development, we return to Earth in a succession of different bodies. Even as my parents fostered the understanding that spirituality is the root and branch of our humanity, religious fundamentalism struck me increasingly as a constrained, kindergarten-level interpretation of the ineffable grandeur that surely embraces the greater world of the soul.

Years later, worn out by deadline angst and daily journalism's terminal cynicism, I decamped from the newsroom of the *Toronto Sun* to Quito, Ecuador, only to find myself bedridden for six weeks with an attack of hepatitis. With time at last for sustained reflection, I entertained the possibility that I may have chosen, before birth, my narrow Christian upbringing. Not in order to emerge as a Bible-thumping evangelist, but, on the contrary, to be inspired to exert my will against this dogmatic vein and, in so doing, to discover a way of being that was less judgmental, more relevant to human destiny, eminently sensible, even sublime. As intimations dawned that rebirth might be a necessary requirement of human evolution, I was drawn to examine its tenets and propositions.

While researching and writing *Coming Back Alive* in 1983, I was attracted by a clutch of blue tin badges on a London market stall. They all bore the same message: *Reincarnation Is Making a Comeback.* Brimming with empathy, I had to buy one. Today, almost fifteen years later, that badge seems more like a prediction than a definition if only because the age-old belief is enjoying a popular revival.

When this book was first published in 1984, reincarnation was still an unusually exotic proposition in the West. The notion was seen as strange because our civilization has been conditioned for hundreds of years by Christian orthodoxy which long ago suppressed the doctrine of rebirth. The controlling church-state alliance considered belief in reincarnation so dangerous that any resurgence of what Henry David Thoreau would call "an instinct of the race" was ruthlessly expunged. The threat to the ecclesiastical autocrats was clear. If the masses expected to live again, believing they were responsible for their own eternal destiny, the church's domination would evaporate.

The hangover born of this age-old oppression was lifting when I began to probe a concept that seemed merely intriguing at the time. In writing an earlier book, *Predictions*, I had been intrigued by the work of the great American clairvoyant, Edgar Cayce. Being a God-fearing man, Cayce was a Sunday school teacher who read his Bible every day and branded reincarnation as the work of the devil. Yet when ushered into self-hypnotic trance he involuntarily spoke of previous existences and their relationship to the present condition of those who sought his advice. At first Cayce wondered darkly about satanic influences but eventually, persuaded by his own unconscious testimony, Cayce accepted reincarnation. This conversion impressed me. If a dedicated Christian such as Edgar Cayce could change his mind, perhaps there was some truth to the Eastern conviction that rebirth is a natural process that envelops each and every one of us.

My plan was to research a book presenting—like a fair-minded judge to a jury—the case both for and against reincarnation. But the more I read about research into claims of successive existences and the more I conducted interviews with medical practitioners and spiritual authorities for whom rebirth made practical sense, the more I was swayed by the large body of evidence supporting the idea. At the same time, those who renounced the possibility of reincarnation seemed compelled to deny the existence of anything beyond the reach of their five senses. In itself, the rejection of sceptics was hardly convincing.

And so I concentrated on delivering the case *for* reincarnation. After all, the nay-sayers had commandeered

public opinion for generations without serious challenge. For that reason, it was hardly surprising when society's jury of the early 1980s was initially reluctant to
give serious consideration to the idea of rebirth. What
would be called The New Age had yet to gain recognition; actress Shirley MacLaine was only in rehearsal for
her role as senior rebirth promulgator; television shows
about the paranormal were not in vogue; and the Internet with its hotwiring to pop culture was just an electronic gleam in the eyes of inventors.

In short, public interest in past lives and reincarnational belief was only just beginning to gather momentum. Mainstream thinking in the West was a long way
from eastern acceptance of reincarnation as a law of life,
a necessary extension of being human. That is why, I believe, His Holiness The Dalai Lama agreed to write the
preface to this book. He wanted the "average westerner"
to understand that we are reborn in different bodies in
order to grow and develop as spiritual beings. And, presumably, he saw my manuscript as a vehicle heading towards this objective. Magically, within a year or two of
publication, it seemed that everyone was talking about
"coming back alive." In North America, Europe, and
Japan, *Coming Back Alive* helped to create—and then
rode—a wave of fascination.

These days, The Dalai Lama must take some satisfaction in reincarnation's progressive rehabilitation in
Western consciousness. But the spiritual leader of Tibet
probably wonders why our still-materialistic society is replete with those who would capitalize on the transcendent
doctrine. Channelers are paid huge sums to give voice to

suspect entities boasting a voluminous history of previous existences. "Empathic counsellors" tout instant psychic past-life readings in person, by telephone, or e-mail. Some banks provide special "next life" services for investors with money to burn even as reincarnation insurance is advertised as "the ultimate financial planning tool."

On television, reincarnation is beguilingly portrayed on shows such as *The X-Files, Psi Factor,* and *Mysterious Forces Beyond.* On the Internet, a company in Illinois offers a "reincarnation systems kit" for $399 to "guide your soul safely. . . . back to the world as we know it." Another Web site promotes a "Next Life Parents" catalogue. And, in the law courts, reincarnation sometimes crops up as a defence against prosecution. In May, 1997 a former teacher—ultimately sentenced to 18 months in jail—told a judge in Santa Fe, New Mexico that his relationship with a 14-year-old student stemmed from their past lives in Tibet more than 1,000 years ago when she saved his life by taking an arrow meant for him.

Laughter may be the best medicine, but a preoccupation with sensationalizing or trivializing rebirth injects dirty oil into what I like to call "the mechanics of immortality"—the very engine room of our spiritual evolution. Reincarnation deserves profound consideration, if only because serious study of the subject yields tentative answers to life's most perplexing questions: Who are we? Where do we come from? And where, if anywhere, are we going? Fyodor Dostoevsky wrote in *The Diary of a Writer*. "There is only a single supreme idea on earth: the concept of the immortality of the human soul; all other profound ideas by which men live are only an extension of it." If immortality is the peerless proposal, reincarnation is its natural means of accomplishment.

This thoroughly revised and updated edition contains much that was not included in the original volume. A new chapter, "Coming Back Alive," presents a succession of recent case studies and research developments. In London, editor Roy Stemman has, since 1994, produced a fine magazine, *Reincarnation International*, which has provided a fount of information. Among the new material, there's a summary of the latest work of Virginia-based Dr. Ian Stevenson, the world's foremost investigator of rebirth, who has continued his painstaking search for evidence connecting current existences with lives that have gone before. The chapter, "The Bardo State: From Grave to Cradle" has been expanded to incorporate, among other additions, the findings of *Life Between Life*, the first contemporary study of inter-life material, which I wrote in collaboration with Toronto neuro-psychiatrist Dr. Joel Whitton. With the help of astrologer Caroline Keenan, the chapter, "Pluto: Planet of Rebirth" has been extensively reworked to incorporate the Earth's extended astrological journey since the first edition was published. Other chapters have newly inserted anecdotes and commentary, especially those chapters addressing past-life therapy and reincarnation in Christianity. Furthermore, marginal "sidebars" that appeared only in the original hardcover edition are now, along with new ones, scattered throughout the text.

Intellectual curiosity drew me to explore the legitimacy of reincarnation. Impressed, in time, with the reasonableness, the justice, and the all-round plausibility of the doctrine, I became mentally convinced that we do return to chisel at our destinies in a variety of bodies. Visceral affirmation—probably detained by deep social conditioning—took much longer, however. But now I cannot help but see people as embodied spirits who have chosen the current lifetime to gain greater love, knowledge, and understanding of themselves and others. An instant affinity or a strong aversion (perhaps even a mixture of both) usually identifies those people in my life with whom I have shared previous existences. Knowing and accepting that I am a member of an extended family cycling in and out of incarnation makes life infinitely fascinating. While we must fashion personal destiny alone, our spiritual journeys are laden with companionship. Today's most loved and trusted friends and relatives will almost certainly have participated in earlier lifetimes. And there's every likelihood that contact will be maintained for a long, long time.

On radio, television, and the lecture circuit, one question crops up repeatedly: If reincarnation is real, why don't earthly conditions improve? Why don't human beings evolve beyond war and greed and selfishness? My answer is always the same. This Earth is like a grade in school. People flow into the grade, learn their lessons, and move on—but the grade remains the same. We return to Earth's training ground as many times as spiritual evolution demands and, once our learning has been accomplished, we graduate to higher planes of existence.

Some people believe that material advances will lead to scientific proof of reincarnation. Some say the day will come when an infant's inventory of past lives can be flashed onto a computer screen as an educational primer, thereby giving parents and child conscious retention of what has gone before in order to enhance the life at hand. While a growing number of people live in expectation of returning to Earth, I cannot see proof of rebirth ever being accomplished in this world. For us to know irrefutably that we have lived before and will live again would be like holding the answers to an examination in mid-session. And let me be clear about the limitations of evaluating a trans-dimensional process from the restricted vantage point of this wordly reality. *Coming Back Alive* cannot prove the existence of rebirth—that's an impossibility for a writer appealing to others who are similarly earthbound. The most that can be done is to present evidence that, over and over again, suggests we must indeed live many times in order to achieve necessary spiritual growth. Whereas the between-life state or *bardo* is our natural home—essentially, a non-material realm of planning, assessment, and reflection—we reincarnate because Earth serves as an ideal crucible for learning and attainment.

As irrepressible as life itself, reincarnation prevails despite the censure of critics mired in materialism. Tribal societies were nourished by its mythic vigour, classical societies graced the doctrine with logic and reason, and the global civilization of the late twentieth century has tested its scientific validity and revealed its therapeutic power.

Witnesses to the process of rebirth will be vocal in the following pages, but the case for re-embodiment will not be relying on subjective testimony. Evidence will be drawn from empirical research, medical assessment, spiritual wisdom, metaphysical investigation, historical record, mystical perception, and wide-ranging contemporary experience. The book pursues the significance of reincarnation for modern humanity, endeavouring to show that knowledge of rebirth expands our vision of who we are as well as granting meaning to our role in the universal order.

As for the personal journey embraced by reincarnation, the following extract from a poem titled *My Law* or *Tieme Ranapiri*—attributed anonymously to a Maori— sums up all our wanderings:

You were. You will be! Know this while you are:
Your spirit has travelled both long and afar
It came from the Source, to the Source it returns—
The spark which was lighted eternally burns.

From body to body your spirit speeds on
It seeks a new form when the old one has gone
And the form that it finds is the fabric you wrought
On the loom of the mind from the fibre of thought.

You are your own devil, you are your own God
You fashioned the paths your footsteps have trod
And no one can save you from error or sin
Until you have hark'd to the spirit within.

– Joe Fisher, West Garafraxa, Ontario.
December 1997

I

A POTTED HISTORY

OF REBIRTH

"The tomb is not a blind alley; it is a thoroughfare. It closes on the twilight. It opens on the dawn."

– Victor Hugo

"Every new-born being indeed comes fresh and blithe into the new existence, and enjoys it as a free gift: but there is, and can be, nothing freely given. Its fresh existence is paid for by the old age and death of a worn-out existence which has perished, but which contained the indestructible seed out of which this new existence has arisen: they are one being."

– Arthur Schopenhauer

FOR OUR ANCESTORS, going to the grave was to return to Mother Earth with her boundless capacity for rebirth. To die was to be reborn, and to be reborn was to be physically refitted so as to express, more appropriately, deathless spiritual energy. Chuang Tzu, the Taoist mystic who lived in the fourth century before Christ, captured the optimism of the process when he wrote: "To have attained to the human form must be always a source of joy. And then, to undergo countless transitions, with only the infinite to look forward to—what incomparable bliss is that!"

As civilization slowly evolved from a scattered tribal lifestyle, primal instincts of renewal, which had inspired sacred myth and lent meaning to the rigours of day-to-day survival, became the doctrine of reincarnation. And the doctrine's professed rationale for everyone's succession of Earth lives is karma; the notion that whatever a person thinks and does acts upon the equilibrium of the universe to create its own reaction. In other words, rebirth never lets up until all imperfection has been eradicated through the complex interplay of cause and effect. Karma's impersonal justice is implicit in the very fabric of the universe. The law of the conservation of energy which decrees that no energy is ever lost, Newton's third law of motion (every action has its reaction which is equal and opposite) and the oft-quoted Biblical phrase: "Whatsoever a man soweth, that shall he also reap" (Galatians 6:7) all testify to karmic accountancy.

> Reincarnation is known in Nigeria as *Ogba Nje*. Traditional belief holds that people can arrange to be reborn together so that they may embark on joint undertakings. Should a person involved in such a contract no longer wish to keep it while alive, he is harassed by his partners. This harassment is said to take the form of mental disturbance which native doctors, after diagnoses by handreading, can heal by freeing the patient from the agreement.

Since the espousal of reincarnation and karma by the wisest spiritual and philosophical sages, the people of the East have remained in awe of the relentless revolutions of the "wheel of life." Not so their counterparts in the Western Hemisphere where reincarnation was buried alive more than fourteen centuries ago. The conspiring undertakers were the church and the state, fearful that their authority could be challenged by a doctrine that made individuals responsible for their own salvation. Since A.D. 553, when the "monstrous restoration" of rebirth was denounced by Emperor Justinian, the faithful have been taught to believe in eternal life while ignoring immortality's spiritual sister, reincarnation. Christians learn that eternity starts at birth. But, since only the beginningless can be endless, one might as well have faith in a table's ability to stand on only three legs!

Such quasi-immortality rendered materialism more attractive as a code by which to live. Consequently, with the growth of Western materialism indirectly ordained by the church, reincarnation's exile was confirmed. For materialism, which later bound fledgling science to its blinkered vision, sanctions no reality outside that which can be measured, weighed, heard, smelled, bought, and sold. Ironically, this trend also hastened the decline of ecclesiastical authority, which relied largely on the manipulation of the intangible.

The church was to remain all-powerful for centuries, even as it carried the seeds of its own decay. Many a rebel reincarnationist was put to death with vengeful fury as the bishops implicitly condemned the rebirth doctrine twice more at the councils of 1274 and 1439 with thunderous assertions about heaven, purgatory, and hell. Yet the ancient belief that many lives are as essential to our spiritual evolution as a succession of years are to our physical development wouldn't be stamped out. When the Dark Ages retreated before the Renaissance, society was reborn in a spontaneous exaltation of individuality. The hold of the papacy was finally broken and, in the Age of Enlightenment that followed, many of the great minds of Europe vented the conviction that reincarnation was an unalterable fact of life which tempered the chaos of an unfair world with justice, meaning, and purpose. Noted Voltaire: "It is no more surprising to be born twice than it is to be born once."

The masses, however, had other things to be surprised about as tremendous excitement was being generated by the rudimentary automation of the industrial revolution. Towards the end of the nineteenth century, the Theosophical movement challenged the prevailing mechanism of the times by rummaging around in the

> "You ask me to plough the ground! Shall I take a knife and tear my mother's bosom? Then when I die she will not take me to her bosom to rest.
> "You ask me to dig for stone! Shall I dig under her skin for her bones? Then when I die I cannot enter her body to be born again."
>
>   – Response of Smohalla, a chieftain of The Great Plains, when urged to have his people take up an agricultural way of life.

treasure chest of Hindu and Buddhist observance to retrieve reincarnation for adoption in the West. Pickled in fundamentalist concepts and skewered by the fear of death with its stark remuneration of either paradise or hellfire, most people weren't to be swayed.

Our own century witnessed the limited response, in the 1930s and 1940s, to the God-fearing mystic Edgar Cayce, who went into self-hypnotic trance to deliver— at first against his own wishes—startling revelations about past lives extending all the way back to the lost continent of Atlantis.

Not until the Bridey Murphy sensation of 1954 did the public imagination accept reincarnation as a reasonable hypothesis. Believers and unbelievers alike were captivated by accounts of how Colorado businessman Morey Bernstein had hypnotically regressed housewife Virginia Tighe to an obscure but historically plausible life in nineteenth-century Ireland as Bridey Murphy. Reincarnation-inspired movies and songs followed. So did pioneering studies that subjected past-life recall to scientific scrutiny. As files of intriguing cases grew, the mid-seventies saw past-life therapy emerge as a dramatic way of curing physical and psychological disorders through the tapping of reincarnational memories under hypnosis. Belief in successive lives was not, however, enjoying its rebirth in isolation. Rather, it was taking place amid a widespread resurgence of spiritual aware- ness and a developing hunger for nonmaterial nourish- ment in what had become a highly technological world.

Polls are reflecting this trend. A Gallup Poll survey in 1994 showed that 27 per cent of all Americans accepted rebirth. A 1997 survey in Britain demonstrated that one in four of 8,000 adults believed in reincarnation.

Sceptics, of course, have never stopped sniping at the "credulous" types who ascribe so many of life's insights and idiosyncracies to echoes of other lives. They dismiss the host of past-life claims as spirit possession, extrasensory perception, or tricks played by the mind which we do not fully understand. Nevertheless, reincarnation continues to divest itself of the banishment so long imposed by the trinity of church, state, and scientific materialism. In the words of Austrian scientist and educator Rudolf Steiner: ". . . Just as an age was once ready to receive the Copernican theory of the universe, so is our own age ready for the ideas of reincarnation and karma to be brought into the general consciousness of humanity. And what is destined to happen in the course of evolution *will* happen, no matter what powers rise up against it."

Sceptics say that reincarnation is merely the wishful thinking of human beings who cannot bear to confront their own mortality. Yet, for Hindus and Buddhists, wishful thinking is daring to believe they can be spared the innumerable births springing from the endlessly revolving wheel of life.

2

OUT OF THE
MOUTHS OF BABES
AND SUCKLINGS

"... The most promising evidence bearing on reincarnation seems to come from the spontaneous cases, especially among children."

    – Dr. Ian Stevenson

"Have you never observed that children will sometimes, of a sudden, give utterance to ideas which makes us wonder how they got possession of them, which presuppose a long series of other ideas and secret self-communings, which break forth like a full stream out of the earth, an infallible sign that the stream was not produced in a moment from a few raindrops, but had long been flowing concealed beneath the ground...?"

    – J. G. Herder

SPONTANEOUSLY, in scattered remarks mixed with mundane chatter about the world around her, little Romy Crees poured out her memories of the man she insisted she once was. As soon as she could talk, the pretty, curly haired toddler from Des Moines, Iowa said she was Joe Williams, husband of Sheila and father of three children. Again and again, she expressed the wish to "go home." Then she went on to describe her death in a motorcycle accident, a description so graphic that her parents were jolted into taking seriously what they had at first dismissed as the drivelings of childhood fantasy. "I'm afraid of motorcycles," said Romy.

So persistent were the three-year-old's "memories" of incidents and personalities from this other, mysterious life that her parents eventually agreed to a visit from Hemendra Banerjee, a professional investigator of "extracerebral memory." Accompanied by his wife and research associate, Margit, and two journalists from the Swedish magazine *Allers*, Banerjee arrived at the Crees' home on a cold winter's day in 1981. Her curls dancing about her rosy face, Romy was playing energetically on the living room's thick broadloom in a blue floral dress. A Roman Catholic image of the Madonna smiled down from the wall as Bonnie Crees, twenty-eight, told how she had tried to distract her daughter, hoping to deflect these disturbing recollections while encouraging more normal conversation. But still the other life intruded. . . .

"I went to school in Charles City," Romy would say. "I lived in a red brick house and I married Sheila and we had children, but we did not live in Charles City then . . ."

"Mother has a pain in her leg—here," she said, pointing to her right leg. "Mother Williams' name is Louise. I haven't seen her for a long time."

"When I lived at home there was a fire. It was my fault, but mother threw water on the fire. She burnt her hand."

Romy's face lit up with concern as Bonnie Crees related her daughter's preoccupation with Joe Williams and Charles City. "I want to go to Charles City," she declared. "I must tell Mother Williams that everything is okay."

So it was that the Banerjees, the Swedish journalists, Des Moines specialist Dr. Greg States and Barry Crees set off with Romy for Charles City, a town of 8,000 people some 140 miles away. For the entire journey, Romy was restless and excitable, and as Charles City was approached—without a word from anyone as to the imminence of their destination—she climbed over from the back seat to squeeze between Dr. States and Hemendra Banerjee. "We have to buy flowers," she said. "Mother Williams loves blue flowers. And when we get there we can't go in through the front door. We have to go around the corner to the door in the middle."

Because Romy was uncertain of Mrs. Williams' address in this modern town of churches and bungalows set among spreading fields close to the Minnesota border, the party consulted the local telephone directory. Soon they arrived, not at a red brick house as they had been led to suppose from Romy's earlier statement, but at a white bungalow on the outskirts of town. There,

> *Samskara* is a Sanskrit word for personal traits that pass from one life to the next. *Samskara* are residual mental impressions left by causes that are no longer operative.

Romy jumped out of the car and pulled Banerjee impatiently up the path that led to the front door and a printed notice: PLEASE USE THE BACK DOOR.

There was no initial response to the ringing of the doorbell, but at last the back door was opened wearily by an elderly woman leaning on metal crutches. Romy's words about "a pain in her leg" were as accurate as her prediction about the front door. For around the right leg of the old woman—who was indeed Mrs. Louise Williams—was a tightly wrapped bandage. Mrs. Williams, however, was about to leave for an appointment with her doctor and wanted neither to talk to the group nor hear their stories. She closed the door, and Romy's eyes filled with tears.

Romy, her father, and the Swedish journalists returned an hour later and were received into the home. There was immediate rapport between Romy and the old lady and kisses and hugs were shared as Mrs. Williams accepted and unwrapped Romy's gift of flowers. Bemused by her visitors and astonished at Romy's choice of bouquet, Mrs. Williams disclosed that her late son's last gift had been a posy of blue flowers. She was even more astonished when Barry Crees, who was also wrestling with disbelief, related Romy's collected reminiscences about the Williams family. "Where did this girl get all this information?" Mrs. Williams wanted to know. "I don't know you or anyone else in Des Moines." The seventy-six-year-old woman then explained why she was living in a white bungalow and why the community must have appeared strange to Romy, even with her uncanny familiarity. "Our house was made of red brick," she said, "but it was destroyed in an awful tornado that damaged much of Charles City ten years ago. Joe helped us build this house and insisted we keep the front door shut in winter."

Mrs. Williams broke off her narrative to shuffle into the next room and Romy rushed after her. Later, they returned, holding hands. Little Romy appeared to be trying to support the old woman who was clutching a framed photograph of Joe, Sheila, and the children taken the Christmas before the accident. "She recognized them," murmured Mrs. Williams, incredulously. "She recognized them!"

Joe's marriage to Sheila, the three children that followed, the names of other relatives, the 1975 motorcycle accident near Chicago in which Joe and Sheila were killed, the fire at home where Mrs. Williams burned her hand: these and other details mentioned by Romy were all confirmed. Her precise description of the injuries sustained in the fatal accident was also found to be accurate. Born in 1937, Joe Williams, who died two years before Romy was born, was the second youngest of seven children.

The case of Romy Crees is the best-documented study in Banerjee's files and, according to the investigator, "demonstrates that reincarnation is real." But as

---

Burmese children who can remember their former lives are known as *winzas*. In Burma, it is the custom to mark children who have died, or are expected to die, in the hope that they will be reborn in the same family to be identified by a corresponding birthmark.

devout Catholics, Romy's parents and Louise Williams couldn't bring themselves to accept that explanation. "I don't know how to explain it," sighed Bonnie Crees, "but I *do* know my daughter isn't lying."

At three years of age, Joey Verwey of Pretoria, South Africa, began talking about her former lives. Her mother, Helge Verwey, started a diary of her recollections—spanning ten lives in all—when she was six years old. Commented South African scientist Dr. Arthur Bleksley: "Before she could write she could draw fashions of ancient times, always supplying the most minute and accurate details. She later described objects, manners, and dress that only someone who had lived in the times could possibly know. Her accuracy is uncanny, and other than the possibility that she had indeed been reincarnated several times, I can find no other explanation of her amazing knowledge."

Hankering for Past Lives

Romy is just one of hundreds of young children from all parts of the world who have spoken volubly, accurately, and with unswerving conviction about previous lives that have been historically verified. In most cases, these guileless witnesses voice their memories between the ages of two and five years, telling, usually, of lives that ended abruptly and with violence. Muttering distractedly or pleading to be heard, they use such phrases as:

"When I was big," and have been known to grumble about the limitations of their small bodies and even to speak resentfully of not being the same sex as before. Often they yearn for the lost companionship of a husband, wife, son, or daughter. They hanker for the food, clothing and lifestyle—even, on occasion, the alcohol, drugs, or tobacco—of a former existence. They suffer phobias that can be linked directly with their unexpected deaths—sharp knives, perhaps, or motor vehicles, or water. Yet these small children have little hope of neutralizing such powerful impulses because they are rarely encouraged to air their past-life memories. In the West, parents tend to dismiss and deflect what they consider to be nonsensical ramblings, while in the East, there's a superstition that those who remember a previous existence are fated to die young. In India, southern Asia, and Turkey, it is not uncommon for parents to react by filling their child's mouth with filth or soap.

Railway clerk B. Ram Ghulam Kapoor may have been too dumbfounded to reach for the soap dish when his five-year-old son, Bishen Chand, launched into a man-to-man chat about sex. "Papa," Bishen wondered aloud one day, "why don't you keep a mistress? You will have great pleasure from her." Managing to conceal his amazement, his father asked quietly: "What pleasure, my boy?" To which Bishen replied: "You will enjoy the fragrance of her hair and feel much joy from her company."

Bishen's memories, recorded in Bareilly, Uttar Pradesh, India in the mid-1920s, were found to correspond with the life of Laxmi Narain, who had died in

1918 at the age of thirty-two in Shahjahanpur, Uttar Pradesh. The only son of a wealthy landowner, Laxmi had overindulged himself in food, clothes, women, and alcohol and had cherished a prostitute by the name of Padma.

When Bishen was twenty-three years old and working in the central excise office at Tenakpore, Padma, then fifty-two, happened to walk across the threshold. Bishen recognized her at once and was so overcome with emotion that he fainted. That evening, he set out for Padma's home with the intent of renewing the relationship Laxmi had enjoyed more than twenty-six years earlier. As Laxmi would have done, Bishen approached the house carrying a bottle of wine even though he was a teetotaller. Padma was not amused. She smashed the wine bottle and sent him back into the night saying: "I am an old woman like your mother."

"I cannot emphasize too strongly that these cases impinge unexpectedly and often in an undesirable way on the lives of the persons concerned. The nagging demands of a four-year-old boy that he be taken immediately to another remote village, his revelations of sordid murders or other crimes, his claim that he has in the "other" home electricity, good food, automobiles, and maybe a wife, cannot possibly increase the pleasure of a poor farmer who must listen to such talk in the morning before he leaves to till the soil and again at night when he returns weary from doing so."

– Dr. Ian Stevenson

In 1971, Bishen Chand told psychiatrist Dr. Ian Stevenson, of the University of Virginia, that he had never drunk alcohol before or since this occasion. But the intensity of his aroused affection for Padma left him eager to abandon his abstemious ways.

"He Killed Me"

There are exceptions, however, to the fondness most subjects feel for past-life personalities, and none is more dramatic than the way Reena Gupta reacted to the last man in her life. When Reena was less than two years old she told her grandmother: "I have a *gharwala* (husband). My *gharwala* was a very bad man. He killed me."

Reena's behaviour was as bizarre as her utterances. She would toddle out onto the balcony of her New Delhi home and stare into the street crowds; searching, always searching. When out in the family car, she was perpetually on the lookout for someone. "I'm looking for my *gharwala* and my children," she would tell anyone who asked what she was up to. Reena's strangeness became exasperating when she began to criticize the way her mother cooked and did chores around the house. It wasn't long before Reena, who claimed to have four youngsters of her own, wandered off during a market outing only to explain later to her worried mother that she had followed a woman "who used to come to my house." The past-life connection wouldn't go away and, to her mother's annoyance, the little girl continued to express affection for her children as well as anguish at her enforced separation from them. Mercifully, the explanation that this double life demanded was on the way. Vijendra Kaur, a teaching colleague of Reena's mother, had heard about a Sikh family in another part of the city that had suffered in a way that seemed to tally with Reena's stories. Her enquiries, conducted five years after Reena had first spoken of her past life, led to the door of Sardar Kishan Singh and his wife, parents of the late Gurdeep Kaur, who had been murdered by her husband on June 2, 1961. Intrigued by a possible link with their dead daughter, the couple called on the Gupta family. Reena was fast asleep but, on waking, she looked up at the Singhs and her face became all smiles as she said: "They are my father and mother."

The next day, the Singhs brought Swarna, Gurdeep's younger sister, to see Reena who immediately called her by her nickname, Sarno. In India, custom decrees that gifts of money may be accepted only by a person younger than the giver. So Reena's response was particularly revealing when Swarna offered her two rupees. "How can I take money from Sarno?" she said. "She is younger than me." Later, Reena visited Kishan·Singh's home where she recognized as herself a photograph of the late Gurdeep Kaur.

"Indian criminal records contain several instances of the women of certain tribes in the country kidnapping children and murdering them, and smearing their own bodies with the blood of the innocent victims, in the hope that the liberated souls will be reborn to them."

    – P. Parameswara in *Soul, Karma and Rebirth*

It was only a matter of time before Surjeet Singh, the husband and killer of Gurdeep, heard of Reena's claims and was drawn to pay a visit of his own. Reena, however, had no wish to see him. "He will kill me again," she said, clearly unenthusiastic that Surjeet Singh, once jailed for life for murdering his wife and her brother, had been freed after ten years because of good behaviour. When they met in 1975, Reena was nine years old and all the good behaviour in the world would not have been enough to allay her fears. Only with the greatest reluctance would she pose—perching uneasily on the armrest of Surjeet Singh's chair—with the man she is convinced was her murderer. In fact, when Surjeet Singh tried to put his arms around her, she tore herself away. But when Reena met Gurdeep Kaur's four children—three daughters and one son—she greeted them as joyfully as she had Gurdeep's mother, father, and sister.

The Russian Bishop of Alaska, I. E. P. Veniaminov, noted in the middle of the last century that the Tlingit Indians always scrutinized birthmarks on the bodies of newborn babies. If the marks closely resembled those of a dead relative, reincarnation was assumed and the child was given the name of the deceased.

Spontaneous Emotional Recognition

Without doubt, young children are the best witnesses to reincarnation. They have yet to be distracted by the information barrage and the crowded memories of later years. Their lack of worldly experience makes them, if not incorruptible, much less inclined to fraudulence than adults. And although parental manipulation can never be ruled out, it's practically impossible to fake the strong identification so commonly felt with the former personality, or the powerful emotional attachment expressed towards surviving past-life relatives and friends. As Banerjee declared: "To witness spontaneous emotional recognition is what convinces me more than anything of a case's validity." In the facilitation of such recognition, there often appears to be another factor at work, something Banerjee described as "the geography of reincarnation." Studies indicate that those whose lives have ended prematurely tend to return to the same general area, drawn back, one can surmise, by a sense of unfinished business and emotional hunger.

Nevertheless, the casebooks of spontaneous past-life memories, well-stocked and painstakingly researched though they may be, cannot prove reincarnation. And they never will. It's no accident that Dr. Ian Stevenson always refers to even his best cases as being "suggestive" of reincarnation. He writes: "All of the cases I have investigated so far have some flaws, many of them serious ones. Neither any single case nor all of the investigated cases together offer anything like a proof of reincarnation. They provide instead a body of evidence suggestive of reincarnation that appears to be accumulating in amount and quality."

Even when a link with a past life is established beyond doubt and in the most precise detail, nobody can *prove* that the child with all the emotion and information was once the person he or she claims to be. Besides, the possibility will always exist that the youngster's memory could have been encouraged by fraud, extrasensory perception, spirit possession, or cryptomnesia, that is, the welling up of forgotten memory originating in the present life. Yet these alternative interpretations are, in Stevenson's opinion, "just as mind-stretching as is reincarnation itself, at least for most Westerners."

Spirit possession is perhaps the most likely rival to reincarnation, but even this theory appears decidedly anaemic when birthmark evidence is taken into consideration. Stevenson has examined well over 200 birthmarks on children claiming to have been killed by bullets and bladed weapons that had pierced the corresponding part of their anatomy in a previous life. In seventeen such cases, medical documents such as hospital records or autopsy reports have been obtained that establish that the past-life individual was killed in the way described.

As the case of William George Jr. attests, violence is not a necessary component of birthmark evidence. Although this case has the air of a tribal folk tale, Stevenson has meticulously documented the evidence by personally interviewing, on separate occasions, family members, relatives, and friends. It all started when William George Sr., a celebrated fisherman of the Tlingit Indian tribe of Alaska, made a vow when he began to doubt the tribe's traditional belief in reincarnation. "If there is anything to this rebirth business," he told his favourite son, Reginald George, "I will come back and be your son." He could be recognized, he said, by the half-inch birthmarks he possessed—one on the left shoulder, the other on the left forearm. Furthermore, he handed over his gold watch with the promise of regaining it should there be another incarnation.

Soon afterwards, the old man was lost at sea and, barely nine months later—on May 5, 1950—Susan George gave birth to her ninth child. The baby was born with two distinctive birthmarks in identical locations to those of his grandfather, though half their size. There was no debate over the baby's name: they called him William George Jr.

Friends and relatives were quick to notice how similar the little boy was to his grandfather. Not only did he look like a diminutive version of the old man, he also walked like him and demonstrated a precocious knowledge of fishing and boats, even while showing more fear of the water than was usual for boys of his age. He called his great aunt "sister," referred to his uncles and aunts as his sons and daughters, and didn't object when his own brothers and sisters called him "grandfather." At four years of age, after wandering into his parents' bedroom where Susan George was sorting through her jewelry box, William spied the gold watch that had belonged to William George Sr. "That's my watch," he declared, picking it up. Eventually, the boy grudgingly surrendered ownership. Even though his past-life memories

---

Taqamus, the romanized Arabic word for reincarnation, means, literally, "Changing one's shirt."

faded in later childhood, he never renounced his claim to "my watch."

Five-year-old Imad Elawar of Lebanon made fifty-seven verifiable claims about his past life as tuberculosis victim Ibrahim Bouhamzy. Fifty-one of them turned out to be "dead right," according to Dr. Ian Stevenson.

Sexual Confusion

Obsession with an existence that has gone before can lead to confusion over sexual identity. Two girls who were sure they were male in former existences—Dolan Mitra of West Bengal and Ma Tin Aung Myo of Upper Burma—insisted, year after year, on wearing boys' clothes and playing boys' games. Dolan, who was born on August 8, 1967, started donning her elder brother's clothes at three years of age and, as she grew older, liked nothing better than to play football and cricket. Thinking she would spoil her brother's clothes, her mother, Konika Mitra, was quick to scold the little girl who replied that she used to be a bigger boy who lived in Burdwan, a community seventy-five miles from her home in Narendrapur. This claim was seen to be justified after Dolan's parents finally agreed to take her to Burdwan, if only to end her crying and distress. Although the first visit, in October, 1971, failed to locate Dolan's former home, a second attempt in March, 1972, was thoroughly

successful. Starting from a local landmark, the Anna-
purna Temple, Dolan led the way through twisty streets
to the home of Anath Saran Dey where she was invited
in by Dey's youngest daughter, Rita. Dolan scampered
knowingly through the house recognizing rooms, and
identifying their contents, and then proceeded to point
out the possessions of Rita's late brother, Nishith, a student and keen sportsman who had died, supposedly of a
brain tumour, in a Calcutta hospital on July 25, 1964.
Dolan also recognized Nishith's mother among a group
of women and, in subsequent recognition tests, correctly
identified a number of relatives and friends.

Ma Tin Aung Myo's male memory made an even
deeper impression. Born in 1953, she first experienced the
shadow of the past as a four-year-old: she had started to
cry when an airplane flew over while she was out walking
with her father. Thereafter, a passing plane would always
make her cower and weep. When reproached about her
behaviour she would say: "What do you know? I was shot
and killed." She began to tell how, as a Japanese soldier
stationed in the family's village of Na-Thul during the last
war, she had been strafed by an Allied plane. She remembered wearing short pants and a big belt. And she recalled
having taken off her shirt in readiness to cook a meal
when the aircraft dived, spraying bullets. As she grew up,
Ma Tin Aung Myo expressed a longing to return to Japan
to see her wife and children, was adamant about wearing
boys' clothes, and enjoyed playing at being a soldier. At
twelve years of age, she dropped out of school when the
authorities demanded that she dress in girls' clothes. By
the age of nineteen she had rejected her sex completely.

Continuing to dress in male garb, she had no desire for a husband but, instead, said she wanted to marry a girl.

By the age of ten, memories of previous existences have usually evaporated in the heat of life like some strange cerebral mist. But by then the extraordinary behaviour of the formative years will have taken its toll. The perplexity and anguish generated by infantile yearning for a different lifestyle in another location certainly does nothing to foster harmony between parent and child. And though many parents manage to resist emotional pressure from their offspring to visit another set of relatives, children have been known to retaliate by running off to the other home they seem to know so well.

Dr. Helen Wambach, a San Francisco psychologist, argued against encouraging children to recall past-life memories because she believed that such "premature immersion" only added needlessly to the burden of adjustment in the present life. She vividly remembered an experience in psychotherapy—long before her involvement in reincarnation research—when she was treating a five-year-old called Peter for hyperactivity. To her astonishment, the boy launched into a monologue about his life as a policeman. At first, Dr. Wambach thought Peter must be relating some episode that he had seen on television, but the more he talked the more she understood that he was reliving experiences he felt had been his own. The boy's mother revealed that he had started to speak about his life as a cop at three years of age but she had told him "not to make up stories." Dr. Wambach, on the other hand, enjoyed listening to Peter's tales of law and order—until his mother reported that a policeman had brought him home because he was out in the middle of the street trying to direct traffic. "I felt slightly guilty," Dr. Wambach confessed, "because he had told me about his traffic assignment in his life as a policeman and apparently was beginning to act out his past-life recall— worrisome behaviour for a five-year-old."

Worrisome also describes the way a two-year-old boy from Waukomis, Oklahoma, insisted his name was Jimmy. "No, it's Jeremy," he would be told. "Your name is Jeremy Anderson."

Leafing through a picture book with his grandmother, Nancy Anderson, Jeremy spotted a wagon and, in so doing, offered another clue to his predicament which went unnoticed at the time. "He told me the wagon hit him," his grandmother recalled. "He said he was dead, and he was angry with the man who drove the wagon. I didn't think any more about it." On another occasion, when Jeremy's grandfather, Jack, was resting in bed with a bad back, he had asked: "What's wrong with your back, Papa? Is it killing you?" Jack replied that while his back hurt, it wasn't exactly "killing him." And Jeremy said: "Well, my back got hurt one time and it killed me."

All this time a gravestone bearing the name of James L. Houser (August 22, 1952 – August 12, 1967) had been

---

"Prince and peasant, bond and free, barbarian and cultured, all share alike whatever weal or woe there is in the world, because all must at some future time change places with each other."

– Professor Francis Bowen, *Princeton Review*, May 1881

standing 90 miles away in a cemetery at Tonkawa, Oklahoma. "Jimmy" Houser, as he was known, was the son of Nancy Anderson and the half-brother of Ron Anderson, Jeremy's father. He was raised by his paternal grandmother in Tonkawa. Jimmy was last seen alive on a broiling August day just ten days short of his fifteenth birthday. A police accident report states that Jimmy Houser, fourteen, and his pal Kevin Lucas, sixteen, were driving at 75 m.p.h. in a Buick sedan with Lucas at the wheel when they struck a truck at a rural intersection. The car skidded 99 feet before bouncing off a second truck and spinning a further 108 feet. Kevin Lucas, who is said to have no memory of the accident or his life before the accident, was seriously injured. Jimmy was killed.

In April, 1980, when Jeremy was five years of age, he was taken to the scene of the accident. Apparently recognizing his surroundings, he became quite emotional and went on to demonstrate how he had fallen out of the car. "I was going like a bullet," he said. "It was like a bomb." Jeremy wasn't surprised when the undertaker who had examined Jimmy's body later disclosed that the corpse had been marked by the type of injuries normally sustained by a driver rather than a passenger. Jeremy, you see, has always insisted he *was* the driver.

In rural Lebanon, where infant chatter about past lives is not discouraged, cases of reincarnation reach an incidence of at least 1 for every 500 inhabitants, according to Dr. Sami Makarem, a member of the Arab Studies Department, American University of Beirut.

Two-Year-Old Plot

Why, then, are these remarkable children alone in their awareness of a previous existence? Dr. Stevenson suggests that the relatively low incidence of past-life recall doesn't necessarily mean that rebirth is restricted to garrulous infants. Reincarnation could be a much more widespread phenomenon with many people retaining only very dim impressions that would need stimulating—perhaps through encounters with certain people or places—to bring them into the conscious mind. *Déjà vu* experiences, so prevalent among adults and children alike, can be explained thus as the activation of the imprint of past-life memory. The same can be said for certain types of dreams.

Dreams and *déjà vu* can provide dramatic personal pointers to a former life. But spontaneous infant testimony, unsullied by self-consciousness or social conditioning, goes much further by carrying the reincarnational suggestion out of the individual mind and into the public domain. Only the most sceptical can fail to wonder about reincarnation when a boy called Ramu, aged only two years and nine months but already inordinately fond of helicopters, is able to give precise, gestured directions to a pilot of the Indian Air Force in the flying of his machine. Only the most insensitive would belittle the screams of another two-year-old, this time in Toronto, who became panic-stricken at the sight of closing elevator doors. "Don't be silly. It won't kill you," his mother told him. "It did before," the child replied.

Traversing the wide world beyond the cradle to collect, test, and collate the past-life tales of toddlers has practically convinced Dr. Ian Stevenson and Hemendra Banerjee that reincarnation is a fact of life. For Banerjee, the irresistible conclusion came after twenty-four years of research. "I'm always finding loopholes and always asking if there is another way to explain the phenomena," he said. "Cumulatively, however, there are patterns in the cases that have made me believe in reincarnation." Stevenson, by nature, has always been more detached and intellectually austere than Banerjee. But even this shy, circumspect professional goes so far as to say that "a rational man can, if he wants now, believe in reincarnation on the basis of evidence rather than simply on the basis of religious doctrine or cultural tradition."

To accept this evidence is to regard all children with new interest and respect. For if a moral emerges from the mouths of these remarkable babes and sucklings it is that infants should be looked upon less and less as the creations and constructions of their parents, and more and more as people for whom the family is merely a setting for their most recent stage of personal development.

Among the Bella Coola Indians of central British Columbia, the occasional infant who is born with teeth is thought to be the reincarnation of an ancestor. The same goes for any child born with dimples in the lobes of its ears. These dimples are regarded as the remnants of holes pierced for earrings.

The Investigators

Infant claims of past-life memory from Alaska to Zaire have lured Dr. Ian Stevenson and Hemendra Banerjee around the world countless times. Although practically alone in their calling, they have little in common. In fact, these two men, who for more than two decades pioneered scientific study into childhood memory that defies ordinary understanding, could scarcely be more different.

Based mostly in Los Angeles, Banerjee was short, plump, dark-skinned, and outgoing, even publicity-hungry. Stevenson, seventy-eight, Carlson Professor of Psychiatry at the University of Virginia, is tall, lean, fair-skinned, and reserved. Although they once worked together, personal and professional acrimony separated them since 1964.

Assisted by a team of researchers, Stevenson has more than 2,500 child cases filed on computer at his Department of Parapsychology. Banerjee, helped only by his wife and research associate, Margit, gathered more than 1,100 cases since 1955 when a university professor in his native India told him: "You will ruin your career this way."

"Twenty years ago," Banerjee admitted in 1982, "people would not touch me with a big bamboo." Even as reincarnation became more widely accepted in the past decade, he had to contend with the scientific establishment's unrelenting exclusion. The books he wrote on the subject were aimed at the popular market while Stevenson's literary output is more staid and scholarly in style and presentation. Founder of the Indian Institute of Parapsychology in 1957, Banerjee lived in the United States from 1970 until his death several years ago. As a researcher, he said he acted like a detective, lawyer, and psychologist rolled into one, his aim being "to create a body of data so that serious-minded people can make up their minds about reincarnation for themselves— from the evidence."

Montreal-born Stevenson, whose work has been published in the prestigious *Journal of Nervous and Mental Disease*, says that "dissatisfaction with modern theories of personality" fuels his investigative persistence. Reincarnation, he feels, could account for certain behaviour not explained by genetics and early environmental influences. Dr. Harold Lief, a friend and admirer of Stevenson, describes him as a methodical, careful, even cautious, investigator with a personality inclined towards obsessiveness. "Either he is making a colossal mistake," Lief has written, "or he will be known as the Galileo of the twentieth century."

3

PUTTING US

IN PERSPECTIVE

"Reincarnation is implicit in the manifested universe and is a basic and fundamental theme underlying systemic pulsation."

– Alice A. Bailey

"Are not all things which have opposites generated out of their opposites?"

– Socrates

T HERE IS INHALATION, there is exhalation; there is death, there is rebirth. Such is the drama of continuity that sustains the all-pervading process in which we are enveloped. As the catalyst of transformation on which the evolution of all matter and spirit depends, reincarnation is ceaselessly within us and around us. From the tiniest micro to the macro most huge, cycles that hinge on rebirth and regeneration are proceeding at every conceivable level of life.

The idea of palingenesis (a word of Greek and Latin origin literally meaning "again, birth") is as old as the human race. Eastern mystics have long viewed the universe in terms of *samsara*, or continuous death and rebirth. Shiva, the four-armed Hindu god of creation and destruction, symbolizes this vision by performing the dance of the cosmos through endless cycles of rise and fall, wax and wane. In ancient China, the *Tao*—meaning the very nature of the life process—was seen to be expressed by relentless cycles of coming and going. The universe swung backwards and forwards between *yin* and *yang*. The rational West, trussed for centuries in a strait-jacket tailored by scientific concepts that impeded any meeting of matter and spirit, looked condescendingly upon this exotic interpretation. Until, that is, science was pushed into a magnificent transformation of its own perceptions. The transformation was triggered by Einstein's theories of relativity which showed there was much more to time, space, and motion in the universe than classical Newtonian physics had allowed. Next came the development of quantum mechanics and its rigorous inquiry into the nature of subatomic phenomena. Imagine the furrowed brows of the old world eggheads when, like a gorgeous butterfly emerging from an earthbound cocoon, this so-called new physics of the twentieth century made the breathtaking discovery that subatomic particles, from which all matter is made, are indeed partaking in the relentless choreography of death and rebirth. Writes Gary Zukav in *The Dancing Wu Li Masters*:

> Every subatomic interaction consists of the annihilation of the original particles and the creation of

new subatomic particles. The subatomic world
is a continual dance of creation and annihilation,
of mass changing to energy and energy changing
to mass. Transient forms sparkle in and out of
existence creating a never-ending, forever-newly-
created reality.

In other words, science advances the hypothesis that
a microscopic form of rebirth underlies everything in
the physical world. In *The Tao of Physics* Fritjof Capra
refers to these subatomic particles as being "destructible
and indestructible at the same time." This is precisely
what is implied by reincarnation: even as we die we
are capable of activating another body. Destructible yet
indestructible. Dead yet very much alive.

A similar process is taking place among the fifty tril-
lion cells in the human body. At a rate that defies imagination, old cells perish and new ones are created from a
mixture of the dead material and freshly absorbed nutri-
ents. Every second, two million oxygen-carrying red
cells are dying and being replaced while the hundreds of
millions of cells in the human gut renew themselves
completely every one or two days. Tracer studies have
shown that, in the course of a year, approximately 98 per
cent of the atoms in the human body are replaced by
other atoms ingested with air, food, and drink. While
the origins of this infinitesimal exchange are lost in the
prehistoric mysteries of evolution, Colin Wilson argues
in his work *The Occult* that true evolution didn't begin
until life managed to overcome its most basic problem
of forgetfulness. Progress became possible only when

the life force invented the trick of coding knowledge into the reproductory processes. He writes:

> The Pre-Cambrian creatures shed old cells and grew new ones in the same way that my body replaces all its old cells every eight years. With the invention of death and reproduction, *they shed old bodies and grew new ones.* . . . Life is not at the mercy of death. It is in control of death. Half a billion years ago, it learned the secret of reincarnation.

Cosmic rhythms in space and time are reflected in human beings. For example, the average number of human breaths in a day (18 per minute x 60 x 24 = 25,920) gives the same figure as the number of years required for the vernal equinox to make a complete circuit in the signs of the zodiac—the greatest rhythm we can survey within our solar system. These 25,920 years are known as the Platonic year.

Macroscopic Rebirth

Shooting far beyond the body into the vastness of space, the same principle appears to be at work in the most macroscopic of worlds. While agreeing to disagree on the finer points of theory, many cosmologists and astrophysicists suggest the universe is oscillating, forever dying in order to be reborn. Big Bang is followed by expansion followed by collapse into another fireball ripe for explosion. Renowned astrophysicist John Gribbin says he believes the universe "rolls on forever in an eternal cycle in which death is merely the necessary prelude to rebirth."

Recent developments in high-energy astrophysics have led to speculation that the stuff of the universe doesn't vanish into enormous cul-de-sacs when sucked into black holes, but is pumped out again on the far side into white holes or quasars. In this way, universes can feed endlessly on one another using black holes as colossal uterine tracts of transformation. Such a recycling of the cosmos was described in picture language in the Bible long before the stirrings of the scientific age. St. Paul, in his epistle to the Hebrews (1:10-12), says that the earth and heavens "all shall wax old as doth a garment. And as a vesture shalt thou fold them up, and they shall be changed." Earlier still, human rebirth was similarly likened to a change of clothes in the great Hindu scripture, the Bhagavad-Gita (2:17): ". . . As a man casting off worn-out garments, taketh new ones, so the dweller in the body, casting off worn-out bodies, entereth into others that are new. . . ."

In the sixteenth century, visionary Italian philosopher Giordano Bruno had the audacity to champion the heretical Copernican theory of the sun-centred solar system as well as the doctrine of reincarnation. To Bruno, rebirth was at the heart of the ubiquitous emanation and return of the "Life of the Universe," embracing atoms, human beings, and worlds. He spoke of the circulation of the blood as reflecting the cosmic scheme and taught that circular movement is the only enduring form of motion. Furthermore, he declared that the planet Earth has a soul and maintained that every part of the globe—mineral as well as plant, animal, and human—is animated by the same elemental soul matter, there being no distinction between what is terrestrial and what is celestial. As a Catholic, Bruno agreed that souls do not pass from body to body, but go to Paradise, Purgatory, or Hell. "But I have reasoned deeply," he wrote, "and speaking as a philosopher, since the soul is not found without body and yet is not body, it may be in one body or in another, and pass from body to body." Such outrageous thinking was not to be tolerated by the Inquisition. For daring to vent his original mind, Bruno was imprisoned by the Venetian authorities for seven years and eventually burned at the stake in Rome in 1600.

Twentieth-century intellectual freedom was on the side of Rudolf Steiner, the founder of Anthroposophy, when he chose to augment the teachings of the cyclic school. Comparing the human life cycle with that of the planets, he wrote: "Just as the human being passes from incarnation to incarnation, passes through repeated Earth lives, so did our Earth pass through other states before it came into the state in which it is today. There are earlier incarnations of a planet just as there are earlier incarnations of a human being. Everything in the great world and in the little world is subject to the law of reincarnation."

Testimony both ancient and modern proclaims the same message. Death and renewal are one. Mind and matter are one. We are the same everlasting energy that assumes a multitude of forms in order to interact with itself unto infinity. In the materialization of this energy, patterns of recurrence manifest themselves in planetary positioning, the seasons, weather systems, tides, organic metamorphoses, and the fortunes of the human, animal, and vegetable kingdoms. Night yields to day; calm gives way to storm; rainwater evaporates to become rain once more. From the ruins of empire are born new civilizations.

Some aboriginal tribes, still cherishing the innate belief of their ancestors, ally themselves with this cosmic procedure by seeing the monthly "death" and "birth" of the moon as a guarantee of their reincarnation. In so doing they are expressing a feeling of integration, of unity, with their farthest surroundings. How ironic it is that the technology which has tended to alienate modern society from the natural rhythms conducive to such experience should be used by the "new physics" to rediscover—intellectually, at least—this Oneness, this ordinary miracle of perpetual rebirth.

"Like last year's vegetation our human life but dies down to its root, and still puts forth its green blade into eternity."

– Henry David Thoreau

4

PRODIGIES, PLATO
AND PRECOGNITION

"The endless legacy of the past to the present is the secret source of human genius."

   – Honoré de Balzac

"Forgetfulness of the past may be one of the conditions of an entrance upon a new stage of existence. The body, which is the organ of sense-perception, may be quite as much a hindrance as a help to remembrance. In that case, casual gleams of memory, giving us sudden, abrupt, and momentary revelations of the past, are precisely the phenomena we would expect to meet with."

   – William Knight

ON A HOT DAY in August, 1971, author Frank De Felitta and his wife, Dorothy, were relaxing beside the swimming pool at their $200,000 Los Angeles home when they suddenly heard brilliant ragtime piano playing coming from the house. Rushing inside, they were amazed to find their six-year-old son, Raymond, dexterously running his hands up and down their piano keyboard which he had never before attempted to play. "Daddy, my fingers are doing it by themselves!" exclaimed Raymond. "Isn't is wonderful?"

At first, his parents weren't so sure. While Dorothy screamed: "What the hell's he doing?" and refused to go near her son, Frank was overtaken by an unaccountable surge of anger. "The impact would not have been greater had we found him floating around the room," he recalled. Raymond went on to be recognized throughout the United States for his accomplished playing which veers toward the strident jazz style of Fats Waller who died in 1945. And Frank De Felitta became "a grudging and cynical convert" to reincarnation—the only logical explanation for what he had seen and heard. His son's behaviour, he said, "was not consistent with anything we had been given to understand. It was beyond my comprehension. From never even experimenting with the piano as some young children do, here was my tiny son playing like a professional for up to five hours a day." The experience moved Frank to write the reincarnational novel *Audrey Rose* which has since been made into a popular film.

Flabbergasting though it must have been, Raymond's impromptu performance was no more than a modern manifestation of an infrequent yet ancient phenomenon, the very existence of which implies that past-life talents can be responsible for innate ability. As long ago as the first century before Christ, Cicero, the Roman orator, statesman, and philosopher, maintained that the speed with which children grasp innumerable facts is "a strong proof of men knowing most things before birth." But the foundations, at least for the modern world, of the teaching that all knowledge is recollection were laid by Socrates and Plato some 350 years earlier. "Knowledge easily acquired," stated Plato's Theory of Reminiscence, "is that which the enduring self had in an earlier life, so that it flows back easily." Which is to say that genius is the flowering of past-life experience. So imbued was the old world with this way of thinking that the word "education" originally meant "to draw from that which already was known." Centuries later, the French philosopher René Descartes played a variation on this hoary theme when he remarked that human beings seem to possess an anterior memory that shows itself in differing intuitions, predispositions, talents, insights, and inspirations, all suggesting the promptings of earlier rehearsals.

When William Wordsworth wrote that "birth is but a sleep and a forgetting" he probably wasn't aware of the world's wonder children with their rare talent for awakening and remembering. Nevertheless, child prodigies and youngsters like Raymond De Felitta, who are seemingly gripped by flashes of their past, bear out the poet's words, and provide strong circumstantial evidence to show that what may be consciously forgotten is not necessarily lost. No Western child prodigy has been known to remember a past life, but reincarnation appears to offer the best explanation for:

Christian Friedrich Heinecken. Known as the "Infant of Lubeck," he is said to have talked within a few hours of his birth in 1721. At one, he knew the main events related in the first five books of the Old Testament; at two, the whole of Biblical history; and at three, he understood the outlines of world history and geography, while speaking Latin and French as well as his native German. Intrigued by the boy's reputation, the King of Denmark had him brought to Copenhagen in 1724. Shortly after this, however, the Infant of Lubeck fell ill and predicted his own death within the year. He died at the tender age of four.

Wolfgang Amadeus Mozart. At four years of age this world-famous composer of the eighteenth century wrote minuets, a piano concerto, and a sonata. His compositions at this age were not only technically accurate but also extremely difficult. At seven, he composed a full-length opera.

Jean Louis Cardiac. Born in 1719, this French wonder child was able to repeat the alphabet when just three months old. At three years, he could read Latin, and at four, he could translate the language into either French or English. He died in Paris at the age of seven.

Miguel Mantilla. An article in a 1928 edition of the *British Journal of Psychical Research* featured the calendar wizardry of this two-year-old Mexican tot. Within fifteen seconds, Miguel could answer such questions as: "In what years will February 4 be a Friday?" and "What date was the second Sunday in 1840?"

"Blind Tom" Wiggins. The sightless child of a Negro slave living in Georgia, Tom played the piano like a consummate professional at four years of age. His master hired a music teacher to encourage the boy's amazing talent. But after hearing Tom play, the teacher refused the appointment, declaring: "That boy already knows more about music than I will ever know." Tom went on to give concerts both in America and abroad. Yet, away from the piano, he remained a near-idiot with a vocabulary of no more than a few hundred words. He died, world-famous, in 1908.

John Stuart Mill. The English philosopher-economist who lived from 1806 to 1873 knew Greek at three years of age and, at six, could read Xenophon, Herodotus, Aesop and Lucian.

José Capablanca. A Cuban prodigy who, by the age of four, was already a brilliant chess player. He seldom lost a game even when playing against experts who had spent years perfecting their moves. He went on to become world champion and died in 1942.

Giannella de Marco. On March 12, 1953, Giannella, an eight-year-old Italian girl, conducted the London Philharmonic Orchestra at the Royal Albert Hall, London, in works by Weber, Haydn, Wagner and Beethoven. A review in *The Times* said: "She plies a clear, generous beat and plainly has the music at her finger-ends. . . . There is an unnerving maturity in her intellectual accomplishment. . . ." The London concert appearance was the 123rd of her career, which began at the age of four.

Carl Friedrich Gauss. When not quite three years of age, the boy who went on to become the greatest mathematician of the nineteenth century is said to have mentally followed a calculation of his father's and spotted a mistake. The calculation was related to the wages of some of his father's employees.

Medical experts have attempted to explain child wonders by pointing to glandular abnormalities that cause certain parts of the nervous system to reach peak activity in advance of other bodily areas. That most prodigies are male and infantile gland disorders are mainly found in boys, tends to support this view. Yet the phenomena can only be partially explained by a purely physical interpretation. It's worth noting that Edgar Cayce and other clairvoyant investigators are in agreement that the glands are the primary agents of karma, the impersonal and ongoing thrust of cause and effect integral to the doctrine of rebirth.

> "Genius is experience. Some seem to think that it is a gift or talent, but it is the fruit of long experience in many lives. Some are older souls than others, and so they know more."
> – Henry Ford

Chang and Eng

The most popular argument against reincarnation as the source of precocious talent is the theory that memory is transferred genetically from generation to generation through what have been dubbed the psychogenes. It is contested that prodigies somehow dip into this genetic material, this anterior thread of DNA molecules, in order to draw on a skill well developed in an ancestor. But if heredity can explain similarities among family members—and there's no denying the hand-me-down pattern of physical resemblance—it cannot pretend to account for the differences. One would think that conjoined or "Siamese" twins, having uniform genetic material and a uniform early environment, would develop similarly as human beings. Not so. Chang and Eng, the pair of conjoined twins whose nationality inspired the term "Siamese twins," developed demonstrably different personalities. Chang, for example, loved drinking liquor and sank into periodic alcoholic debauches while Eng was a teetotaller. Chang and Eng are not alone in their variance. "Siamese twins are almost without exception more different in various ways than any but a very few pairs of separate one-egg twins," wrote H. H. Newman in *Multiple Human Births*. "One of the most difficult problems faced by the twinning specialist is that of accounting for this unexpected dissimilarity of the components of Siamese twin pairs." Such glaring disparities, which are also reflected in identical twins, quadruplets, and quintuplets, continue to plague geneticists, most of whom are loath to consider the possible explanation of divergent past-life experience.

Studies showing the ability of tiny babies to mimic adults within hours of their birth appear to underline the Platonic assertion that all learning is remembering. Research from the University of Miami Medical School reported in the *Brain Mind Bulletin* of November 22, 1982, detected the "remarkable ability" of infants averaging thirty-six hours old to imitate happy, sad, and surprised expressions modelled by adults. "Because of their early appearance and apparent universality, these basic facial expressions may reflect innate processes," the study concluded. Dr. Tom Verny, a Toronto psychiatrist not given to metaphysical speculation, tells in *The Secret Life of the Unborn Child* how the animated faces of researchers in Seattle, Washington, were imitated by a nursery full of babies—some of whom were only one hour old! "When a researcher stuck out his or her tongue, made a face, or wiggled fingers in front of a baby, the child often responded in kind," writes Verny. "This (and other experiments like it) demonstrates conclusively the presence of well-developed (one could say adult) thinking, including the handling of abstract ideas in the newborn."

Naturally, the question that shrieks for reply is: Where does such behaviour come from? Dr. Verny is not a reincarnationist, but he does allow that reincarnation could provide the answer. He revealed that certain case material gathered for his book, material which demonstrates how the thoughts and feelings of pregnant mothers affect their unborn children, "could not be explained in terms of physiological and behavioural communications." His studies and clinical experience suggest that, besides the memory of the central nervous system which becomes functional between the fifth and sixth months of pregnancy, there is another memory system which cannot be accounted for. Nevertheless, being pragmatically scientific in his approach, Verny is uncomfortable with rebirth as an explanation, preferring to believe such recollection is cellular, coded in the DNA molecules. While he has had "inklings of something mystical and spiritual while working with my patients," Verny admits to being "doubly careful that I'm not reduced to accepting a world of fantasy, make-believe, or wish fulfillment." Yet even this self-imposed safeguard cannot invalidate the experiences of several of Verny's patients who have slipped unbidden into "past lives" when lulled with music and hypnotic suggestion for exploration of the prenatal state. One patient, John Kerr, reported being aware of his parents' contrasting emotions at the moment of his conception. Another, commercial artist Denise Maxwell, vividly experienced three past-life deaths in the course of an hour: first, as a young woman in a Central American tribe, then as a primitive Scandinavian hunter buried in the sitting position with his knife and spear, and finally, as a poverty-stricken male artist in eighteenth-century Europe.

While the thrust of Verny's research demonstrates how maternal emotions can profoundly affect the child in the womb, Dr. Ian Stevenson has shown, as an offshoot of his child studies suggestive of reincarnation, that the foetus can provoke reactions in the mother by making her conform to its tastes of the previous lifetime. In a number of cases studied intensively by Stevenson, the mother of a child subject reported that, during pregnancy, she had been seized by an unusual craving for a food relished by the previous personality subsequently claimed by her child. In other cases, the mother had experienced revulsion for a food which also happened to fall foul of the tastebuds of the claimed previous personality.

In one case from Sri Lanka, the mother of Gamini Jayasena experienced a marked aversion for meat during her pregnancy in 1962—an aversion not encountered while carrying her three other children. Gamini later claimed to have lived as Palitha Senewiratne who had died at eight years of age on July 28, 1960. Palitha had given up eating meat at five years of age and, after making this decision, had vomited while reluctantly trying to comply with a family request to go back to his meat-eating ways.

In another Sri Lanka case, the mother of Sujuth Lakmal Jayaratne suddenly developed, in the course of her pregnancy, a fascination for wade—a hot spiced food made of dhal, chillies, and coconut oil—and manioc, a type of yam. It so happened that Sujuth, who was born on August 7, 1969, remembered the life of Sammy Fernando who had been struck and killed by a truck roughly six months earlier. Fernando had been particularly fond of the food Sujuth's mother craved. In the words of Walter Pater: "Taste is the memory of a culture once known."

Heredity can only explain so much about human succession and the range of predispositions which we suppress or develop in the course of a lifetime. Thomas Henry Huxley, one of the most outstanding scientists of the nineteenth century, was convinced that "every one of us bears upon him obvious marks of his parentage, perhaps of remoter relationships." But he didn't rule out the possibility of rebirth working in tandem with this hereditary influence. In his essay *Evolution and Ethics*, written in 1897, Huxley argued that "none but very hasty thinkers" will reject reincarnation on the grounds of inherent absurdity.

The Russian writer and lecturer P. D. Ouspensky found the "various ingenious theories" of heredity, hidden instincts, and unconscious memory all acceptable, but he also found that they left very much unexplained. "Until we find it possible to recognize that we have lived before," he declared, "very much will remain in us that we shall never be able to understand."

According to the insights of those who have taken LSD under experimental conditions, the laws of reincarnation operate independently of the subject's biological lineage and the genetic transfer of idioplasma. "The assignment of an individual spiritual entity to a particular physical body and a specific life seems to bypass biological hereditary lines and violate genetic laws," Czechoslovakian-born psychotherapist Dr. Stanislav Grof has noted.

> "Now we are ready to understand the startling statement that there is no such thing as heredity . . . No one ever 'inherits'' anything from his parents or his ancestors. He already had certain mental tendencies before he reincarnated this time and these tendencies guided him to a family where similar tendencies existed—that is all."
>
> – Emmet Fox

Electing for Birth

A 1978 research study in which 750 subjects were hypnotized and guided back to a state just before birth satisfied clinical psychologist Dr. Helen Wambach that heredity

and reincarnation operate independently but comple-
ment each other. She found that the individual entity
opts for materialization in a specific body in a particular
hereditary line. Eighty-one per cent of Dr. Wambach's
subjects said they chose to be born, most choosing reluctantly after consultation with spiritual advisers. Although 90 per cent of the group spoke of death as being
pleasant, only 26 per cent looked forward to the coming
lifetime. Noted one participant: "My feelings about the
prospect of coming into the current lifetime were, 'Well,
guess I'll go get stripped down some more.'" (Case A-418)
Another said: "It was something that had to be done, like
washing the floor when it's dirty." (Case A-285)

Eighty-seven per cent reported knowing parents,
lovers, relatives, and friends of the current lifetime in
varied relationships both in past lives and in the state between lives. "Blood may be thicker than water," wrote
Dr. Wambach in her book *Life Before Life*, "but judging
by my results, past-life ties are a lot thicker than blood."
As farfetched as the idea of group reincarnation might
seem to some people, the meeting of cells in all the right
places within the human body is surely no more miracu-
lous a proposition. Time and time again, Dr. Wambach's
subjects emerged from their trance to relay the same
story—that we come back with the same souls to share a
variety of relationships not only with those we love but
also with those who inspire fear and hatred. Such statements can only lead to further conjecture: perhaps the
individual must know *from personal experience* life's
every vicissitude; perhaps spiritual evolution demands
our rotational embodiment so that we may truly under-

stand the host of conflicting human perspectives. Perhaps we can learn and grow only by being rich and poor, beautiful and ugly, healthy and disease-ridden, master and slave, murderer and murderer's victim. . . .

Research undertaken by the world's leading expert on death and dying, Swiss-born psychiatrist Dr. Elisabeth Kübler-Ross, lends credence to the suggestion that there is an evolutionary requirement to plunge repeatedly into the brackish water of earthly existence. Dr. Ross wrote from her Shanti Nilaya foundation in Escondido, California, that the purpose of life on the physical plane is "to learn and grow and to participate in the spiritual evolution of man. In order to fulfill our destiny we have to learn certain lessons and pass certain tests. And we can regard death as a graduation from the physical plane only when we have learned all these lessons and passed those tests. In our present society, where negativity is so overwhelming and evident in every area from raising children to the killing of our fellow humans in war, in violence and crime, it is practically impossible to fulfill our destiny in one lifetime. When we have not learned our lessons or if we have broken some universal law like 'Thou shalt not kill' we have a chance to return into a physical body of another human being. . . . We then choose our own parents, our place of birth, and an environment that will make it most likely to learn the lessons that ought to be learned. . . ."

Dr. Richard Alpert, an American social scientist and spiritual teacher who often goes under the name of Ram Dass, expressed his perception of the guiding role of the subconscious in selecting lives of appropriate experience when he wrote that, before birth, people "know just what they're buying into. They say, 'I'm buying into these parents, this experience. I'm going to be in this life, I'm going to have one eye, I'm going to be a cripple, I'm going to end up being beaten to death on the street in Benares and that's what I need. Okay, here I go.' You dive down in, and the veil is lowered. There you are, and here we are, and we run through this one, and then we get all finished and we come back out of it and we wake up. Okay, you ran that one off; now let's see what's next. What I need to be now is a duke, and I might have to wait thousands of years for that one."

Reincarnationists like to speak of the Earth plane as a training school to which we, the pupils, return lifeterm after lifeterm, each of us bearing our own spiritual satchel of inclinations, wisdom, and experience garnered from previous existences. So many are the past glories and graduations, trials and reversals, that to remember them all in each successive life could overwhelm to the point of inertia—just as knowing the fortunes of the future could sap all desire for living. "It is nature's kindness that we do not remember past births," remarked Mohandas K. Gandhi, the great Indian philosopher and apostle of non-violence. "Life would be a burden if we carried such a tremendous load of memories."

Yet it is possible, even therapeutically helpful, to reach into the fathomless past to retrieve some of this obscured recollection. Knowing and accepting crucial events of the past can transform present experience, as the next chapter will show.

"Our innermost being is more valuable than all titles and honours. These are coloured rags with which we try to cover our nudities. Whatever is of value in us we bring from our previous lives that were spiritual."

– Queen Elisabeth of Austria (1837–1898)

5

HEALING THE SCARS
OF CENTURIES

"There is no disease known to man the cause of which is entirely determined in what is called his own lifetime."
 – Dr. Arthur Guirdham

"Past-lives therapy allows you to stop doing things to people because you have to and to start doing things with people because you want to."
 – Dr. Morris Netherton

T HE CLINICAL VALIDITY of past-life therapy has been established beyond doubt. With increasing regularity over the last forty years, hundreds of thousands of suffering people have been lulled into altered states of consciousness and guided through the veil of time to relive, or view with detached wonderment, critical episodes of former existences. What they experience is another, superimposed reality fraught with all the immediacy of the therapist's couch—it might be a workhouse in nineteenth-century England, a mud hut in ancient Somalia, or a Mayan temple courtyard deep in the Central American jungle.

To match the onrushing change of scene, the clients of past-life therapy find that they assume appropriate identities from out of the amnesia of hundreds, even thousands, of years. Anything can—and does—happen. A hearty-voiced plumber might become a lisping peasant girl; a placid secretary could take on the persona of a fierce warrior. Some people observe their transformation as if they were seated in the front row of a theatre of the mind; others enter the very body of the character. And then there are those who sense or feel events unfolding from afar. However a past life is perceived, the aim of the therapy is to mine the experience of the soul; to heal through self-understanding.

Having ensured that the source of a patient's troublesome condition cannot be detected in the current lifetime, the therapist knows the canker is lurking somewhere in the individual's repertoire of past lives. This buried trauma invariably reverberates in the life of today as physiological pain or mental anguish, or both. For past-life therapy confirms that mind and body share the closest of relationships, that a psychological component exists for every physical disease, and vice versa. While many hours spent probing successive lives may be required to locate the source of the aggravation, healing is often rapid and dramatic once the pertinent information has been wrested from the subconscious. No one can state with certainty how this remedial effect is wrought, but it would appear that the very act of confronting and accepting negativity long trapped in the psyche provokes some alchemy of liberation. The release of blocked energy seems to encourage the evaporation of the cause of the ailment which could be cancer, multiple sclerosis, ulcers, arthritis, obesity, stuttering, migraine headaches, depression, learning disability, epilepsy, every conceivable form of phobia, addiction, allergies, sexual inadequacy—the lot! The end of the regression isn't necessarily the end of the experience. Confused memories, emotions, and expanded awareness of the trauma can invade the patient's dreams and waking consciousness for weeks or even months afterwards.

So past-life therapy often works where conventional treatment fails, but does that mean reincarnation is responsible for the plethora of "past lives?" Not necessarily. Telepathy, the uncharted ocean of the collective unconscious, spirit possession, ancestral memory, intricate sub-personalities created by the ever-inventive mind, and pure fantasy are some alternative explanations. Yet the rebirth hypothesis, being the most straightforward interpretation, keeps bobbing up like an apple in a bucket of water. Patients' oft-expressed strong identification with the personalities assumed under hypnosis as well as the fact that many a past-life individual has been historically verified, strengthens the case for reincarnation. So does the research of Dr. Helen Wambach whose subjects, regardless of their sex in the current lifetime, have divided strictly according to biological fact by recalling 50.6 per cent male and 49.4 per cent female lives when regressed to time periods as far back as 2000 B.C.. The studies of Dr. Wambach—even though her subjects were primarily white, middle-class Americans—also accurately reflect race, class, and population distribution in the real historical world as well as the clothing and footwear worn across the centuries and the type of food eaten and utensils used.

Nevertheless, proof of reincarnation is no more accessible to past-life therapists than it is to investigators of infant recall. "Even if every detail given by a patient under hypnosis is shown to be an accurate statement about a person who had once lived," says hypnotherapist Dr. Edith Fiore, "you are not proving the patient actually lived the life. You are just showing that someone lived and died. The patient could be tapping into someone else's thought forms." Which isn't to say that Dr. Fiore, a clinical psychologist from Saratoga, California, discounts reincarnation. Far from it. In the first eight years of using hypnosis as the mainstay of her practice, she swung from disbelief to a 99 per cent conviction in rebirth. "If someone's phobia is eliminated instantly and permanently by the remembrance of an event from the past, it seems to make logical sense that the event must have happened," she declares.

Certainly, this viewpoint is disputed by hypnotherapists who don't believe in reincarnation. Such a man is Dr. Gerald Edelstein, a staff psychiatrist at Herrick Memorial Hospital in Berkeley, California, who has found that, despite his ideological prejudice, several of his patients have slipped into past lives—with terrific results! He admits candidly: "These experiences, for reasons I cannot explain, almost always lead to rapid improvements in the patients' lives."

Says Dr. Morris Netherton, a pioneering Los Angeles practitioner: "Many people go away believing in reincarnation as a result of their experience; others see it as symbolic, metaphorical. But what is the logical answer? That it actually happened! It took nature ten million years to build the Grand Canyon and that's just a big hole in the ground. I can't believe it takes just seventy or eighty years to build a man's soul."

What Netherton does believe is that "everything in the mind comes from what has gone on before." He defines imagination as "the sum total of everything that ever happened to you in every lifetime you ever lived." It's a grand vision, created and corroborated by the testimony of more than ten thousand patients. This chubby, energetic personality whose coffee mug bears the slogan "World's Greatest Doctor" was raised a fundamental southern Methodist. He hardly considered the idea of reincarnation until thirty-one years ago when, beset by unemployment, a chronic bleeding ulcer, and feelings of emotional inadequacy, he turned in despair to conventional therapy. "In the third session I talked about the pain I was feeling," he said, "and the next thing I knew I was in a different place." Suddenly, spontaneously, Netherton visualized himself in a Mexican institution for the criminally insane. The year was 1818. A guard had kicked him in the stomach in the exact spot where his ulcer had flared. He understood that his lands had been seized by his wife and her family who had conspired to have him committed. At the same time, he was intuitively aware that his wife in that life was also Carol, the woman he is married to today. (Being told of this later at a local restaurant, Carol "passed out in her mashed potatoes," to quote her husband.)

Whatever the truth of this flashback of confrontation, Netherton was at once granted "amazing relief" from pain that has never returned. Hired as a probation officer, he went on to win a master's degree in counseling, and a doctorate in psychology. Yet he was not converted instantly to a belief in reincarnation. Conversion came slowly as a by-product of his self-development as a therapist in which he personally underwent more than 1,200 hours of past-life examination. The Netherton Method, expounded in the best-seller *Past Lives Therapy* and since practised not only in Los Angeles but also in training offices in Montreal, São Paulo, Brazil, and Stuttgart, West Germany, is unique in that it relies, at the outset, on a patient's use of specific recurring or out-of-place phrases. Guided by these key phrases, for example, "It's hopeless" or "They're holding me down," Netherton attempts to unlock the unconscious by asking the patient to concentrate on repeating them. This repetition jogs the patient's mind to an image, the starting point for a detailed reconstruction of pain, guilt, and trauma. Netherton says his patients *must* relive traumatic experiences of the past in order to clear up their current problems. "You have to bring it into the body," he declares. "That's the only way you can be assured you're getting accurate information." And so, often screaming, writhing, moaning, weeping, and breaking into foreign languages, Netherton's subjects enter their battened-down ugliness in order to leave it all behind. Past births and deaths—common sources of behavioural disorder—are commonly re-enacted. And Netherton insists that no past-life trauma is completely erased without detecting the unresolved prenatal incident, or incidents, that activates a track of problematical past lives in the individual. Noting that the foetus is extremely sensitive to the mother's thoughts and feelings (an observation substantiated by the findings of Dr. Tom Verny) Netherton writes in *Past Lives Therapy*:

> The unborn child, awaiting the beginning of conscious life, is profoundly affected by this prenatal awareness. With no conscious mind to discern or interpret, the unconscious plays back any past-life incidents triggered by events in the mother's life. These incidents shape the behaviour patterns of the child. At birth the infant will begin a life of trying to resolve those past-life events without ever knowing what they are.

It matters not whether Netherton's patients, who range from priests to physicists, believe in reincarnation: the recall flows just the same, restricted neither by creed nor colour. Whites, for example, hark back to existences as Negro slaves; Chicanos remember fighting as British soldiers in World War II, and as if to invalidate the genetic memory interpretation, many have described being alive during their parents' lifetimes! "Some patients start by feeling that they are 'making up' parts of what they tell me," Netherton has written, "but they soon discover that they cannot change the content of their past-life incidents, and must reveal the most personal and painful aspects of the stories they had thought were imaginary. This is what most quickly convinces the sceptic. He begins by saying the first thing that comes into his head simply to placate me. But the moment he comes face to face with his pain, he can no longer deny the validity of the therapy."

Among the conclusions Netherton has gleaned from his patients' testimony is that each individual returns to Earth at the identical state of development reached at the time of death. He urges people, wherever possible, not to enlist artificial support at death "unless you want to come back in that way, being supported. You come back as you went out. It's a continuous journey." Abortion, according to Netherton's findings, is "the killing of something that has feeling." Time and again, he has

---

"If you dream of travel, being regressed is a wonderful way to go. For you may chance upon Rome, Athens, Paris, Pompeii or Babylon, find yourself shopping in the bazaars of ancient Persia, seeing China when she was young, Egypt before it was ancient, or maybe even lost Atlantis, not to mention the countless quiet villages around the world.... Imagine participating in such sports as gladiating, tiger-hunting (with a spear) and mountain climbing; or how about sailing the world's oceans on a three-masted schooner, building the pyramids, or leading the quiet life of a Grecian scholar. If food is your thing, there is always a delicious Polynesian pig, a rare mammoth steak and the old-fashioned favorite—gruel (ugh!) .... If nothing else, a regression is a sure cure for boredom in today's push-button world."

– Bryan Jameison in *Explore Your Past Lives*

asked patients who have regressed to aborted embryos whether they have a message for their mothers and often that message is a haunting "I'll be back." The act of abortion appears to set up a pattern of incompletion for the protagonists which can exert a domino effect from life to life. In fact, the recurrence of similar patterns and problems over a sequence of lives is a common phenomenon perceived by Netherton as the unconscious mind's way of resolving specific issues through repeated trials of close resemblance.

Victims of the Self

Dr. Edith Fiore singles out guilt as the architect of the most profoundly negative effects in her patients' experiences. "When I see someone with four or five symptoms, when they are losing in the game of life, it's as if they are saying: 'I don't deserve this, that, and the other,'" says the author of *You Have Been Here Before*. She also finds that "nobody is ever a victim without a cause": her patients have always earned their discomfort by their own actions.

Illustrating this system of cause and effect, which mirrors the Hindu and Buddhist doctrine of karma, is one of Fiore's most dramatic cases. A woman in her mid-thirties, who booked therapy in desperation after undergoing twelve operations for bone cancer, saw herself, under hypnosis, as a priestess in an ancient cult which practised human sacrifice. Her role was to drink the blood of the sacrificial victims, a chore she detested.

But, as the choice was drink, or be sacrificed yourself, she hardened herself to the task. After the regression, the woman submitted to a blood test prior to yet another expected operation. The test revealed there were no longer any living cancer cells in her body and the operation was cancelled. Now that several years have elapsed and the woman appears to be completely healed, it's interesting to reflect that blood is manufactured in the bone marrow—the very site of her affliction.

Speaking to the second annual conference of the Association for Past Life Research and Therapy in Los Angeles in October, 1982, Fiore declared: "Other therapies address the symptoms and leave the cause untouched. Past-life therapy attacks the root cause. There isn't a single physical problem that can't be resolved by good past-life treatment." This statement was the product of her clinical experience which has shown that all sorts of ailments can be traced back to past lives. She has found that practically all patients who are overweight by more than ten pounds have had a lifetime in which they starved to death or suffered food deprivation for long periods. Irrational fears of snakes, of fire, of being alone, of flying, of darkness, of crowds, of natural cataclysms such as earthquakes and storms, have been relieved by coming to terms with terrifying past-life misfortunes. One teenage boy, for example, was troubled by only being able to fall asleep if he was alone and in total silence. His difficulty was traced to his having been bayoneted to death by a Japanese soldier while sleeping on the beach of a Pacific island during World War II. The origins of migraine headaches have been variously determined as clubbing, guillotining, shooting, stoning, hanging, or scalping in another existence. Those with chronic abdominal pains have relived having their bellies run through with swords, bayonets, or knives. Even menstrual problems have been seen to stem from past-life sexual trauma, while instant attractions, dislikes, and feelings of familiarity or distrust have become perfectly understandable after a glimpse of events in former existences.

"Are they putting on an act?" Fiore asks rhetorically of her patients in *You Have Been Here Before.* "If so, most should be nominated for Academy Awards. I have listened to and watched people in past-life regressions under hypnosis for thousands of hours. I am convinced there is no deliberate, nor conscious, attempt to deceive. The tears, shaking, flinching, smiling, gasping for breath, groaning, sweating, and other physical manifestations are all too real."

It's fitting that Californians, with their legendary affluence and fixation for self-discovery, should be the world's greatest patrons of past-life therapy, which can cost as much as $300 an hour in the redwood state. Yet the origins of hypnotic regression—which gripped California in the mid-seventies and has failed to let go—can be traced to turn-of-the-century France and the experiments of the enigmatic Colonel Albert de Rochas. Conducting transverse and longitudinal passes with his hands in the style of Franz Anton Mesmer, the Austrian physician who gave his name to hypnosis or "mesmerism," Rochas swept his subjects back into a succession of past lives.

One of these subjects was eighteen-year-old Mlle. Marie Mayo, an engineer's daughter, who was first taken back to the age of eight when, having attended a school in Beirut, she wrote her name in Arabic. Beyond her birth, she called herself Lina, the daughter of a fisherman in Brittany. She related how she married, at twenty, a fisherman called Yvon, how her only child died at the age of two, and how, in a fit of despair after her husband's death in a shipwreck, she threw herself into the sea from the top of a precipice. Marie Mayo relived the convulsions of drowning before passing into another incarnation, this time as a man—Charles Mauville, a clerk and murderer who lived during the time of Louis xvi. Still further back, she became Madeleine de Saint-Marc, whose husband was a gentleman of the French court.

As fascinating and as plausible as most of Rochas' subjects were, they never gave precise information which could be checked out with historical fact even though the places and families mentioned were often known to have existed. This frustration caused Rochas—who tried in vain to divert his subjects' recall so as to counteract any suggestion that he was prompting

---

Research into the past-life testimony of hypnotized subjects has undermined many a historical stereotype. "When the images contrast with what we believe to be true and yet prove on careful study to be accurate, then we must look anew at the concept of past-life recall as fantasy."

– Dr. Helen Wambach

telepathically the experimental evidence—to reflect upon "the darkness in which all observers have to struggle at the beginning of every new science."

The Power Within

For years, psychiatrists and psychologists interpreted their patients' occasional spontaneous recall from other lives as mental derangement. But there were always investigators knocking at the door of the unknown. Sweden's John Björkhem (1910–1963) advanced the fledgling science by conducting hundreds of regression experiments in which the previous lives claimed under hypnosis were frequently verified. And in 1950, Dr. Alexander Cannon, an Englishman awarded degrees by nine European universities, grudgingly gave in to the evidence of rebirth produced by 1,382 volunteers who, when regressed, spoke of living in various time periods as far back as several thousand years before Christ. He wrote in *The Power Within*:

> For years the theory of reincarnation was a nightmare to me and I did my best to disprove it and even argued with my trance subjects to the effect that they were talking nonsense. Yet as the years went by one subject after another told me the same story in spite of different and varied conscious beliefs. Now well over a thousand cases have been so investigated and I have to admit that there is such a thing as reincarnation.

Cannon specialized in discovering hidden complexes and fears engendered by traumatic incidents in past lives. Holding that the work of the great psychoanalyst Sigmund Freud had been "out-flanked" by reincarnation, he declared: "The majority of people do not benefit from psychoanalysis because the trauma lies not in this life but in a past life."

Similar conclusions were reached independently by English psychiatrist Dr. Arthur Guirdham through what he called "a purely intellectual process." Verifying and cross-referencing over many years a torrent of obscure suggestions, medical symptoms, psychic revelations, automatic writing, and recurring dreams, Guirdham came to believe that he was one of a group of people who have reincarnated together in five separate time periods. Having completed forty-four years of medical practice and written fourteen books, Guirdham maintained he had remained a sceptic ever since being nicknamed "Doubting Thomas" as a boy. But he declared quite emphatically: "If I didn't believe in reincarnation on the evidence I'd received I'd be mentally defective." The evidence—vast in quantity and complex in nature—does not involve hypnotic regression, but it does point to disease originating in past incarnations. Guirdham cited many examples of the "anniversary phenomenon" in which illness or depression is suffered on days coinciding with tragic happenings in previous incarnations. He argued that while the short duration of symptoms often corresponds to brief incidents in previous lives, longer disturbances will have a more lasting counterpart in a previous existence.

The case of Bonnie Brown, a Toronto fashion model who was regressed to a sickly past life in a concentration camp, backs up this viewpoint. At twenty-nine years of age, Bonnie had been plagued with repeated attacks of bronchitis every winter since childhood. Induced into an altered state of consciousness by hypnotherapist Beverly Janus, she encountered five different lifetimes in the space of an hour. Then she found herself as a young woman in a small East European town wearing drab clothes and a head scarf. With her neighbours, she was taken from her earthen-floored hut and led to a train by soldiers wearing World War II uniforms. There was no food or water on the train and she was cold and racked with coughing. (Bonnie coughed throughout the regression and felt so cold she had to be wrapped in blankets.) After several days' journey, Bonnie and her fellow captives were herded into a camp fenced with barbed wire. "I was standing at the fence with my hands on the wire," Bonnie recalls. "I was coughing blood. I remember thinking: 'I don't want to live anymore.' No one seemed to care. I was coughing and coughing until the end." It was then that Beverly Janus instructed her hypnotized patient that she would no longer be affected by the bad effects of the past. Since that regression in 1972, when she confronted her sickness in what appeared to be her previous incarnation, Bonnie hasn't experienced a trace of bronchial trouble. She says: "I feel that reincarnation is the best explanation for what happened. But if it was only an exploration of my psyche to show me that I no longer need to have bronchitis, who cares? The main thing is that it works."

Shirley Kleppe-Moran, a research subject of Dr. Helen Wambach, was similarly relieved of periodic seizures for which there was no medical explanation or salvation. The seizures, lasting from fifteen minutes to an hour, made her body "feel like it was going a million miles an hour" and had afflicted her since the age of seven. Under hypnosis, she entered the life of a young French girl living on the coast of Normandy in the sixteenth century. Suspected of being a witch because she was seen visiting a sick boy who had subsequently died, she was chased by torch-carrying villagers to a line of cliffs where she jumped to her death. Shirley relived her leap into mid-air as the intense, emotional equivalent of her seizures which, since that day in 1977, have never returned.

By no means confined to the seekers and self-analysts of the West, past-life therapy is earnestly pursued behind the Iron Curtain. Moscow specialist Varvara Ivanova, held in high esteem by Soviet scientists and writers, has found that regression allows people not only to perceive the reasons for their sufferings and the educational goal of their "chain of life," but also to understand their habits, idiosyncracies, and unconscious gestures. In a statement that could have come from the lips of Morris Netherton or a hundred other Western therapists, she avers that similar difficulties will crop up in successive lifetimes "until one learns to fight adversity. You have to solve them. If you don't solve them in this lifetime, they appear again and again in different forms and situations in the same life, and in other ones, till you learn to master them in the right way."

"A hundred years ago Bedlam would have been the place for anyone who voiced the fact that in the future we would be able to communicate with countries across the sea by seeing and hearing—or with men on the moon. In a century to come perhaps science and regressive hypnotism will have finally proven the fact of our many lives."

– Clarice Toyne

Children as Regression Subjects

Being placed closer than adults to the source of past-life memories, children are particularly good candidates for regression. In 1995, American hypnotherapist Carol Bowman argued against the prevailing belief that past-life regression is an inappropriate strategy for children because of their fragile ego structures. "On the contrary," she declared in an article in *The Journal of Regression Therapy*, "it is highly appropriate in some cases. Many children benefit greatly, and sometimes effortlessly, from past-life therapy." Bowman appeared on America's top-rated *Oprah Winfrey Show* to encourage other parents to treat their children's past-life stories with seriousness. And in her 1997 book *Children's Past Lives*, Bowman tells how her own children, Chase and Sarah, benefitted hugely from regression. This is the story of how hypnosis carried Chase Bowman back into an earlier life, bringing complete recovery from a besetting phobia. . . .

Chase was five years old when it became obvious that he suffered from an apparently irrational fear of loud noises. The year was 1988 and his parents, Carol and Steve, were hosting a big Fourth of July party at their home in Asheville, North Carolina. The party ended with the guests taking a short walk to a municipal golf course which granted a superb view of the town's annual Independence Day fireworks display. As soon as the sound of exploding fireworks began reverberating against the hills, however, Chase—who had been eagerly anticipating the colour and excitement of the display—started to cry. No amount of comforting and reassurance stemmed his tears and Carol Bowman felt obliged to take him home, leaving Steve with nine-year-old Sarah and their party guests. Even when he was back home and away from the noise, Chase continued to sob deeply. His hysteria only grew worse when his mother asked whether the noises had scared him. All she could do was rock him gently in her arms until the sobbing stopped and he fell asleep.

This episode was set aside until the family visited the town's indoor swimming pool a month later. Chase loves the water, but as soon as they entered the noisy pool he began crying desperately. He grabbed his mother's hands and pulled her towards the door, refusing to listen to reason. Later, Carol Bowman realized that the sound of the diving board thudding off the bare walls of the pool building may have sounded, to Chase's ears, like the booming of the firework explosions. But she was still at a loss to understand why her son should react with such fear.

The source of the phobia was discovered a few weeks later when a skilled hypnotherapist, Norman Inge, was staying as a house guest with the Bowmans while conducting past-life regression workshops in Asheville. Carol mentioned Chase's irrational fear while the family were enjoying afternoon tea with their visitor. Inge then suggested an experiment in which both mother and son readily agreed to participate. That moment, Bowman writes in *Children's Past Lives*, "was a turning point in my life." On Norman Inge's instructions, Chase climbed onto his mother's knee, closed his eyes, and began describing what he saw when he heard the loud noises that frightened him. Nothing, admits Bowman, could have prepared her for what she was about to hear. "Young Chase immediately began describing himself as a soldier—an adult soldier—carrying 'a long gun with a kind of sword at the end.' My heart was pounding in my ears, and the hair on my arms stood up as I listened. Sarah and I glanced at each other in wide-eyed amazement."

"What are you wearing?" Norman asked. Chase replied: "I have dirty, ripped clothes, brown boots, a belt. I'm hiding behind a rock, crouching on my knees and shooting at the enemy. I'm at the edge of a valley. The battle is going on all around me." These words were coming from a child who had never shown any interest in war games and had never even owned a toy gun. He went on to describe his activity behind the rock. "I don't want to look, but I have to when I shoot. Smoke and flashes everywhere. And loud noises: yelling, screaming, loud booms. I'm not sure who I'm shooting at—there's so much smoke, so much going on. I'm scared. I shoot at anything that moves. I really don't want to be here and shoot other people."

There were more surprises in Chase's testimony, including the assertion that he had been black in that life. Despite his mother's scepticism, research would show there were black soldiers who fought in the American Civil War. Chase said he was shot in the wrist, taken to a field hospital where his wound was bandaged, and then sent back to operate a cannon. His description of the hospital tallied with accounts of that time, but it was his sister who remarked that the wrist in question had been marked with eczema since he was a baby. Whenever he became tired or upset, he would scratch that wrist until it bled and Bowman often had to bandage it to prevent him from causing further aggravation.

Bowman writes: "To our astonishment and relief, within a few days of his regression to the lifetime of a soldier, the eczema on Chase's right wrist vanished completely, and it has never returned. Chase's fear of loud noises also totally disappeared. Fireworks, explosions,

---

"The unresolved trauma at death is a primary cause of behavioural disorder," writes past-life therapist Dr. Morris Netherton. "Most of the problems I encounter have their source in past-life deaths; when the impact of these deaths is erased, many disorders simply evaporate." In the same vein, Dr. Helen Wambach maintains: "It is quite common for my subjects to tell me that after they have experienced death in a past life, a phobia or symptom they have had has gone away."

and booming sounds never scared him again. In fact, soon after the regression, Chase began showing an intense interest in playing the drums . . . Now he's a serious drummer, filling the house with loud booming sounds every day."

Bridey Hysteria

Not all regression has a therapeutic objective. Which is just as well because past-life therapists, with healing as their aim, care little for shouldering the burden of dissecting the mystery behind the daily miracle. Usually, regressionists interested in the phenomena for its own sake are the ones who scrutinize their labours for any leads which might provide detailed evidence for rebirth. Certainly, the sole objective of part-time hypnotist Morey Bernstein in 1952 was to test his ability to probe memories before birth—a phenomenon he had only read about. Imagine his excitement when his subject, Colorado housewife Virginia Tighe (a name to be quickly submerged by the alias Ruth Simmons) slipped into what was to become her celebrated Bridey Murphy persona from nineteenth-century Ireland. Bridey took the world by storm when the story of Bernstein's regressions were splashed across newspapers and magazines. "Come as You Were" costume parties were held, Reincarnation Cocktails were mixed in bars, songs about rebirth crowded the airwaves, and Paramount Pictures produced a Bridey Murphy movie. *The Search for Bridey Murphy*, Bernstein's account of his adventures in hypnotism by candle flame, went on to become a million copy best seller. On at least one occasion the past-life fever got out of hand. A teenager in Shawnee, Oklahoma, was so carried away by the mass enthusiasm that he shot himself, leaving a note saying that he intended to conduct his own investigation of reincarnation.

Although the landmarks of Bridey's existence (born in County Cork, 1798, the daughter of Duncan and Kathleen Murphy, she married Brian MacCarthy and died childless in Belfast at the age of sixty-six after falling down some steps) were clearly stated in Irish brogue, the dates of her birth, marriage, and death were impossible to confirm because no records were kept in Ireland before 1864. Nevertheless, the stores mentioned by Bridey—Caden House, Farr's, and John Carrigan's— were found to have existed. A host of obsolete Irish words, among them "flats" for platters and "slip" for a child's pinafore or frock, had been used accurately. Local events and details of household furniture, domestic articles, food and kitchen utensils, coinage, books, popular songs and dances, farming practices, and the street lighting of Belfast—"poles with lights on them"—were all graphically described. She even related the correct procedure for kissing the Blarney stone and, being particularly fond of dancing, rounded off one hypnotic session by performing *The Morning Jig* complete with its finale of a stylized yawn. At her funeral, Bridey was aware of the playing of the Uilleann pipes—a popular instrument of the day owing to its soft tone.

More than anything, it is the accumulation of minor verifications that gives the case its core of credibility.

For a while, sceptics made great play of Bridey's child-hood reference to a metal bed because such beds were thought to have been unknown in Ireland before 1850. Further inquiry, however, showed that metal beds were advertised as early as 1802. "Research," wrote journalist William J. Barker, who travelled to Ireland to prepare a 19,000-word report entitled *The Truth About Bridey Murphy*, "is Bridey's best ally." In the summer of 1995, the woman whose regressions made headlines around the world passed away. Virginia Tighe, who remarried as Virginia Mae Morrow, died in Denver at the age of 70.

Since the Bridey Murphy sensation, regressionists around the world have been eager to emulate the feat with distinctive cases of their own. From the Cheshire home of Joe Keeton, Britain's busiest regressionist, to the corporate office in Malibu, California, of Dick Sutphen, a man who markets reincarnation like soapsuds, the tapes and casebooks of rebirth are swollen with evidence for all who are willing to be persuaded.

There are few cases more convincing than teacher Margaret Baker's remarkable recall of the life and death of gypsy horse dealer Tyzo Boswell. In 1978, during a taped regression in which she was suspicious of her *gorgio* or non-gypsy interviewer, Margaret spoke in coarse language of Boswell's life and work from 1775 until his death by lightning in 1831 at the Horncastle, Lincolnshire, fair. When the tape was played back at the end of the session, Margaret "was totally unaware of anything she had said, and was astonished to hear that she had changed sex," said hypnotherapist Maurice Blake of Norwich, England. Margaret's next move was a pilgrimage to the neighbouring county of Lincolnshire to see whether there was any truth to her ramblings. It wasn't long before she had the eerie sensation of standing next to the grave of Tyzo Boswell in the graveyard of St. Mary's Church at Tetford. The tombstone confirms that Boswell was "slain by lightening" [*sic*] on August 5, 1831, and the burial of his remains, two days later, is duly recorded in the parish register. Once on Boswell's home territory, Margaret felt great familiarity with her surroundings. "I'd never been to the area before," she said, "but I knew exactly where the grave was." Neither Margaret nor Maurice Blake had had the slightest contact with gypsy life and yet Margaret's regression was replete with Romany words, for example, "motto" meaning drunk, "mello," for dead, and "chopping greis," meaning selling horses, all of which were later verified.

The Reincarnation Experiments, a stunning television documentary in which four housewives from Sydney, Australia, gave details of past lives under hypnosis and then verified the evidence—in front of TV cameras and independent witnesses—by travelling thousands of miles to the scenes of these bygone lives, was screened before the Australian public in March, 1983. Even atheistic reviewers were compelled to admit that reincarnation appeared to be the only logical explanation for these remarkable journeys through time which followed hypnotic regression conducted by hypnotherapist Peter Ramster.

Cynthia Henderson, for example, who had voiced her past-life memories in colloquial French, led a film crew to a bomb-ravaged, 300-year-old chateau near the village of Fleur in Normandy—her home as French aristocrat Amélie de Cheville. The experience was so powerful that she burst into tears. Helen Pickering, another member of the experimental quartet, journeyed to Aberdeen where she had lived as James Archibald Burns, who had been born in 1807 in Dunbar, Scotland. While still in Sydney, Helen had drawn a detailed sketch of Aberdeen's Marshall College of Medicine that was verified by the only man alive who knows precisely how the building used to be, local historian David Gordon, collector of every plan and drawing from the college's beginnings. That a woman who had no access to his work and didn't even know the plans existed could possess such historical knowledge was "inexplicable," said Gordon. Inexplicable, that is, unless Helen Pickering walked the college's forgotten corridors and staircases as the medical student James Burns a century and a half ago. Aside from these structural revelations, Helen's recall of Burns' life was authenticated by records in the county library at Blairgowrie, the town where Burns had set up a successful medical practice.

Verification isn't always accomplished so easily. Most regression material doesn't contain the specifics sorely needed by researchers if only because the dates and the names of towns and streets usually lack the emotional charge that inspires recall. Also, most past lives, having been lived long before the establishment of Marshall McLuhan's global village, were so removed from the mainstream of history that even such basics as time period and country of origin would have been of little account to the ordinary person. Preoccupation with time is a modern development. Moreover, many nation-states have experienced frequent boundary changes. These difficulties are compounded by the fact that names and dates are stored in the speech centres of the brain, usually the left hemisphere in the temporal lobe, whereas sensory memory recall seems to be a function of the right hemisphere.

Reassuringly, there are ways to establish whether subjects are reporting from genuine altered states of consciousness and not merely spouting the wildest imaginings that enter their conscious minds. EEG (electroencephalograph) studies show that past lives are being tapped when brain levels measure 8.3 cycles per second. Flickering eyelids or REM (rapid eye movement) accompany this state. Some regressionists enlist the aid of a galvanic skin response device which records pore activity when wired to two of the subject's fingers. Once subconscious memory is reached, the device's needle moves away from the horizontal position. "It's like a very unsophisticated lie detector," said hypnotist John Hainlen, who found the biosonometer increased productivity at his Sacramento clinic. "If the conscious mind starts to interfere, we know at once."

Actor Glenn Ford has relived five past lives under hypnosis. At first, he was shaken by the experience of regression. "It conflicts with all my religious beliefs," he said, "I'm a God-fearing man and proud of it, but this has got me mixed up."

The Search Goes On

As the journeying into past lives goes on, the search intensifies for more and better evidence to provide an unshakeable interpretation of the phenomena. Be that as it may, many of the researchers in the field have already convinced themselves that reincarnation underlies and makes possible the reams of testimony from other existences. Dr. Helen Wambach, who in 1975 resolved to determine whether past-life recall is fantasy or reality, said after regressing thousands of volunteers to past lives: "I don't believe in reincarnation—I know it." Pressed to explain her statement, she added: "If you are sitting in a tent on the side of the road and 1,000 people walk past telling you they have crossed a bridge in Pennsylvania, you are convinced of the existence of that bridge in Pennsylvania." On the other hand, Joe Keeton, who has conducted more than 20,000 regressions and claims to have removed several cancerous conditions by hypnotic suggestion, can make no sense of the phenomena. "I'm just as puzzled now as when I started," he said. "I'll keep on prospecting till I die but I doubt whether I shall find the answer." Then he added: "Apples were falling off trees for millions of years before Isaac Newton came along and asked the right question. What we need are questions, not answers."

With the year 2000 just around the corner, past-life therapy largely remains an enigma even as the curious and the afflicted are drawn increasingly to sample the experience and the rewards of being transported to another place and time. In 1995, a new College of Past-Life Regression Studies was established in London under the direction of psychologist Dr. Keith Hearne. Apart from training people in the use of therapeutic past-life and spirit-releasing techniques, the college runs seminars and workshops designed to assist individuals to rediscover lifetime goals planned before birth. In 1992, the Office of Alternative Medicine was opened as a component of America's National Institute of Health (NIH) near Washington, DC. The office includes past-life therapy among its recognized treatments.

Despite the proven benefits of past-life regression, however, there's an ongoing debate about the value of regressive hypnosis for the population at large. *Reincarnation International* editor Roy Stemman—a man who has dedicated his life to gathering and probing evidence for rebirth—is among the cautionary voices. "It does concern me," he wrote in a 1994 editorial, "that if we cannot remember past lives normally then we may be wrong to force open the door to our memories using hypnosis. Surely we have enough phobias and fears in this life without adding to them the guilt of past-life actions?" American past-life therapist Janet Cunningham, however, solidly defends the value of exploring previous existences. "From my point of view it does not serve any of us to learn that we were, perhaps, a nun in France or a monk in Tibet," she declared. "On the other hand, if I understand the effect a past life has on me today, that can benefit me now . . . If we can tap into the energies of who we were it tells us who we are. So, I might bring from one past life a talent that can be expanded in this life, or a relationship issue that I need to work on. It might be a fear and a blockage of my abilities and energies that I need to move through. That is, I believe, the value of the healing that can come through past-life therapy: that I can recognize the different aspects of the energy that I carry today and hopefully move beyond that energy where there have been blockages."

At the May, 1997 annual conference of the Association of Past-Life Research and Therapy (APRT), Dr. Winafred Lucas—author of *Regression Therapy: A Handbook for Therapists*—spoke of past-life therapy's special value in healing abusive relationships. "As we extend our consciousness," she said, "we become able to perceive others in a way that encourages understanding and acceptance."

The overall success rate of past-life therapy is difficult to gauge, although a study by APRT's Dr. Hazel Denning between 1985 and 1992 serves as a pointer. Of 450 patients of eight therapists who could be tracked down after five years, 24 per cent reported they had been relieved of all symptoms; 23 per cent had benefitted from considerable and dramatic improvement; 17 per cent had experienced noticeable improvement; and 36 per cent claimed no appreciable gains. In 1994, Ronald Vander-Maessen of NVRT, the Dutch association of past-life therapy, conducted a research program which investigated the results of regression therapy involving 401 clients of 32 therapists. Six months after therapy, 50 per cent reported their problems had been largely or completely solved, some 30 per cent showed some improvement, while roughly 20 per cent did not improve.

Not recommended for the faint-hearted, past-life excursions may help to ease discomfort, alleviate anxiety,

and enlarge understanding. And while some would say
that to be a tourist of far memory is just another way of
describing the self-examination of the psyche, what *is*
the psyche but the sum total of an individual's experience in action? As Hazel Denning, executive director
emeritus of the Association for Past Life Research and
Therapy, points out: "You are everything you have ever
been—right now."

"I believe that the West has bastardized reincarnation. In
the East, incarnations are for God to know Himself; reincarnation is a vehicle for spiritual evolution. But in the
West there's more emphasis on ego. This is like concen-
trating on the way you dress rather than on the person
beneath the clothes. People are more interested in the
content of the images than in the process of spiritual
evolution."

– Dr. Ronald Wong Jue, Clinical psychologist

6

SO LONG AGO:

THE ROOTS OF BELIEF

"Rebirth is an affirmation that must be counted among
the primordial affirmations of mankind."
   – Carl Jung

"The origin of the philosophy of reincarnation is prehistoric. It antedates the remotest antiquity all over the
world."
   – E. D. Walker

THERE WAS A TIME when all human beings, being
clairvoyant, perceived the process of rebirth as
clearly as they understood physical reality. Having a direct line to the supersensible worlds, people were fully
aware of the cosmic circumstances, including the necessity of repeated earth lives. But somewhere in the lost
reaches of prehistoric antiquity, having arrived at the
crossroads of choice, humans elected to tread the path of
spiritual degeneration—fossilized in legend as the Fall
of Man—and gradually surrendered this preternatural
power of clairvoyance. From then on, knowledge of

reincarnation gave way to faith and to belief. This believing, a direct consequence of the fallen state, came to be known as religion, a yearning and striving for the sublimity that had been left behind.

Ancient myth and fable, tribal memory, lingering belief among adherents of the great religions, and some grotesque archaeological discoveries all testify to ages long forgotten when reincarnation, much more than the intriguing conjecture it is today, was a commonly accepted law of life. Buried remains of Neanderthal society dating from roughly between 200,000 B.C. and 75,000 B.C., indicate the earliest known belief in rebirth. Skeletons have been found pressed into a flexed fetal position, as if in expectation of the next incarnation, with evidence showing that the deceased had been interred with supplies and sacrifices of animals such as bison and wild goats. Corpses were placed in line with the sun's east-west axis, hinting at recognition that the sun itself rises daily from the womb of Earth.

Shamanic belief, which reaches back into the Upper Paleolithic period between 15,000 and 25,000 years ago, held that the essential life force animating humans and animals resides in the skeletal form: it was from their very bones that creatures were reborn. An Aztec myth

---

The colour green, representing the resurgence of vegetation in springtime, symbolized rebirth to the ancient Britons. After ceremonies of initiation into the Mysteries, neophytes were clothed in a robe of sacred green—the garment of spiritual rebirth.

tells of a new human race being fashioned from the ground-up bones of the dead impregnated with blood drawn from the penis of the god Quetzalcoatl. And, as recently as this century, German ethnologist Leonhard Schultze-Jena when studying the Quiché Maya of Guatemala between the world wars, was told that the bones contain the vital essence of human life. Flesh, it was explained, is like the flesh of fruit that soon withers and decays, whereas the skeleton resembles the seed from whose tough shell life is born anew.

Across the world, legends of godlike men who managed to rise, in a state of perfection, to other realms of existence hark back to an era before human beings had cast away from the divine source. W. Y. Evans-Wentz, writing in *The Fairy Faith in Celtic Countries,* maintains it is logical to assume that there have been other human races in past aeons of time who have evolved completely out of the physical world into the divine plane of existence. "Hence the gods are beings which once were men, and the actual race of men will in time become gods," he declares. "Man now stands related to the divine and invisible world in precisely the same manner that the brute stands related to the human race."

A strikingly similar pattern of myth and legend, in which great kings and heroes were considered to be reincarnations of gods or divine beings from other worlds, is to be found in the records of ancient civilizations as diverse as Egypt, Britain, India, Greece and Latin America. To the Gaels and Brythons King Arthur was a reincarnated sun-god who had returned to educate and inspire the human race. In Egypt, the Pharaohs were thought to be divine appointments of Osiris, ruler of the underworld and judge of the dead. Among the Aztecs and Incas in the New World, the belief persisted that their great heroes had moved on to celestial lodgings in the sun which they would occasionally forsake to reclaim a body and renew the instruction of their people. In ancient Greece, Zeus, the mythological ruler of gods and people, was said to be reborn in the great national heroes that succeeded from age to age, Alexander the Great being one of them. The noblest inspiration in the venerable literature of India is attributed to such figures as Rama and Krishna who are both gods and men. "I produce myself among creatures," Krishna, masterful teacher of the Hindus, says in the Bhagavad-Gita, "whenever there is a decline of virtue and an insurrection of vice and injustice in the world; and thus I incarnate from age to age, for the preservation of the just, the destruction of the wicked, and the establishment of righteousness."

Countless echoes from the great tradition of reincarnational belief merge to form a global chorus of yearning for what has been and for what could be again. The richest voices in this wistful choir are those of the great initiates of India who, still in possession of the fading clairvoyance, poured their revelations into scripture. Although Hinduism, the oldest religion in the world, dates back to the fourth millennium B.C., reincarnation was not clearly enunciated in its teachings until the sixth century B.C. No one can vouch for the source of the doctrine, but it was supposedly handed down, not by the Brahmins, but by an older, red race who were kin to the ancient inhabitants of Egypt and Chaldea. The suggestion is made that their teachers were a race of demigods, or divine beings in human form, who might well have had their origins in Atlantis where reincarnation, it is said, was known rather than believed in.

> A well-known proverb among Hindu families is *anta mata so mata*, or a man's next birth is dependent upon the ideas held at his death.

The Wheel of Life

The pervasive Hindu belief in reincarnation holds that all human beings, animals, plants, and minerals are strapped to the wheel of life which repeatedly turns its charges through revolution upon revolution of birth and death. The destiny of human beings, who are thoroughly responsible for their own rise and fall in this voyage of rotation, is dictated by their karma. This means that it is human actions that influence, for good or ill, not only personal fate but also the equilibrium of the universe. Karma has produced the present from the deeds of past lives, and prepares for eternity through the actions of today. The hope of Hindu believers lies in working through their karma so that they may attain eventual deliverance or *moksha* from the dread bondage of the wheel. However, the chances of such release are slim indeed, liberation being won only through immense difficulty. Again and again, desire for the sensuous pleasures of terrestrial life pulls the soul back to successive lives on earth. And being sinful, human beings cannot even be reassured that they will reincarnate next time in human form: severe transgressions can lead to rebirth as an animal just as an animal can succeed in winning a future life as a human. The rough road of consequences is sharply delineated in the *Svetasvatara Upanishad,* 5.11:

> As the body is augmented by food and water, so the individual self, augmented by its aspirations, sense contact, visual impressions and delusion, assumes successive forms in accordance with its actions.

The Lord of Death in the *Katha Upanishad* metes out a sardonic word of warning to those who hoodwink themselves with their own selfishness and seem to think they can avoid the repercussions that must follow:

> Ignorant ones, due to their deep attachment toward wealth and enjoyment, get deluded and blinded to think that this planet alone exists and that there are not other *lokas* [dimensions]; that one need not think about any good actions or preparations for life after death for this Earth alone is everything and there is no other universe. Such foolish ones come under My rod again and again by revolving in the birth-death cycle.

So deep-seated is belief in rebirth among the hundreds of millions of Hindu worshippers today that, according to Nancy Ross in *Three Ways of Asian Wisdom,* "the idea of a succession of lives for each human creature would be no more debatable to the average Hindu than a Westerner's fixed belief that continuity from childhood to adulthood exists in a single life, even though the past may be largely forgotten." Such conviction is shared, moreover, by those who have chosen, or have been chosen by, the other great religion of the East, Buddhism.

The profound Buddhist teachings of reincarnation and karma followed the wisdom of the Upanishads within a century. To Gautama Buddha, who is believed to have lived from 563 to 483 B.C., reincarnation and karma explained the seeming meaninglessness of life and pierced the absurdity of all the apparent inequality in the world. Buddhism differed from Hinduism, however, in denying that there is a soul that persists from one incarnation to the next. The newly born human is the result of the preceding entity only so far as merging waves or candle flames bear relation to one another. For this reason, Buddhists prefer the term "rebirth" to "reincarnation," the Pali word for rebirth being *punabbhava*, which literally means "an existence again." Buddhists do maintain, nevertheless, that an individual's fundamental thought at death becomes the very thought that imbues the nucleus of the new existence.

In *The Tibetan Book of Living and Dying*, Sogyal Rinpoche tells how Buddhist teaching declares that if people do not assume the fullest possible responsibility for themselves in this life, suffering will be prolonged not only for a few lives but for thousands of lives. "It is this sobering knowledge," he argues, "that makes Buddhists consider that future lives are more important even than this one, because there are many more that await us in the future. This long-term vision governs how they live. They know if we were to sacrifice the whole of eternity for this life, it would be like spending our entire savings on one drink, madly ignoring the consequences."

The consequences are plain for all to see. "Is karma really so hard to see in operation?" asks Sogyal Rinpoche rhetorically. "Don't we only have to look back at our own lives to see clearly the consequences of some of our actions? When we upset or hurt someone, didn't it rebound on us? Were we not left with a bitter and dark memory, and the shadows of self-disgust? That memory and those shadows are karma. Our habits and our fears too are also due to karma, the result of actions, words, or thoughts we have done in the past. If we examine our actions, and become really mindful of them, we will see that there is a pattern that repeats itself in our actions. *Whenever we act negatively, it leads to pain and suffering; whenever we act positively, it eventually results in happiness.*" As Gautama Buddha is quoted as saying: "If you want to know the past, look at your present life. If you want to know the future, look at your present."

Doctrinal idiosyncracies aside, the Hindus and Buddhists have similar conceptions of the painfully slow journey of purification from body to body. Craving and ignorance are the great obstacles to enlightenment and human beings, loath to change their ways, revolve incessantly on the wheel of rebirth, bound fast by the chains of karma. In the words of a Buddhist text:

To be born here and to die here
to die here and to be born elsewhere,
to be born there and to die there
to die there and to be born elsewhere—
that is the round of existence.
  (Milinda's Questions, 77)

Gautama Buddha, who is said to have lived 550 previous lives over more than 25,000 years, stressed that attachment to earthly existence confined human beings to the treadmill of rebirth. Teaching that to give up clinging desire is to surrender the need to return, he told his disciples:

For that which clingeth to another thing there is a fall; but unto that which clingeth not no fall can come. Where no fall cometh, there is rest, and where rest is, there is no keen desire. Where keen desire is not, naught cometh or goeth; and where naught cometh or goeth there is no death, no birth. Where there is

There are many references to reincarnation in the *Diamond Sutra*—the oldest printed book known today. Printed by Wang Chieh in A.D. 868, the *Diamond Sutra* was discovered in 1907 by Sir Auriel Stein in the Cave of the Thousand Buddhas at Tunhuang, China, and is now preserved in the British Museum. The book takes the form of a dialogue between Buddha and his disciple Subhuti. "I recall," says the Buddha, "that during my five hundred previous lives . . ."

neither death nor birth, there neither is this world
nor that, nor in between—it is the ending of sorrow.

Esoteric Teachings

Long before the birth of Buddha, and even antedating
its adoption by the Hindus, reincarnation was a central
theme of the Eleusinian Mysteries which, named after the
small town of Eleusis lying fourteen miles west of Athens,
are traditionally thought to have originated as long ago as
the fifteenth century B.C., before the Greeks had settled
their native land. The mystery rites were strictly secret,
but it is thought that by participating in a rebirth ritual,
which sounds like an artificially induced precursor of
today's much reported out-of-body experiences, neophytes were given glimpses of life after death and the onward momentum of the soul. At her loom, the goddess
Persephone was said to weave new bodies for old souls.
And, on Earth, some corpses were interred with special
instructions reminding the souls they carried to ask for
the water of remembrance that flowed from a spring in
Hades. This would enable them to recall, in their next
incarnation, details of the life they had left behind.

Reincarnation, known by the Greeks as metempsychosis, crops up again in the Orphic Mysteries of the
seventh century B.C., with an Orphic text referring, in
classical Indian fashion, to "the sorrowful weary wheel."
The doctrine was antiquated indeed by the time of
Pythagoras and Plato, though its age was anybody's
guess. The Greek historian Herodotus, who lived in the

fifth century B.C., pointed to the Egyptians as the first reincarnationists, while the Egyptians themselves acknowledged that the teaching had come out of the East in the unfathomable long ago. Their writings tell how the god Osiris, who personified esoteric knowledge, was driven to Egypt from India in the form of a spotted bull.

Whether the doctrine was likewise driven into Western Europe where the Druids, Celts, and Gauls wove colourful rebirth tales into their fabric of mythology is beyond documentation. Suffice to say that there's a strong affinity between the Eastern round of existence and the circles of becoming described in the *Barddas* of the Welsh Druids. According to the *Barddas*, there are three life circles of which the intermediate, *Cylch Abred*, is the circle of rebirth. The soul dwells successively in each one, materializing in all possible forms of matter and spirit before entering a state of perfection and bliss comparable to the Indian *nirvana* which awaits those who finally manage to wrest themselves from the wheel of life. The ancient Europeans, it is said, were so confident of rebirth that they wept in commiseration at the birth of a child and greeted death with rejoicing. The Druids, in an even stronger statement of conviction, accepted that if borrowed money could not be repaid in this life, the debt could be made good in the next incarnation!

Orthodox Islamic, Jewish, and Christian belief all deny reincarnation, yet each of these great schools of religious thought have accommodated streams of reincarnational teaching. Transmigration or *tanasukh* is viewed as inconsistent with the teachings of the prophet Mohammed, but the Koran says, quite explicitly:

And Allah hath caused you to spring forth
from the earth like a plant;
Hereafter will He turn you back into it
again, and will bring you forth anew—
   (Sura 71:17-18)

The wellspring of Judaism's esoteric mysticism is the Kabala and that is where reincarnation or *gilgul,* the Hebrew for "circuit" or "rotation," is to be found. Everything follows from the creation of a limited number of souls which gradually achieve purification and reunion with other purified souls. *The Zohar,* a Kabalistic classic believed to date back to the first century A.D., states:

> The souls must re-enter the absolute whence they have emerged. But to accomplish this end they must develop all the perfections, the germ of which is planted in them; and if they have not fulfilled this condition during one life, they must commence another, a third, and so forth, until they have acquired the condition which fits them for reunion with God.

Reincarnational teaching in the Bible is largely "taken for granted, cropping out here and there as a fundamental rock," to quote from E. D. Walker's classic nineteenth-century work *Reincarnation.* Several Biblical passages only make sense if they are interpreted in the context of repeated Earth lives. The following New Testament extract is one of several allusions to the same kind of hard-fought struggle for the godhead as that envisaged by the Hindus and Buddhists:

Him that overcometh will I make a pillar in the
temple of my God, and he shall go no more out.
  (Revelation 3:12)

Yet reincarnation spelled nothing but strife for the
early church. Factions sprang up siding for or against
the doctrine and, tragically, Christianity was turned into
the battleground of a vicious, protracted dispute. The
next chapter will examine the circumstances surrounding the withdrawal of Christian belief in reincarnation,
a belief held strenuously by several early church fathers
as well as the Gnostics (from the Greek *gnose*, meaning
"knowledge") who prided themselves on seeking the
inner, mystical meaning of the Christian message.

The idea of rebirth inspired long-gone hunting rituals. The
Indians of the Plains would symbolically place the heads
of slaughtered bison towards the renewal of the rising
sun, while in ancient Finland, the local shaman carried a
slain bear's remains to a hilltop where they were placed
in the crown of an old pine tree, facing east.

Tribal Memory

As religious belief in reincarnation was passed down
from generation to generation in the old civilized world,
tribal obsession with the very same idea, in differing
forms, was rife across vast tracts of the inhabited territory that remained. Virtually all the tribal groups in

North and South America, Indonesia, Australia, Asia, and Africa lived with the conviction of immortality which, to most of them, implied reincarnation. "However it has been arrived at," wrote Sir James George Frazer in *The Belief in Immortality* (1913), "this doctrine of the transmigration or reincarnation of the soul is found among many tribes of savages; and from what we know on the subject we seem to be justified in conjecturing that at certain stages of mental and social evolution the belief in metempsychosis has been far commoner and has exercised a far deeper influence on the life and institutions of primitive man than the actual evidence before us at present allows us positively to affirm." Over the past century, tribal customs and traditions have been flouted as a result of the incursions of modern materialism, and often all that remain are stories and superstitions—the fading residue of a devout and binding creed.

One of the most commonly shared beliefs was that ancestors return to their families in succeeding incarnations. Among the Yoruba tribe of West Africa, a child born shortly after the death of a grandparent is still likely to be called *Babatunde*, meaning "Father has returned," or *Yetunde*, "Mother has returned." The Llo tribe of southeast Africa aim to find out exactly who is being reincarnated by repeating names of ancestors as soon as a newborn baby is held to its mother's breast. The name being uttered at the instant the baby begins to suck is considered to be the relative who has returned. In a variation on this theme, bones held by members of the Yukagir of Siberia would suddenly decrease in weight when the correct ancestral name was mentioned, although today the deciding factor is the baby's first smile.

A custom widespread among North American tribes was to give a pregnant woman charms made of the hair of the dead relative whose rebirth was hoped for. In the Marquesas, a South Pacific archipelago where a grandfather's soul was thought to be transmitted into the body of his grandchildren, a wife who was having difficulty conceiving reinforced her chances of becoming a mother by placing herself under her grandfather's corpse. Among the Tlingit of Alaska there was even further communion with the dead. At the burial of a loved one, a pregnant woman of the tribe would hold one of the corpse's hands against her breast while wishing with all her might that her unborn child would inherit its spirit. After circling the grave eight times, she scraped a line leading about seven feet from the graveside. She then squatted to urinate at the end of this line and beseeched the spirit to be reborn through her.

Sometimes, the living made careful preparations for their own rebirth. It was customary for an elderly Inuit (Eskimo), sensing the beginning of the end, to approach a young couple in the neighbourhood and request that he be reborn into their family. If he was a likable, respectable old gentleman, the husband and wife would probably tell him they would be delighted to have him for their first child. The elder, his destiny assured, would then await his death with patience and contentment.

In Northern and Central Australia the souls of the dead who were waiting to be reborn were said to haunt certain natural features of the parched landscape—a lone withered tree, say, or a pool of water at the foot of a ravine. The Aborigines, believing that every person is reincarnated, felt that these spirits were just waiting for a woman to pass by so that they could enter her womb. Knowing the spirits' preference for nubile maidens, young women who had no choice but to pass these landmarks but didn't want to become pregnant would make themselves look like old hags and hobble past, whining in a thin, cracked monotone: "Don't come to me. I am an old woman."

The mythical Rainbow Serpent is the Aborigines' link with the sky-world and symbolic maker of the road along which pre-existent spirits pass to the wombs of the mothers who will bring them back into the world. Often, the Serpent's huge body is pictured as a great conveyor of souls bound for rebirth. Some native Australians pin their hopes on reincarnating in the privileged white race. A black convict, about to be executed in Melbourne in the second half of the last century, went to his death full of such anticipation. "Very good!" he exclaimed. "Me jump up Whitefellow!"

Before immigration made white men a common sight in Australia, the Aborigines were convinced that pale-skinned visitors were reincarnations of their people. Not having any idea of leaving their own lands, they couldn't imagine others doing so and consequently believed that whites, in choosing particular locations, must have formed an attachment for these sites as dark-skinned tribesmen in a former existence. The explorer Sir George Grey told in his *Journals of Two Expeditions of Discovery in North-West and Western Australia* (1841) how he was "wholly unprepared" for the scene that followed the approach of an aboriginal processional led by two women whose cheeks streamed with tears:

The eldest of these came up to me, and looking for a moment at me, said: "*Gwa, gwa, bundo bal*"—"Yes, yes, in truth it is him"; and then throwing her arms round me, cried bitterly, her head resting on my breast; and although I was totally ignorant of what their meaning was, from mere motives of compassion, I offered no resistance to her caresses, however disagreeable they might be, for she was old, ugly, and filthily dirty; the other younger one knelt at my feet, also crying. At last the old lady, emboldened by my submission, deliberately kissed me on each cheek, just in the manner a Frenchwoman would have done; she then cried a little more, and at length relieving me, assured me that I was the ghost of her son, who had some time before been killed by a spear-wound in his breast. The younger female was my sister; but she, whether from motives of delicacy, or from any imagined backwardness on my

When Tibetans saw the likeness of Queen Victoria on English coins they were convinced she was the reincarnation of the "Green Dölma," a Tibetan goddess. Furthermore, they believed that the Green Dölma—who is also thought to have incarnated as the Nepalese-born wife of the first Buddhist king of Tibet—had returned to rule the world in the person of the stately monarch. "Owing to this belief," wrote W. Y. Evans-Wentz, "the British representatives of the Queen then met with an unusually friendly reception in their negotiations with Lhasa, although probably unaware of the origin of the friendship."

part, did not think proper to kiss me. My new mother expressed almost as much delight at my return to my family as my real mother would have done, had I been unexpectedly restored to her.

Rites and Initiations

Scalping and cannibalism, two of the most brutal expressions of tribal life, may well have been attempts to prevent the reincarnation of the enemy. Hair had great significance to North American Indians and a dead man without his hair would be at a considerable disadvantage in the spirit world. The primal idea behind cannibalism could have been the absorption of the victim's soul matter, the aggressor taking on the new strength of another soul even as he blocks his adversary's chances of rebirth. The reasons why Peking man of half a million years ago broke open the bases of skulls, presumably to eat the brains, are still being debated. Since the discoveries were made at Choukoutien, a cave site in the suburbs of Peking, archaeologists haven't been able to agree on the nature of this custom. Were these early people trying to assimilate the souls of their ancestors? Or were they performing some benevolent rite aimed at preventing rebirth?

The death of small children—common enough in the Third World—was usually fraught with meaning. Stillborn babies, for example, were thought by the African Ibo tribe to be the outcome of one who decides, on entering a new life, not to resume the struggle on the same old unhappy plane. In many a primitive society, particularly in Northern India and Central Africa, parents would bury a dead child under the threshold of the family home in the hope that its returning soul would be reborn to them. For the same reason, the Hopi of Arizona made a road from the grave of a child to its old home and the Canadian Huron Indians buried their babies alongside a thoroughfare so that they would be reincarnated in women who passed by.

But there were deeper, darker interpretations applied to infant mortality—especially if a family was afflicted by the death of one child after another. Either to induce the soul to remain longer at its next incarnation or to discourage it from making another attempt at rebirth, the bodies of children who died young were subject to mutilation in parts of Africa, America, and India. Toes, legs, and fingers were broken; faces, noses, and ears cut; and ears and fingers amputated. Sometimes, the mother would swallow a piece of lopped-off ear in the hope of drawing the baby's spirit back to her body. And in the dissimilar nations of Estonia and Nigeria, families suffering a string of stillbirths shared the custom of burying the most recent body face downwards in the hope that the errant soul would not see the way to be born again.

The Reverend John Martin, a Wesleyan missionary in West Africa from 1843 to 1848, witnessed a rowdy crowd carrying a very dirty-looking child about the streets of Accra in a basket. He wrote in his diary some time in 1845:

> On enquiry I learned that the mother had lost two or three children previously, who had died when about the age of this. When such is the case they believe that

the same soul which was in the first child returns, and enters the next, and that the child, of its own will through mere spite, dies. Hence these steps are taken. The child while alive is besmutted with charcoal, put into a basket, and carried round the town, when the people take care to abuse it for its wickedness, and to threaten it, should it die. Every ill-usage that can be offered, short of murder, is shown it. Should it afterwards die, its head is sometimes crushed with stones and the body, refused a burial, is thrown either into the sea, or in the bush. These things are done to prevent its coming again in another child.

Death and rebirth pervade the ancient rites of initiation that reach back through the centuries in many parts of the world. Initiatory death was an indispensable preliminary to the awakening of spiritual life. In jungle and forest, initiatory cabins were built to signify personal and cosmological rebirth, the cabin representing "the maw of the devouring monster in which the neophyte is eaten and digested. . . [and] also a nourishing womb, in which he is engendered anew," writes Mircea Eliade in *Rites and Symbols of Initiation.* The initiatory hut, preserved in popular tales from Europe to New Guinea where a huge raffia dummy of a monster's belly called *Kaiemunu* is still constructed, reveals a periodic, primitive need to unify, if only briefly, human experience with cosmic grandeur.

But just how primitive is primitive? Perhaps the time-twisted legacy of tribal memory bears in its rites and rituals the seed of higher knowledge once known and now forgotten. And perhaps we human beings, bound to the pendulum of evolution as surely as we are to the wheel of life, are even now on our way back to the garden. Whether or not we get there is up to us, as Pico della Mirandola observed at the close of the fifteenth century in his *Oration on the Dignity of Man*. He put these words into the mouth of the Creator:

> We have made you a creature neither of heaven nor of earth, neither mortal nor immortal, in order that you may, as the free and proud shaper of your own being, fashion yourself in the form you may prefer. It will be in your power to descend to the lower, brutish forms of life; you will be able, through your own decision, to rise again to the superior orders whose life is divine.

The most celebrated among eight so-called Chinese saints of the popular Taoist religion is "Mr. Li with the iron crutch." According to legend, he was an exponent of the magic arts and would often send his ego-soul to confer with spirits in distant places. On one occasion, he sent his ego-soul away for a week and asked his disciple to guard his lifeless body until its return. The disciple, however, soon wearied of the task and the body was buried by puzzled relatives. So it was that the returning soul of Mr. Li, confounded at not being able to find its body, started looking around for a suitable alternative. But the only body available at such short notice was that of a beggar with a lame leg. And that's how Mr. Li reincarnated—as a beggar obliged to use an iron crutch.

7

THE LOST CHORD
OF CHRISTIANITY

"Reincarnation is assumed in the Bible teaching . . ."
   – *Dictionary Of All Scriptures And Myths*

"Put not off from day to day and from cycle to cycle, in
the belief that ye will succeed in obtaining the mysteries
when ye return to the world in another cycle."

   – Jesus Christ (From the Gnostic scripture, *Pistis Sophia*)

E VERYONE KNOWS the annals of religious history
are stained with blood and corruption. Few appreciate, however, that the ruthless expulsion of reincarnation from Christian thought and theology has left some
of the deepest and most shameful stains of all. Time has
since worked its healing of forgetfulness and today most
Christians are unaware that reincarnation was ever considered seriously by the church. But the fact remains
that before Christianity became a vehicle for the imperial ambitions of Roman emperors, rebirth was widely
accepted among the persecuted faithful.

Taught by a number of early church fathers and trea-
sured by the Christian Gnostics, a movement in the
apostolic tradition dedicated to preserving and promul-
gating the esoteric teachings of Jesus Christ, reincarnation was seen to be consistent with Old and New
Testament scripture and complementary to the idea
of personal salvation through Jesus Christ. From the
earliest days of primitive Christianity, repeated earthly
existences were a fact of life to many supplicants so long
as they soldiered on in the quest for enlightenment.
Yet they also believed that the monotonous cycle of
birth and death could be transcended through the
inspiration of Jesus Christ whose promptings towards
spiritual perfection were able to exalt the individual to
reconciliation with God and relief from the burden of
the body.

The principal architect of this theological edifice was
Origen, called "the prince of Christian learning in the
third century" by St. Gregory of Nyssa, and hailed by
the *Encyclopaedia Britannica* as "the most prominent of
the church fathers with the possible exception of Augustine." While devoted to scriptural authority, Origen was
also very much inclined towards the Platonic philosophy that had prevailed in Alexandria, the city of his
birth, for more than four hundred years. He emphatically agreed with Plato that the divine eternal soul is cast
into the corruptible body in order to prove itself superior to the inclinations of the flesh. Thus he wrote in a
letter published in *A Select Library of the Nicene and Post-
Nicene Fathers of the Christian Church:*

If it can be shown that an incorporeal and reasonable being has life in itself independently of the body and that it is worse off in the body than out of it; then beyond a doubt bodies are only of secondary importance and arise from time to time to meet the varying conditions of reasonable creatures. Those who require bodies are clothed with them, and contrariwise, when fallen souls have lifted themselves up to better things their bodies are once more annihilated. They are thus ever vanishing and ever reappearing.

In *De Principiis*, his major work and the first systematic theology of Christianity, Origen declared:

Every soul . . . comes into this world strengthened by the victories or weakened by the defeats of its previous life. Its place in this world as a vessel appointed to honour or dishonour, is determined by its previous merits or demerits. Its work in this world determines its place in the world which is to follow this.

For Origen, whose faith brought him torture and imprisonment at the hands of the Romans in the last years of his life, and for other church fathers such as Justin Martyr, founder of the first Christian school in Rome, the scriptures were to be interpreted in the most expansive, allegorical way. The visionary breadth of Origen's cosmic theology was not always appreciated by fundamentalists who cherished a narrow, literal reading of the scriptures. But the most telling opposition to the doctrine of reincarnation in Christian theology only developed once the church had evolved, in the fourth century, from harried bands of secret worshippers to an institution that could be exploited for political advancement and control.

> Glanvil, the chaplain to King Charles II of England, petitioned for Christian adoption of reincarnation when he wrote that pre-existence was "the constant opinion of the Jews and therefore accepted by Christ and his apostles" (*Lux Orientalis*, 1662). Furthermore, he declared: "The soul came prejudiced into this body with some implicit notions that it learned in another."

The Abuse of Christianity

The seeds of reincarnation's banishment were sown when Constantine the Great, the first Roman emperor to become a Christian, perceived his faith as the reason for his military supremacy. Before triumphing over the mightier forces of Maxentius at the Battle of Milvian Bridge in 312, he saw a cross of light superimposed on the sun, a vision that led him to believe he was Christianity's chosen defender. As an expression of gratitude for this success, religious freedom was granted to all for the first time. And just as bemused Christians were beginning to accept that they were at last being tolerated by the authorities, Christianity was established as the state religion! Within twenty years, Christianity had progressed from an illegal cult, whose members were hounded, abused, and exterminated, to the official religion of the empire. Yet there was a high price to be paid for the gifts and favours Constantine lavished on the church: the ecclesiastical rock was to be sculpted strictly according to the emperor's political designs. Ethics, faith, and devotion became subordinate to the allure of personal interest and political power. Bishops were appointed not for their spiritual leadership but for what they could do to further Constantine's aim of unifying the empire. For the first time in history, the church began to attract nominal Christians, those who attended for social, economic, or political reasons rather than for the pursuit of righteousness.

Eager to safeguard what he understood to be the authentic Christian message, Constantine kept up the political pressure by calling the Council of Nicea in 325 to determine and define Christian orthodoxy. From then on, the powerful union of church and state—always dominated by the emperor's wishes—decreed what was acceptable and what was heretical. Two lives were all that orthodoxy allowed—one life in the natural body and one hereafter in the form of resurrection. Bishops who disagreed with the council's findings, and there were some notable renegades, were quickly deposed. Meanwhile, those devout Christians who were disenchanted with the secularization of the church initiated their own monastic movement. Tending to settle in the deserts not so much to get away from the world as to escape the worldly church, they set themselves the task of trying to preserve the Christian prototype, a religion as pure and simple as the Saviour's life.

This cleaving of the early church was accentuated in 380 when the establishment acted to outlaw and chastise freethinking Christians. The Edict of Thessalonica, decreed by Emperor Theodosius without consultation with the ecclesiastical authorities, vowed that "all peoples who fall beneath the sway of our imperial clemency should profess the faith which we believe to have been communicated by the Apostle Peter to the Romans and maintained in its traditional form to the present day." The edict went further still:

> And we require that those who follow this rule of faith should embrace the name of Catholic Christian adjudging all others madmen and ordering them to be designated as heretics, condemned as such in the first instance to suffer divine punishment and therewith the vengeance of that power which we, by celestial authority, have assumed.

In other words, heresy was no longer merely sinful; it was a crime, punishable by death. (Ironically, the word "heretic" means, at root, nothing more pernicious than one who is "able to choose.") In 385, the first of a long line of reincarnationist martyrs fell to the barbarism of the church-state alliance when seven Spanish adherents of the Priscillian sect were found guilty by a Christian magistrate of erroneous belief. Yet for another 150 years or more, there was no official edict condemning the doctrine of reincarnation across the empire. These desert Christians, many of them Gnostics or, at least, subscribers to Origen's interpretation of the scriptures, led their lives with little interference from the prime movers of church policy. In the sixth century, however, increasing hostility towards Origen's teaching culminated in the Emperor Justinian being asked to adjudicate in a dispute between Origenist and anti-Origenist factions in Palestine. Justinian gave his answer by convening a synod at Constantinople in 543 which condemned the teachings of Origen. (There must have been little doubt as to the outcome because Justinian had, in 529, closed the University of Athens, the last stronghold of Neoplatonism and, as such, a centre of reincarnational study.) The emperor later issued fifteen "anathemas"—formal ecclesiastical curses involving excommunication—against Origen, four of which were aimed directly at pre-existence and, by implication, reincarnation. The first read:

> If anyone assert the fabulous pre-existence of souls, and shall assert the monstrous restoration which follows from it: let him be anathema.

It is thought that Justinian submitted these official curses to a preliminary session of the unconstitutional Second Council of Constantinople in 553. Pope Vigilius, who had been Justinian's prisoner for eight years, refused to participate in the deliberations and it was left to the attending bishops (representing, overwhelmingly, the Eastern church) to sanction the autocratic emperor's wishes. Although there is no evidence that the curses against reincarnation were even discussed at the full ecumenical gathering, historians have for centuries mistakenly assumed that the Second Council proceeded to adopt them. In a sense, however, the question of official ratification is irrelevant. What matters is that ever since the ecumenical council of 553, the church has shunned the doctrine of rebirth.

Just why belief in reincarnation incurred the wrath of institutional authority is open to interpretation. But it seems likely that reincarnationists caused greatest offence by their self-reliance, which had the effect of minimizing the sway of their totalitarian masters. Believers in reincarnation were neither to be induced by promises of heavenly bliss nor intimidated by threats of hellfire; they didn't need priests and ritual devices such as the confessional to guide them along the straight and narrow path to God. In toiling for their own salvation, they looked upon the church's cultivated dependence of the masses as unnecessary. And this left the church fiercely intolerant of professing Christians whose subservience could not be guaranteed. Writes Hans Holzer in *Patterns of Destiny*: "The church needed the whip of Judgment Day to keep the faithful in line. It was therefore a matter of survival for the church not to allow belief in reincarnation to take hold among her followers."

So it was that any departure from the official line was brutally punished by the guardians of orthodoxy. And yet, despite the menace of the most severe reprisals, including mass torture and execution, Christian sects clinging to their "heretical" beliefs proved themselves irrepressible. These sects were grouped together under the umbrella of Catharism (the religion of catharsis or purification), a term originally applied by St. Augustine to the reincarnationist Manicheans of Mesopotamia. The Cathars, who always believed themselves to be the true Christians, included the Paulicians of Thrace, the Bogomils of Bulgaria, the Patarenes of the Balkans, and the Albigensians of southern France, while other groups flourished in northern Italy and Germany. Despite the fearsome vengeance of the Inquisition, which spared no effort to root out the rebels, Catharism "spread so rapidly and resisted so stubbornly the sternest efforts of suppression that at one time it may be fairly said to have threatened the permanent existence of Christianity itself," comments Henry Lea in his *History of the Inquisition of the Middle Ages.* Linked with the Cathars were the Knights Templars, a Christian military order founded to protect pilgrims visiting the Holy Land, and the troubadours, traveling minstrels who wandered around Europe between the eleventh and thirteenth centuries popularizing the doctrine of reincarnation in their ballads. Simple love songs acted as lyrical disguises for tales of how well-spent lives were rewarded by rebirth in bodies suitable for further spiritual development.

As the church's crusade of terror and slaughter was pursued to its bloody finale, the next life was increasingly all that was left to sing about. In 1244, the Albigensians were massacred to the last man, woman, and child at their fortress of Montségur in the Pyrenees. The church councils of Lyons in 1274 and Florence in 1439 drove home Justinian's anathemas by affirming that souls go immediately to heaven, purgatory, or hell. So thorough was the destruction of heretical works that most of what remains of Origen's disputed discourses is only available because it was quoted in the arguments of his opponents! And much of that was first "smoothed" by his Latin translator, Rufinus, who admitted that he didn't want to offend the church authorities. By the sixteenth century, reincarnational thinking had been routed from the public consciousness and the responsibility for smuggling the belief forward to the modern age was left to mystical groups such as the Alchemists and the Rosicrucians.

In her 1997 book *Reincarnation: The Missing Link in Christianity*, Elizabeth Clare Prophet pares away layers of errant dogma, scriptural camouflage, and wilful misconception to expose the theological divide separating reincarnation teaching from orthodox Christianity. "During the first few centuries of Christian thought, the Church Fathers excavated a great chasm between the soul and God," she writes. "As explained by Catholic theologian Claude Tresmontant, the Church concluded that 'the human soul is not . . . by nature from the divine substance. . . . It is called to share the life of God, but by grace.' For the Catholics, this grace can be accessed only through the Church. The Catholic view is that the soul cannot return to God since it has never been a part of God. 'We are not parts of the divine substance, but creatures of God,' writes Tresmontant."

Prophet explains that when the Church Fathers defined the soul as separate from God, it became impossible for them to accept the reincarnationist idea that the soul can unite with God. Their definition also threw up a roadblock for Christian mystics since mysticism is the search for either direct contact with God or union with God. These mystics, along with reincarnationists of other traditions, were linked in their belief that infinite opportunity equals infinite possibility. "If we have the time and space to become God," writes Prophet, "we also have the ability to do so. Reincarnation gives us that time and space."

"Say, Lord, to me . . . say, did my infancy succeed another age of mine that died before it? Was it that which I spent within my mother's womb? . . . And what before that life again, O God my joy, was I anywhere or in any body? For this I have none to tell me, neither father nor mother, nor experience of others, nor mine own memory."

– Saint Augustine

Biblical Testimony

Confirmation that reincarnation is indeed "the lost chord of Christianity" (a phrase attributed to William Q. Judge, a founder of the Theosophical Movement which has roots in Gnostic philosophy) can be found in the pages of the Bible. While the Old and New Testaments hardly trumpet the belief from the rooftops, there are numerous references to rebirth in both books. James M. Pryse asserts in *Reincarnation in the New Testament* (1900) that to dispute that the doctrine is distinctly taught in the New Testament "is to deny that the authors of that collection of writings meant what they said in unmistakable language."

Several of the most explicit statements are made by Jesus Christ who affirmed his own pre-existence with the words "Before Abraham was, I am." (John 8:58) In the presence of a man who was born blind, Jesus was asked by his disciples: "Master, who did sin, this man or his parents, that he was born blind?" Jesus answered: "Neither hath this man sinned nor his parents: but that the works of God should be made manifest in him." (John 9:1–3) Although the disciples were clearly attributing prenatal existence to the blind man, Christ does nothing to correct or dispel this presupposition as he goes on to prepare a salve that restores the man's sight. By refusing to challenge the disciples' thinking, Jesus acknowledges the fact of pre-existence with its undeniable implication of reincarnation.

In the Gospel according to Matthew, chapter eleven, Jesus identifies John the Baptist as being Elijah reborn. Referring to the Old Testament prophecy that Elijah would appear before the coming of the Messiah, Jesus said: "This is he of whom it is written. . . . For all the prophets and the law prophesied until John. And if ye will receive it, this is Elias, which was for to come. He that hath ears let him hear." Further on in the gospel account, Jesus underlines this assertion by declaring that "Elias has come already." The disciples, Matthew points out, "understood that he had spoken of John the Baptist." Both men, being big, boisterous, and frenetically inspired, not only looked and dressed alike but also possessed the same character traits. Certainly, anything less than the absolute fusing of Elijah's identity with John the Baptist undermines Christ's claims to be the Messiah. The poet Robert Graves commented in a *Playboy* article in December, 1967: "No honest theologian can therefore deny that his acceptance of Jesus as Christ logically binds every Christian to a belief in reincarnation—in Elijah's case, at least."

St. Paul's statement in his Epistle to the Galatians, ". . . whatsoever a man soweth, that shall he also reap" (Galatians 6:7) hints strongly at rebirth because one life is plainly insufficient for a perfect balancing of accounts. Likewise, verse ten in chapter thirteen of Revelation indicates karmic reprisal with all the portentousness of Hindu and Buddhist scripture: "He that leadeth into captivity shall go into captivity: he that killeth with the sword must be killed with the sword." Given that many soldiers die quietly in their beds, these words suggest that retribution must be experienced in a future life.

The rebirth of Jacob and Esau is mentioned several times in both the Old and New Testaments. Before the children were born, "neither having done any good or evil," God declares in Romans 9:13: "As it is written, Jacob have I loved but Esau have I hated."

To complete this Biblical selection is a prayer of Moses, evocative of cosmic timelessness as well as the recurring cycles of human beings and nature:

> Thou turnest man to destruction; and sayest, Return, ye children of men. For a thousand years in thy sight are but as yesterday when it is past, and as

a watch in the night. Thou carriest them away as
with a flood; they are as a sleep: in the morning they
are like grass which groweth up.

(Psalm 90:3–5)

If the Bible does little more than assume reincarnation
this is because its contributors "might just as well give information regarding the digestive process, sleep, or any
other natural vital function," according to G. A. Gaskell's
Dictionary of All Scriptures and Myths. More straightforward in its approach is the Gnostic gospel *Pistis Sophia*
(meaning "knowledge-wisdom" and claiming to be the
secret teachings of Jesus to Mary Magdalene) which
quotes Jesus as saying that "souls are poured from one
into another of different kinds of bodies of the world."

The Aquarian Gospel of Jesus The Christ, having been
transcribed from the Akashic Records during the last
century by Levi, a pastor and medical doctor of Belle-
ville, Ohio, cannot be classed as having the same scriptural authority as gospels with historical pedigrees.
Nevertheless, the authenticity conveyed by the pages of
this psychically transmitted work extends to a reincarnational passage in which Jesus, after listening to a group
of youthful singers and musicians in Lahore, makes the
following comment:

These people are not young. A thousand years
would not suffice to give them such divine expres-
siveness, and such purity of voice and touch.

Ten thousand years ago these people mastered
harmony.

In days of old they trod the busy thoroughfares
of life, and caught the melody of birds, and played
on harps of perfect form. And they have come again
to learn still other lessons. . . .
(Chapter 37:13-15)

Today's leadership of the Protestant and Roman
Catholic churches, although by no means eager to consider reincarnational belief for Christian adoption,
must be well aware of the growing empathy it generates
in ecclesiastical circles. Perhaps this warming trend
harks back to the conversion of the Reverend William
Alger in the second half of the last century. An energetic
Unitarian minister who devoted half his lifetime to a
work on immortality called *A Critical History of the
Doctrine of a Future Life*, Alger dismissed reincarnation
as a plausible delusion in the book's first edition, published in 1860. But after further concentrated study
he was so overpowered by the "peerless sublimity" of
the doctrine that he gave rebirth his heartiest endorse-
ment in the final edition, published in 1878. More
recently, a number of leading clerics have spoken out in
favour of reincarnation. In a 1957 lecture titled *The Case
for Reincarnation*, Dr. Leslie Weatherhead, a former
president of the Methodist Conference of Great Britain,
declared:

The intelligent Christian asks not only that life
should be just, but that it shall make sense. Does
the idea of reincarnation help here? . . . If I fail to
pass those examinations in life which can only be

taken while I dwell in a physical body, shall I not
have to come back and take them again?

A 1979 survey by the University of Surrey sociology
department on attitudes among Britain's Roman
Catholics reported that an astonishing 27 per cent of
Catholics believe in rebirth. An indication of the seriousness with which the establishment viewed this resurgence of the old heresy was the subsequent publication
by the London-based Catholic Truth Society of a pam-
phlet titled simply *Reincarnation* by Father Joseph Crehan. Crehan states tersely: "Our faith has no room for
theories of reincarnation." Nor, it must be said, has the
faith of fundamentalist Christians who, according to a
September, 1982, editorial in the American magazine
Reincarnation Report, are "using the same age-old ma-
nipulative fear-guilt superstition formula to control the
masses and perpetuate their own power." Yet many
Christians are not being hoodwinked by these traditional scare tactics. According to a 1990 Gallup Poll, the
percentage of Christians in America who believe in reincarnation is about the same as the percentage of believers
in the general population. In 1980, 21 per cent of Protes-
tants and 25 per cent of Catholics held the belief—an
estimated 28 million Christian reincarnationists!

The battlements of the old guard will always be vigorously defended. But there's no denying the undercur-
rent of partiality for reincarnation that will, unless
confronted sympathetically, create quite a disruption in
the halls of conformity. California theology professor
Dr. Pascal Kaplan—who in 1972 was refused permission

to write his Harvard doctoral dissertation on rebirth because, in the words of his rejecter, "no-one connected with theology in the West since the third century has taken reincarnation seriously"—is fascinated by the recent surge of reincarnational interest. He points out that there's a growing network of priests, nuns, and ministers who, in accepting reincarnation, believe that an understanding of rebirth "provides a framework for a deeper, truer understanding of their religion and of the essence of Christian spirituality." According to Kaplan, many advocates play "very significant" roles within the church hierarchy.

It may be just a matter of time before one of these individuals argues his or her position too loudly to be ignored by the establishment church, thus precipitating the public airing this bottled-up issue has long demanded. Meanwhile, the lost chord awaits its rehabilitation in the symphony of the ages.

"Because we fear to be naked and unashamed, we scuttle back in search of another garment of flesh. But eventually we shall love enough, and be sufficiently lovable, to accept who we were, and are, and will be: for fig leaves are worn only by exiles from Eden."

– Joan Grant

8

THE BARDO STATE:
FROM GRAVE
TO CRADLE

"The past situation has just occurred and the future situation has not yet manifested itself so there is a gap between the two. This is basically the bardo experience."
    – Chogyam Trungpa, *Rinpoche*

"The Soul-Ego takes its flight into Dreamland."
    – Madame H. P. Blavatsky

A CROSS the threshold of death lies a realm beyond our conscious understanding, a fourth-dimensional commonwealth of spirit in which the human entity, released from bodily constraints, is steeped in the quintessence of being. Ancient Tibetans referred to this profoundly mysterious condition as the *bardo*, the plane of consciousness between lives. In the eighth century, Tibetan scribes compiled and condensed the out-of-body journeyings of generations into a guidebook mapping out the psychic territory to be negotiated once the body has perished. For centuries, the *Bardo Thödol,* better known to Westerners as *The Tibetan Book of the Dead,* has been recited into the ears of the dying and the deceased in hope of steering the liberated soul across the "dangerous ambush" of the *bardo* (literally, *bar* "in between"; *do,* "island") and away from the necessity of rebirth.

According to *The Tibetan Book of the Dead,* the experience that lies in wait at death ranges over a symbolic forty-nine days, from blissful envelopment in "Clear Light" to the most terrifying, gory hallucinations. If the *bardo* traveller can only accept the absolute beauty and truth of the Clear Light or, failing this, if he or she refuses to be intimidated by the evil visions which, after all, are only born of personal *karmic* thought forms, then it is possible to merge with the Godhead and escape "the muddy swamp of *samsara*." Most human souls, however, are unequal to this task and gradually descend from the gloriously intense brightness that greets them at death to confrontation with their personal devils and, eventually, yet another earthly body. The three *bardo* stages in which self meets self in ever-degenerating encounters are:

Chikhai Bardo: The supreme serenity of the between-life state is reached right at the beginning. Death yields to the Clear Light which is simply, if overwhelmingly, "the radiance of thine own true nature." The book describes the Light as being "like a mirage moving across a landscape in springtime in one continuous stream of vibrations." Everything, it seems, is bright, blissful, and boundless. To quote the book once more, "all things are like the void and

cloudless sky, and the naked, spotless intellect is like unto
a transparent vacuum without circumference or centre."
As welcome as this transcendent state must be, the Light
usually overpowers the doubting, guilt-ridden human
ego. And the consciousness principle falls away to the . . .

Chönyid Bardo: Here, the living consciousness of the
dead person views its abandoned body and, on hearing
the mourning of friends and relatives, tries in vain to
contact them. The discarnate entity experiences sounds,
lights, and rays which awe, frighten, and fatigue the flag-
ging soul surprised by its bodily transformation. Next
come visitations from peaceful and wrathful deities—
post-mortem dreams brought on by the karmic reflexes
of actions committed in the physical world. In a sense,
nothing has changed. The book intones: "As men think,
so are they, both here and hereafter, thoughts being
things, the parents of all actions good and bad alike; and,
as the sowing has been, so will the harvest be." Which is
to say that if the previous life has been loving and honest,
the hallucinations will be correspondingly heavenly; if
nasty and deceitful, horrifying visions will rear up to
match. Most people's lives will have been an amalgam of
good and ill—hence the book's description of two kinds
of projection. The wrathful deities are vile indeed; they
advance tearing heads from corpses, drinking blood, and
threatening all manner of infliction. And so to the . . .

Sidpa Bardo: Much to its surprise, the entity finds it
can "instantaneously arrive in whatever place" by travelling through rock-masses, hills, or houses. But the soul is

cautioned neither to desire these "various powers of illusion" nor to grieve for the loss of the body which, in any event, becomes more and more dim as the last life is left behind and the next life is approached. Pursuit by sounds and hallucinations leads to a confrontation with the Lord of Death, yet another psychological projection, who consults his Mirror of Karma "wherein every good and evil act is vividly reflected." In more contemporary terminology, this is where the individual reviews and judges the thoughts and deeds of the past life. At last, as the time for rebirth draws near, visions are seen of a man and woman in sexual union—the entity's parents in the forthcoming life. If about to be born male, the soul feels intense jealousy towards the father and acute desire for the mother; the reverse being the case if the future gender is female. This, in turn, thrusts the entity into the path leading to the womb to experience "self-existing bliss in the midst of the meeting of the sperm and ovum." Consciousness is cloaked in forgetfulness as the embryo grows and grows to emerge from the womb as a reborn human.

> "Wherever the ether pervadeth, consciousness pervadeth."
>
> – Tibetan Book of the Dead

Choosing the Next Life

Until 1975, *The Tibetan Book of the Dead* was generally considered to be an instructive yet essentially symbolic allegory, as quaint, moralistic, and old world as a fairy tale by the Brothers Grimm. But a burst of medical research into near-death and out-of-body experiences has justified a more literal interpretation of much of the *Bardo Thödol*, mainly because the testimony of modern accident victims and hospital patients who have come back from the dead bears near-identical witness to certain stages of the venerable *bardo* state. Studies by Dr. Elisabeth Kübler-Ross, Dr. Raymond Moody, Dr. Kenneth Ring and others demonstrate that the after-death state is alive with commonly reported phenomena—a powerful, welcoming Light, a sense of peace and timelessness, freedom of movement and the ability to travel through objects, increased clarity of perception, surprise at being out-of-the-body coupled with the capacity to see and hear people nearby, strange sounds, the granting of a rapid review of the life that has gone before, a loss of the fear of death combined with a heightened sense of purpose, and the inadequacy of words to describe the overall experience. How humbling it must be for medical scientists to accept that these dramatic findings had been set down on parchment in remote Tibet more than eleven centuries earlier.

Dr. Raymond Moody marvelled in *Life After Life*, his best selling account of near-death research, that the correspondence between the early stages of death related in *The Tibetan Book of the Dead* and the reports of his subjects "is nothing short of fantastic." The obvious conclusion to be drawn from this tallying of testimonies is that the survivors of out-of-body experiences have ventured part way into the between-life state, their reports reflecting the earliest, predominantly positive aspects of the *bardo*. "What may happen *after* the initial stages of death . . . remains an open question," comments Dr. Ring. Yet many of the witnesses seem to have travelled far enough to become aware of the process of reincarnation. One of Ring's subjects, a man who survived a serious car accident, said:

> I got to see a movie of basically my life, of what *had* happened and what *was* happening. It was like, I have a *mission* here to do, let's say, and I had a choice of what basically I call going on with the physical body or starting over again with a new one.

The woman who, according to Ring's statistical measuring gauge, had the most profound near-death experience of all his subjects, wrote:

> I really believe that death is just part of a continuous cycle. . . . Not an end *at all*. . . . I know that whenever I have another grandchild, I look at him and think, "Could you be papa? Could you be mama? *Who* could you be?" And it's very exciting.

After a cardiac arrest left New York film maker Victor Solow clinically dead for twenty-three minutes, he was revived by a medical team's final desperate effort. Formerly sceptical of any life beyond the grave, Solow related his *bardo* adventure in the *Reader's Digest* (October, 1974):

There was no time for fear, pain or thought. . . . I was moving at high speed toward a net of great luminosity. . . . The instant I made contact with it, the vibrant luminosity increased to a blinding intensity which drained, absorbed, and transformed me at the same time. There was no pain. The sensation was neither pleasant nor unpleasant but completely consuming. . . . The grid was like a transformer, an energy converter transporting me through form and into formlessness, beyond time and space. . . . This new "I" was not the I which I knew, but rather a distilled essence of it, yet something vaguely familiar, something I had always known buried under the superstructure of personal fears, hopes, wants and needs. This "I" had no connection to ego. It was final, unchangeable, indivisible, indestructible, pure spirit. While completely unique and individual as a fingerprint, "I" was, at the same time, part of some infinite, harmonious, and ordered whole. *I had been there before. . .*

Near-death experiences, the first glimpses of the *bardo*, became commonplace by the 1980s. But in 1986 *Life Between Life*—a book claiming to be a scientific exploration into the void separating one incarnation from the next—emerged as the first modern study of the nonmaterial world straddling earthly lives. The groundbreaking researcher was Dr. Joel Whitton, a Toronto neuro-psychiatrist who presented compelling testimony from more than thirty hypnotic subjects studied over a period of twelve years.

Whether they believed in reincarnation, disbelieved, or were rebirth agnostics, Dr. Whitton's patients reported entering, at death, a timeless, spaceless, light-filled realm in which they had shed their bodies yet felt intensely alive. One subject commented:

> It's so bright, so beautiful, so serene. It's like going into the sun and being absorbed without any sensation of heat. You go back to the wholeness of everything.

To enter metaconsciousness, as Dr. Whitton dubbed between-life awareness, is to be one with the timeless oversoul which is the invisible cornerstone of the powers of the individual. Because this oversoul contains a multiplicity of personalities that have materialized in previous existences, subjects are able to understand their level of spiritual development in the context of other lives.

Guides, instructors, deceased loved ones, and a board of judgment are commonly encountered in the life between lives. The board of judgment—a group of discarnate elders who know everything there is to know about the individual appearing before them—give supportive counsel during a review of the most recent lifetime and recommend plans for the next earthly expedition.

Perhaps the most significant finding of Dr. Whitton's research is the discovery that many people prepare a "karmic script" in the *bardo* for the life to come, often specifying, for example, their parents, marriage partners, and careers. It is as if we are artists who make a rough sketch of a fresco in the between-life state. Once incarnate, we set to work on the intended masterpiece, working at close range day by day to execute, in minute detail, a general idea. At death, confronted with the accomplished work, we realize how faithful we have been to our objectives.

When people regain normal consciousness after deep-trance travelling in the interlife, they are frequently shocked, disorientated, and dismayed. Like tiny tots who have been snatched from the candy store of their dreams, Dr. Whitton's subjects ache to return to the land of perfect understanding, the land where meaning is self-explanatory and the soul and its immortal purpose are as diaphanous as glass. "You've woken me up in an unreal world," one subject complained. "Now I know where the true reality lies." Even a glimpse of the "true reality" brings understanding that the *bardo* experience is bound to recur, if only because one is contained in a bodily vehicle that must perish. This, in turn, removes all fear of death.

All who return from the *bardo* have a different tale to tell. While similar in theme, their accounts vary as to the degree of light or enlightenment at the threshold, the number and appearance of judgment board members, the extent to which the karmic script may be examined while incarnate, and many other details. But in one fundamental aspect the privileged few who have visited the interlife receive the same unrelenting message: *We are thoroughly responsible for who we are and the circumstances in which we find ourselves. We are the ones who do the choosing.*

As Gladys Archer wrote in the March, 1996 edition of *Reincarnation International*: "I believe that a 'blueprint' of the life to come is imprinted in the subconscious. We decide, before we pass through the gates of birth, which parents, which country, and which colour will give us the opportunity to progress to the next rung of the ladder of evolution."

Dutch writer and therapist Hans TenDam maintains that many people choose a "feeding" past-life personality in preparing for the current incarnation. In his book *Deep Healing* (1997), TenDam writes: "Women who want to make a social career often have as a feeding personality a man who was socially prominent, because that experience is one that they can use well. If you want to become a composer and you were once a flutist in ancient Greece, you will take that earlier life with you. When people plan their next lifetime, the feeding personality that has most to offer for the coming life usually gets the leading role and becomes the root personality."

"We choose our parents," TenDam adds, "mainly because we have karmic business to finish together, or because we recognize them as old friends."

In 1995, American hypnotherapist Dr. Michael Newton added to contemporary *bardo* literature with *Journey of Souls*, a book of case studies from hypnotized subjects ushered into the between-life state. The cases mirrored, and enlarged upon, the testimony of Dr. Whitton's patients and reinforced the notion that groups of souls tend to congregate for shared experience both in and out of incarnation.

"It seems ironic that most people on Earth want to cling to their earthly existence with all their might, while all those on the other side of life look forward to their new corporal existence with just as much fear."
— Thorwald Dethlefsen

LSD *and Shamans' Visions*

Documented evidence from medical after-care is not all that points to the verity of the *bardo* state. In a study of 127 cases of spontaneous past-life memory reported in the book *Lifetimes*, New York professor Frederic Lenz noted that the occasional between-life remembrances of his subjects not only contained common phenomena in exactly the same sequence but were also "strikingly similar" to the death and rebirth process portrayed by *The Tibetan Book of the Dead.* The LSD experiments of Dr. Stanislav Grof show that many of his subjects experience vivid and profound rebirth visions much like those described in the *Bardo Thödol.* "The human unconscious, activated chemically, actually tends to enact spontaneously a powerful confrontation with death that can result in transcendence," Grof has written. With a little help from lysergic acid diethylamide, volunteers have sat through the most shattering hallucinations, seeing themselves wallowing in excrement, drowning in cesspools, crawling in rotting offal, or slurping blood. Visions of murders, torture, mutilations, sadomasochistic orgies, and cruelty of all kinds are commonplace. But there are also psychedelic blasts of brilliant white or golden light during which the subjects feel absolutely purified as they glide in a timeless, indescribably beautiful universe.

Varieties of transpersonal experience, which Grof defines as an expansion or extension of consciousness beyond the usual ego boundaries and the limitations of time and space, are also brought on by the hallucinogenics mescalin (the active ingredient of the peyote cactus) and psilocybin, derived from a mushroom, sacred to Mexican Indians, called *teonanacatl* or "the flesh of God." The anaesthetic ketamine hydrochloride has the power to transport its users into a bright world totally dissociated from the body. "It's impossible to describe," said a medical doctor who has experimented with ketamine. "The 'you' that you know is not there. You forget your name and identity. There's only experience—and it can be terrifying if you're unprepared." According to anaesthetist Dr. Howard Alltounian, who conducted ketamine experiments with his late wife, Marcia Moore, the drug opens up the mind to the larger designs of the universe. "We see the reasons for which we came to birth, why we had to die, and why we decided to be born again—and we know these reasons to be good," he said.

Clinical work with schizophrenics has led psychiatrists to conclude that their patients' visions often represent, not denial of death or wishful fantasy, but unadorned experiential reality. The actions of Old Testament prophets and yogis of the East also testify to communion with this state of being. While Ezekiel sometimes remained in a trance for days, and Daniel spoke of his visions throwing him to the ground and making him physically sick, advanced yogis have demonstrated their ability to leave their bodies at will, to exist for weeks without food, and even to merge with water and flame. Prisoners and monks confined to solitary cells, explorers subsisting in conditions of extreme isolation, and sufferers of epilepsy, which the Greeks called "the sacred disease" for its capacity to inspire body-free timelessness, have all experienced comparative states of higher awareness. They're all dipping into various levels of the *bardo* to be rejuvenated by the knowledge that rebirth proceeds from the very jaws of annihilation.

Just as modern scientific findings can be referred back for comparison to *The Tibetan Book of the Dead*, so the *Bardo Thödol* echoes the earliest experiences of non-physical awareness; experiences that gave human beings their primal notion of heaven and hell. Shamanism, a primitive religious practice of the Ural-Altaic peoples of northern Asia, has long incorporated a profound rite of annihilation and rebirth at the core of its initiation trials. Novice shamans, willing themselves into trance, lie alone and close to death for between three and seven days. In this state, they suffer the most hellish visions, including personal dismemberment and the scraping of flesh from their bones, before receiving new flesh and blood, spiritual enlightenment, and rapturous transport to the heavenly realms. The shaman's vision, to quote from Joseph Campbell's *The Masks of God*, reveals "that sense of an immortal inhabitant within the individual which is announced in every mystical tradition." This obscure dweller-in-the-body "neither dies nor is born, but simply passes back and forth, as it were through a veil, appearing in bodies and departing." There's substantial evidence that hallucinatory drugs have been used for millennia to encourage the onset of shamanistic perception. The *Rig-Veda*, India's earliest religious document, glorifies a psychedelic mushroom called *soma* and, during excavations of a shaman's grave at the New Stone Age settlement of Catal Huyuk in Turkey, pollen analysis revealed that psychedelic plants had been placed beside the medicine man's corpse.

The ancient Mysteries of the old civilized world were rife with death and rebirth rituals, and myth and fable from around the globe is coloured with tales of that free-floating state after death where the human spirit has yet to shed the thoughts and appetites of the Earth-world but must do without the satisfaction afforded by the physical body. In Scandinavian mythology, for example, the *Song of Olaf Ostesen* conjures up graphic images of disembodied discontent:

> In other worlds I lingered
> Through the length of many nights;
> And God alone can ever know
> How great the sorrow of soul I saw—
> In Brooksvalin, where souls
> Are subject to the cosmic judgement.

A number of renowned historical figures, Cicero and Virgil among them, have written glowingly of out-of-body experiences. Cicero, having rejoined his frame with renewed vigour, wrote: "We at last possess reasons why we should live; and we are not only eager to live, but we cherish a better hope in death." Plato, in the tenth book of the *Republic*, recounts the legend of Er who, twelve days after being killed in battle, returned to life as he lay on a funeral pyre to tell of his adventures in the other world. Er observed how, after undergoing judgment, each soul was granted the opportunity to choose the form of its next incarnation, a selection process determined by the individual's wisdom, or lack of it. Plato writes: "Most curious . . . was the spectacle— sad and laughable and strange; for the choice of the souls was in most cases based on their own experience of a previous life." The choice being made, the souls drank of the River Lethe (Greek for "forgetfulness") which erased all conscious memory in readiness for the next incarnation. Such enforced oblivion crops up again and again as a between-life theme.

Jesus Christ in the *Pistis Sophia* speaks of the soul drinking from a cup "filled with the water of forgetfulness" and, in Chinese Buddhism, Meng P'o, the presiding goddess of the underworld, ensures that souls quaff a bitter-sweet broth to drown all memory of their previous existence before returning to earth. "Body," wrote the Greek philosopher Plotinus, "is the true River of Lethe; for souls plunged into it forget all."

Modern medicine might have discovered an explanation for this amnesia in a hormone called oxytocin, which controls the pregnant woman's rate of labour contractions. Research studies have established that large quantities of oxytocin produce loss of memory in laboratory animals and cause even well-trained animals to lose their ability to perform known tasks. Because a woman's oxytocin floods her child's system it is not unreasonable to suppose that this natural drug flushes away memories of former incarnations along with conscious remembrance of birth. Not that smearing of the slate of memory doesn't occur in life outside the womb. The inability of keen-minded adults to remember their earliest years and the frequent loss of recall among the elderly is, perhaps, nature's way of imparting the relative insignificance of conscious memory.

Forgetfulness of the previous life, according to the Kabalists, happens in the between-life state when the night angel Layela gives the hovering soul a little pinch on the nose while applying light pressure to the upper lip. So it is said that we all bear the mark of the angel's finger on our lips. Sholem Asch writes in *The Nazarene* that our senses are haunted by fragmentary recollections of another life when the Angel of Forgetfulness forgets his mission. These recollections "drift like torn clouds above the hills and valleys of the mind, and weave themselves into the incidents of our current existence. They assert themselves clothed with reality, in the form of nightmares which visit our beds. Then the effect is exactly the same as when, listening to a concert broadcast through the air, we suddenly hear a strange voice break in, carried from afar on another ether-wave and charged with another melody."

From Amenthe to Gusho

All sorts of names and conditions have been ascribed to the between-life state, the popular conception of which is largely decreed by culture and custom. The ancient Egyptians spoke of sensitive souls passing through the gate of the gods into the *amenthe* where they dwelt in continuous pleasure until descending once more to animate a new body. Similarly, the Hebrews of old envisaged a spell in *pardish* or paradise—the place where fruit ripens and is gathered or, esoterically, where the spirit matures from seed sown in earthly incarnations. Souls whose time in *pardish* has nearly expired are given instructions for the next life, explains the *Zohar*, before being sent out "sorrowing in exile; to a place where there is no true happiness because only in the presence of God can this state be attained." The Australian Aborigines of Queensland's Pennefather River believe that between incarnations the spirit resides in the haunts of Anjea, a mythical being who causes women to conceive by putting mud babies in their bodies. To the Okinawans of the South Pacific the interim kingdom is called *gusho* to be entered on the forty-ninth day after death by spirits who, though fleeing their dead bodies, remain in their homes until this time. There's an intriguing parallel here with the *bardo's* forty-nine stations of planetary existence. Be that as it may, the Okinawans believe that the entity returns to earth within seven generations in the form of an individual closely resembling the previous incarnation. Not mind but spirit reincarnates, the mind being inherited from ancestors. Some spirits, nevertheless, remain in *gusho* indefinitely to act as hosts and tour guides for new arrivals.

More than one hundred years ago the Russian noble-woman Madame Helena Petrovna Blavatsky and her Theosophical movement rifled Eastern mysticism for two terms to describe the after-death state: *kama loka*, meaning the "plane of desire," and *devachan*, a Tibetan word meaning "the blissful." According to Theosophy, *kama loka* is the astral region penetrating and surrounding the Earth where the soul is purged of its impurities before rising to the unalloyed spiritual joys of *devachan* where it rests—for up to fifteen centuries, according to Madame Blavatsky—until being drawn back to the chores of earthly existence demanded by the ceaseless, universal law of *karma*. The between-life process, argue the Theosophists, is remedial, restful, and beneficial, as vital to the spirit as sleep is to mortals. Were the adoption of another body to follow immediately upon death, the soul, being thus deprived of the necessary opportunity for reflection and consequent development of its higher nature, would soon become utterly exhausted.

Rudolf Steiner, who headed the German section of the Theosophical Society before founding the Anthroposophical Society based on his own metaphysical researches, also spoke of *kamaloca* (his spelling) and *devachan* as both essential and complementary to physical existence. For evolution to proceed, the body must be repeatedly eliminated. In Steiner's words: "In order to sustain consciousness and to keep it active, we have been continually destroying our corporeal sheath." In *kamaloca* (recognizable, though most inaccurately presented, as the Roman Catholic purgatory, says Steiner) the soul weans itself of all desires, appetites, and passions. Here, every past-life deed committed in relation to a fellow human being is re-experienced as if the acting individual were that other person. Simultaneously, the soul is drenched in the "spiritual rain" of the sympathies and antipathies of higher beings who pass judgment on these deeds. All the while, the entity is passing through the planetary spheres where a vision is presented of all its previous earthly incarnations spread out in a tableau. Work then begins on the creation of the next physical body in exact accordance with the experience, lessons, and karmic propensities assimilated from the past life. "Nothing that you can ever do on earth," Steiner told an audience in November, 1922, "can be as great and manifold as what you have to do when from the starry worlds you build this temple of the gods, the human body." Before the spiritual seed of the physical body descends to the parents who have been chosen to receive it, the soul is granted a vision

"In a myth of the New Hebrides, the soul runs along the line of hills till he reaches the end of the island, and then he comes to the place of recollection, the Maewo name for which is *vat dodona*, the stone of thought; if he remembers there his child or his wife, or anything that belongs to him, he will run back and come to life again. In the same place are two rocks with a deep ravine between them; if the ghost clears this as he leaps across he is forever dead, but if one fails he returns to life again."

– R.H. Codrington, *In The Melanesians*

of the life to come. Sometimes, says Steiner, this preview is so shocking that the self draws back in horror. Should this happen, the soul might never truly incarnate in the body it prepares for itself, an eventuality which can lead either to so-called prenatal defects or to epilepsy, which reveals lack of full control over the organism.

The Bardo's Duration

The time spent between lives seems to be as variable as the length of the lives themselves. Reports range from whistle-stops of several hours to extended settlements of hundreds of years. Those who suffer violent or otherwise premature deaths appear to return faster than those who die of old age, personal choice being the overriding factor in establishing length of residence in the immaterial world. When Seth, the famous spirit guide who communicated through the mediumship of author Jane Roberts, was asked by a minister to reveal what determines the time between incarnations, he replied:

> You. If you are very tired, then you rest. If you are wise, you take time to digest your knowledge and plan your next life, even as a writer plans his next book. If you have too many ties with this reality or if you are too impatient, or if you have not learned sufficiently, then you may return too quickly. It is always up to the individual. There is no predestination. The answers are within yourself then, as the answers are within you now.

Despite its obvious capacity to terrify, the *bardo* state is a most seductive realm. Dr. Raymond Moody tells how many people, having drifted free of the body, resist the return to physical existence. It must be wrenching indeed to leave a state of relaxation described enthusiastically by a racing car driver as one thousand times greater than that induced by a sauna and massage! Virginia Tighe, as Bridey Murphy, told of basking in "just satisfaction" in "a place of waiting" between lives where all have knowledge of the future. Chicago-born past-lives specialist Bryan Jameison reports that most people he regresses to the interim are lulled by a euphoric, floating sensation, a feeling of being surrounded by soft clouds. "Some people go over and find pure energy and light," commented hypnotherapist Dr. Edith Fiore. "And yet I have many who say they see beautiful lakes, beautiful scenes, gleaming cities. . . ." After such an abundance of sweetness and light, the sexual vortex that draws the soul back to the physical plane—described by a subject of German hypnotherapist Thorwald Dethlefsen as "the big vacuum cleaner"—comes as a jarring shock. Consequently, it's hardly surprising that Dr. Helen Wambach's research subjects, who report the average time spent in the *bardo* is fifty-two years, speak of birth being pervaded by an abiding sense of sadness and dislocation. As much as they would like to stay, the patients of Dr. Morris Netherton are rarely allowed to linger in the between-life state because, for all its mystery and promise of sudden revelation, he finds that nothing can be accomplished there to improve the present-life situation. In a pessimistic aside on the perversity of the species, Netherton writes:

We are no different out of the body than in; unwilling to learn from our in-the-body experience, we repeat our patterns out of the body, until we can find a body to enter that will allow us to repeat in-the-body patterns all over again.

But if a person's mental traits and limitations are borne out of incarnation by the self, so the between-life state has continuing application to physical existence. It was always the intention of the Tibetan sages that the *Bardo Thödol* serve as much as counsel to the living as a guidebook for the dying. Chogyam Trungpa in a modern commentary on *The Tibetan Book of the Dead* pursued this theme by remarking that the *bardo* experience is part of our basic psychological make-up. At every moment, birth and death are recurring. In fact, the *bardo* state could be said to be the experiences of paranoia and uncertainty in everyday life; feelings of not being sure of our ground, of neither knowing what we have asked for nor what we are getting into. More emphatically, states Trungpa, the *bardo* experiences can be seen "purely in terms of the living situation."

A forgotten gem of a book first published in 1891, *In the Forest of Arden* is an extended metaphor for between-life consciousness. Perfect love, unspoiled nature, and

---

". . . Believing as I do in the theory of rebirth, I live in the hope that if not in this birth, in some other birth I shall be able to hug all humanity in friendly embrace."

– Mohandas K. Gandhi

non-material existence are all one in this tale of other-
wordly exploration where "we felt the delight of a sudden exchange of poverty for richness, a swift transition
from bondage to freedom."

Author Hamilton Wright Mabie tells of feeling . . .

. . . the vast irresistible movement of life rolling,
wave after wave, out of the unseen seas beyond,
obliterating the faint divisions by which, in this
working world, we count the days of our toil, and
making all the ages one unbroken growth; I felt the
measureless calm, the sublime repose, of that unin-
terrupted expansion of form and beauty, from
flower to star and from bird to cloud; I felt the
mighty impulse of that force which lights the sun in
its track and sets the stars to mark the boundaries of
its way. Unbroken repose, unlimited growth, inex-
haustible life, measureless force, unsearchable
beauty—who shall feel these things and not know
that there are no words for them! And yet in Arden
they are part of every man's life!

Mabie writes of being convinced that everybody
who loved the place had been born there and that this
explained the "home feeling" that filled the soul on entering the Forest. "It is, in fact, the only place I have
known which seemed to belong to me and to everybody
else at the same time; in which I felt no alien influence."

If one continues to inhabit a body, however, The Forest of Arden cannot be roamed indefinitely. Nevertheless,
returning visitors are blessed with a "great consolation,"

according to Mabie. "Those who have lived in Arden and have gone back again into the world, are sustained in their loneliness by the knowledge of their fellowship with a nobler community. Aliens though they are, they have yet a country to which they are loyal, not through interest, but through aspiration, imagination, faith, and love."

The unbodily rapture of the between-life state, it must be stressed, is simply the manifestation of a higher level of consciousness. William James, the American psychologist who used nitrous oxide and ether to "stimulate the mystical consciousness in an extraordinary degree," wrote that our normal waking consciousness "is but one special type of consciousness, whilst all about it, parted from it by the filmiest of screens, there lie potential forms of consciousness entirely different." Unfrequented, except in dreams, by the majority of the human race, these other realities are there *all the time* and can be experienced voluntarily by those rare beings who are spiritually self-realized. Some pay a visit with the help of drugs; others get there through hypnosis or by plumbing the deepest meditative states, or without wanting to, through schizophrenia or extremes of illness and isolation. And then there are those accident victims for whom traumatic flirtation with death leads inadvertently into the *bardo*. The rest of us, waiting patiently until our time expires, at least have something to look forward to—a sustained cosmic adventure that, in dissolving mortality's frustrating limitations, surveys the grandeur of innermost being.

"I think, as we die, that we go through a process of retaining some fairly close identification with the personality we have last been on earth. The larger personality absorbs the recently experienced personality but discards the unimportant things such as race, social security number, and belief systems. Then, I believe that the soul or deeper self can plan a new expedition into physical reality in order to experience emotions, develop knowledge, and, most important of all, to live with other souls so as to straighten out past mistakes."

– Dr. Helen Wambach

7

THE GHOST
OF FUTURE PAST

"The Oversoul is before Time, and Time, Father of all else, is one of His children."
  – Ralph Waldo Emerson

"One level out, you see that who you are isn't moving in time. Time is describing the incarnations, the packaging changes."
  – Ram Dass

SOMETIMES, thinking obstructs understanding: that's the way it is with human conception of time. Thought, being sequential by nature, presents the three-dimensional world in terms of past, present, and future—an interpretation that is convenient, essential, even, for coping with the physical world. But time, being a product of our mundane consciousness, is no more than a convenient illusion. Visitors to the *bardo* state, as we have seen, are well aware that time doesn't really exist. Freed momentarily from the Earth-plane, they know that everything is happening at once. As confusing as this might sound to an aging individual watching the seconds tick by on the clock surmounting a local historical monument, everything *is* taking place in the eternal *now*. Past lives, therefore, are transpiring simultaneously; only thought's way of viewing the world informs us otherwise.

Although wise men from Huang Po to St. Augustine have remarked on the unreality of time, reason has always balked at surrendering the linear view. Ken Wilber writes in *The Spectrum of Consciousness*:

> Thought is sequential, successive, one-dimensional, while the real world presents itself as a multi-dimensional, non-successive, simultaneous pattern of infinite richness and variety; and trying to make the one grasp the other is like trying to appreciate a beautiful landscape by looking through a narrow slit in a fence or trying to take in a Renoir painting by microscope alone.

Only when memory is no longer imagined to be real knowledge of the past but, instead, is understood to be current experience will the time illusion evaporate. Because the present moment contains all time, it is therefore timeless. And this timelessness is eternity. Of course, it is much less taxing to abide with past, present, and future, but a more than superficial understanding of reincarnation insists upon broader horizons. As René Guénon declared: "He who cannot escape from the standpoint of temporal succession so as to see all things in their simultaneity is incapable of the least conception

of the metaphysical order." Joan Grant, an English-
woman whose far memory has recalled a long succession
of past lives, does her best to make this idea of simultaneity easier to grasp by suggesting that time be seen as
the centre of an orange, equidistant from its segments
which are likened to the soul's various lives. Consequently, for Miss Grant, ". . . it is no more difficult to
recall an episode which took place several millennia ago
than to recall one from the current or the preceding century." Subjects regressed to former existences also find
that recent lives are no more vivid or emotionally intense than those from the deep past. Seth, the spirit
guide who appeared earlier in these pages, hammered
home the eternal present's relevance to reincarnation in
this communication:

> Because you are obsessed with the idea of past, pre-
> sent, and future, you are forced to think of reincar-
> nations as strung out one before the other. Indeed
> we speak of past lives because you are used to the
> time sequence concept. . . . You have dominant
> egos, all a part of an inner identity, dominant in
> various existences. But the separate existences exist
> simultaneously. Only the egos involved make the
> time distinction. 145 B.C., A.D. 145, a thousand years
> in your past and a thousand years in your future—
> all exist now.

The illusory nature of time is perhaps best perceived
by thinking of dreams which can telescope the experience of years into seconds. No time whatsoever passes for

the dreamer. Nor, indeed, for one who is asleep or under hypnosis. Why? Because the inner self lives outside the temporal state. In the same way, a helicopter pilot lives outside the vehicles he is observing far below on a traffic-jammed highway. Suppose the pilot is the oversoul while the driver of each vehicle is a separate ego-soul experiencing a different life. The oversoul, being in the time-less state, can see all the various lives happening at once, but the separate souls, restricted in visibility and aware-ness, can see only their particular traffic problem.

The approaching years, with all their events, may be out of sight but only in the same way that higher vibra-tions of sight, sound, smell, taste, and feeling are beyond the limitations of physical consciousness. The future is here and has always existed. That is why gifted clairvoy-ants can foretell what will come to pass; by psychically tuning in to a higher frequency they are able to perceive the everlasting present. Alan Vaughan, the editor of *Reincarnation Report*, argued in a February, 1983, article that the more we know about this "future," the better our chances of making the best choices in the present moment:

> By learning more about our unconscious blueprint of life, we bring to the surface more of our reasons for choosing to be born. We can never, I suspect, know *all* of our blueprint, for that would remove our zest for life. In fact, the reason for the barrier between our unconscious and conscious minds may well be to prevent foreknowledge from completely robbing us of the thrill of our daily encounters.

> "The mind of man is capable of anything—because everything is in it, all the past as well as all the future."
> – Joseph Conrad

Future Lives

Hypnosis, nevertheless, is able to pierce the barrier cleaving the conscious from the unconscious. Theoretically, this means that, for a skilled hypnotist, future lives are no more inaccessible than past lives. Practically, however, progressions aren't conducted nearly so frequently as regressions. Future lives are impossible to document; information doesn't flow as readily, and subjects, once adrift in the future, tend to switch spontaneously from one scene to another. Perhaps the mind, conditioned to see the future as forbidden territory, tries to block or jumble the store of images.

Dr. Helen Wambach undertook a pilot study called "Mass Dreams of the Future" in which hypnotized subjects were carried forward to the years 2100 and 2300 respectively. Eighty-nine out of 1,100 participants found themselves incarnate in one or both of the designated years and went on to describe "remarkably common" experiences. "Many more *wanted* to go into the future," said Dr. Wambach, "but they found they were not humanly alive in these time periods."

Perhaps they were not alive because of a dire shortage of bodies to accommodate them. The study pointed to a

96 per cent reduction in the earth's population by the year 2100 when subjects reported they were living in the aftermath of widespread destruction. The planet had been rendered barren and poisonous with roughly half of those alive in 2100 describing life in domed cities which they could leave only by donning a form of gas mask. One domed city was reported to be in Arizona; another in Tunisia. The other half of the population lived as space colonists eating mushy, artificial food with the aid of a strange utensil shaped like a fork and spoon combined. All vegetables had disappeared, but so had pain, violence, and disease. By the year 2300, the subjects testified, vegetables had reappeared, people were living all over the solar universe and earth's population had doubled.

Progressions conducted by Dr. Bruce Goldberg, a Baltimore hypnotherapist, have encountered none of this apocalyptic material—at least, not until the twenty-fifth century when a major nuclear war apparently causes a "tremendous decrease" in the world's population. The "numerous consistent observations" reported by Goldberg in his book *Past Lives, Future Lives* range from major geographical changes during the next century to underwater cities and information pills in the twenty-sixth century. On February 2, 1981, Goldberg hypnotized Baltimore television newscaster Harry Mar-

"If you don't believe in karma or reincarnation, don't worry. You probably will in your next life."
  – Bruce Goldberg

tin and asked him to "read" the news one week hence. The WBAL newscast of February 9, 1981, showed that Martin had scored a number of minor successes, including a near-identical description of a road accident in the Baltimore area. Later, Harry Martin was moved forward to a life in the twenty-second century where he saw himself working as a scientist inside a solar-powered glass pyramid. Not a word is spoken among the three hundred people who live inside the pyramid; their appointed task is to explore thought transference. Progressed to the last day of this future life, Martin describes a high-tech version of euthanasia which he understands will lead to his rebirth:

GOLDBERG: Where are you?

MARTIN: I'm reporting to the termination room.

GOLDBERG: Are you still in the pyramid?

MARTIN: Yes

GOLDBERG: Why are you in the termination room?

MARTIN: It's my turn to change units.

GOLDBERG: Can you describe this procedure?

MARTIN: I lie down on a table and they put something on my fingers and you just go to sleep.

GOLDBERG: What does this do to you?

MARTIN: It takes all of your energy out of you.

To dwell on the subject of progression is to addle the mind. Dick Sutphen, who has progressed subjects as far as the year 4000, once mused that, in different bodies disseminated across the future, people are probably interacting with many of the same souls they knew in past and present incarnations. And in 1976 he speculated: "Could it possibly be that, somewhere in time, my future self is being regressed to 1976 to find out about his spiritual roots? I wonder. . . ."

Time is freely given to all who accept the doctrine of reincarnation. And that's very attractive to people only too conscious of their limitations and shortcomings. For if perfection is beyond all reasonable expectation in this life then there's always the next existence, and the one after that. . . . With time and rebirth operating in tandem, there is no goal that cannot be reached; no virtue that can remain forever unattainable. An old Buddhist tale hints at the enormity of time required for expeditions of multitudinous incarnations. An image is presented of a granite mountain six miles high, six miles long and six miles wide. Every hundred years a bird with a silk scarf in its beak flies past this mountain, running the scarf over the rock-face. The time it takes for the silk scarf to wear away the mountain is likened to the dimension of our being in round after round, in form after form, on plane after plane.

Yet if time doesn't exist, has anything really changed? Perception, that is all. Rational order falls away to the grandest vision imaginable. And the sands of timelessness are seen to be even more vast and imponderable than the sands of time.

"If you could see that the Supreme works not in Time and Space, but that both these are in its Being . . . then you would see that the changeful process of Samsara is a Frozen Dream"

– Vasishta Ramayana

10

LESSER LIVES:
REBIRTH IN THE
LOWER KINGDOMS

"We can only get away from the necessity of an animal
past by denying all soul to subhuman nature."
  – Sri Aurobindo

"A stone I died and rose again a plant,
A plant I died and rose again an animal;
I died an animal and was born a man.
Why should I fear? When was I less by dying?"
  – Jalalu' L-Din Rumi

IVINE SPIRIT, says the ancient wisdom of the
East, permeates all matter. Manifesting as units of
consciousness, this spiritual power embarks on an immense journey of progressive embodiment. Incarnation
after incarnation as various minerals is followed by innumerable lives as plants followed by successive births and
deaths as animals. When, at last, the human form is
attained, the relentless cycle won't be stilled. Time rolls

ever onward, fertilizing unto eternity the seeds of rebirth.

What Eastern sages had to say about the ascending consciousness of this Great Chain of Being was echoed by the *Barddas* of Celtic antiquity, a document which expounded a scheme of evolution in which the monad or soul passes through every phase of material embodiment before entering the human kingdom. The Rosicrucians, a mystical order of indeterminately ancient origin, have long held that every mineral contains an "eager fire" or "jewel of light"—the essence of evolutionary development. Furthermore, the findings of modern science support these claims that consciousness abides within all types of corporal envelopes. IBM scientist Marcel Vogel has shown through infrared photography that quartz crystals store and release energy, and he has also demonstrated that crystalline growth can be modified by human thought patterns. Various experiments have shown that plants are "living, breathing, communicating creatures endowed with the personality and attributes of soul," to quote from *The Secret Life of Plants* by Peter Tompkins and Christopher Bird. As for animals, their possession of mental and emotional faculties is self-evident; the nonphysical difference between the human and animal kingdoms being intellectual rather than spiritual.

At first glance, however, this progression of consciousness is hard to accept on sheer numerical grounds. The mind wrestles with an image of, say, trillions of sand-grain souls competing among themselves for the eventual tenancy of a lone human body. Yet the apparently prohibitive logistics of funnelling the vast soul matter of minerals into plant existences and henceforth into the less plentiful bodies of animals and humans is explained by Manly P. Hall, president-founder of the Philosophical Research Society based in Los Angeles. He argues that only the physical aspects of minerals, plants, and animals are individualized, their entity and mind being collective. Whereas humans must grow separately, the types and species that comprise the lesser kingdoms develop through the evolution of group consciousness.

Dorothy Maclean, whose psychic communication with plants was one of the major inspirations behind the spectacular Findhorn community in the north of Scotland where enormous flowers and vegetables flourished on land that had harboured only gorse bushes and spiky grass, has the same perception of the group soul concept. Writing of this woman's remarkable ability to converse with plants for the betterment of their welfare, Paul Hawken, in his book *The Magic of Findhorn*, noted: "It became apparent that what was coming through was not a spirit attached to one particular pea plant or tomato bush but rather a spirit which was the plan, the mould, and architect of all peas on the Earth."

The various natural kingdoms are linked by what Manly Hall calls pronounced "transitorial forms." Between the mineral and the plant there are lichens and mosses; between the plant and the animal there are certain carnivorous plants as well as plants with elementary nervous systems. Between animals and human beings lie the anthropoids and between human beings and the next order stand the great initiates and teachers—the demigods of classical antiquity.

Confirmation of our animal heritage can be found not only in Charles Darwin's *Origin of Species* but also in the case histories of past-life therapists, many of whom find that patients, if carried back far enough in an altered state of consciousness, will feel and see themselves in animal bodies. Dr. Morris Netherton says that whenever he delves into the earliest source of a patient's particular problem that patient "almost always" describes an animal wound or death. Lying on the couch in Netherton's office, people commonly regress to lives as rodents, shrews, insects, and, every so often, prehistoric creatures. Many of Joe Keeton's subjects do likewise. Among the most convincing re-enactments he's observed have been those of a woman who saw herself covered in reddish-brown fur and lying under a boulder; another who envisaged herself picking insects from a dead tree trunk; and a builder who told of being close to the ground and covered in scales. Although Dr. Helen Wambach never tried to retrieve data from animal lives, some of her subjects found themselves on four legs whether they liked it or not. "They look down and see their little furry paws," she said.

Participants in Dr. Stanislav Grof's LSD experiments have also reported identification with various animal ancestors. These feelings of identity usually apply to other mammals, birds, reptiles, amphibians, and various species of fish. Grof says that his subjects can have "illuminating insight into what it feels like when a snake is hungry, when a turtle is sexually excited, or when a salmon breathes through its gills." Less frequently, plant and mineral existences are related. Grof's subjects have experienced themselves as germinating seed, as roots reaching out for nourishment, and as the consciousness of such material as diamond, granite, and gold. "Similar experiences," he writes, "can reach even the microworld and depict the dynamic structure of the atoms. . . ."

In India, the swan—*hamsa* in Sanskrit—symbolizes the liberated soul. The holiest of sages are known by the title *paramahamsa* which literally means "supreme swan." Plato told how Orpheus, after being torn to pieces by the Ciconian women, refused to be reborn through the body of a woman and instead took incarnation as a swan. And the composer Jean Sibelius once said: "Millions of years ago, in my previous incarnations, I must have been related to swans or wild geese because I can still feel that affinity."

The Laws of Manu

Once human, is it possible to be reborn into lesser lives? The Hindus of antiquity believed that people lacking in virtue would surely be reincarnated as beasts and the dread Laws of Manu spelled out precisely how this involution could occur. Manu, a legendary legislator and saint who lived more than two thousand years ago, decreed that each person's life was influenced by one of three overriding qualities—goodness, activity, or darkness. Those endowed with darkness, which he defined as the craving after sensual pleasure, were destined to be reborn as some form of animal, insect, or plant. "In consequence of attachment to the senses, and in consequence of the nonperformance of their duties, fools, the lowest of men, reach the vilest of births," Manu declared. And he gave pointed examples of the specific deeds that lead to particular bodies of the lower kingdom: thieves of grain become rats; thieves of honey, stinging insects; thieves of milk, crows; thieves of meat, vultures. The "violator of a guru's bed" enters a hundred times the forms of grasses, shrubs, and creepers. A woman who is "disloyal to her husband" is born in the womb of a jackal—the list of crimes and punishment goes on and on.

In the old days, Brahmin priests found the Laws a great help in enforcing caste practices; there was nothing quite like the threat of subhuman rebirth to encourage obedience. But modern Hindus tend not to take the Laws of Manu quite so literally, preferring to believe that base appetites and inclinations, rather than individual souls, are reincarnated in animal form. They argue that as neither plants nor animals are capable of degenerating into lesser species, human beings, though they might lapse into a savage state, must never be less than human.

The ancient Hindus—who believed there were 8,400,000 different kinds of birth culminating in the human race—were not alone in anticipating lower lives. The Buddhists held a popular doctrine of rebirth in subhuman realms which may well have led them to institute the first hospitals for the care of animals. Initiates and adepts of the faith, however, regard this teaching to be symbolic rather than literal, believing that karmic hardship can be experienced more profitably in renewed human form. They would rather not accept, at face value, the warning in *The Tibetan Book of the Dead* that when a bestial birth is imminent, the soul ". . . will see, as if through a mist, rock caves and holes in the ground and straw huts."

In ancient Egypt, magic spells from *The Egyptian Book of the Dead* were buried with the newly deceased so they would be empowered to change themselves into "whatever form they please." The Egyptians believed they must spend a cycle of 3,000 years migrating from species to species before they were finally able to be reborn as human beings. This idea resurfaces among the Inuit. Dr. Hartley B. Alexander in his *North American Mythology of Arctic Tribes* tells how souls may be reborn as both human and beast "and some have been known to run the whole gamut of the animal kingdom before returning to human shape."

The unenviable fate of King Nebuchadnezzar is central to the Jewish tradition of transmigration. The Book of Daniel (4:33) describes how the King "was driven from men, and did eat grass as oxen, and his body was wet with the dew of heaven, till his hairs were grown like eagles' feathers and his nails were like birds' claws." In the Kabala, the souls of the wicked were said to migrate into animal bodies—an adulterer, for example, was destined to pass into the body of a stork as it was believed that storks punish adultery with death. Moreover, the mixing of various seeds and the crossbreeding of animals was prohibited so as not to cause suffering to the souls they contained.

The Greek thinkers were similarly captivated by rebirth as an agent of human degeneration. While Plato explained the evolution of birds and animals by saying they arose from the deterioration of human souls, Pythagoras was said to have exclaimed on hearing the yelping of a beaten dog: "Beat him no more! His soul is my friend's as I recognized when I heard his voice." But it was Plotinus, the founder of Neoplatonism, who, like Manu, dared to be most explicit about the kinds of bestial bodies that would result from human actions and desires:

> Those who have sought only to gratify their lust and appetite pass into the bodies of lascivious and gluttonous animals. . . . Those who have degraded their senses by disuse are compelled to vegetate in the plants. Those who have loved music to excess and yet have lived pure lives, go into the bodies of melodious birds. Those who have ruled tyranically become eagles. Those who have spoken lightly of heavenly things, keeping their eyes always turned toward heaven, are changed into birds which always fly toward the upper air. He who has acquired civic virtues becomes a man; if he has not these virtues he is transformed into a domestic animal, like the bee.

In the first century before Christ, the Roman poet Ovid put himself in the place of a victim of transmigration in penning his poem *Metamorphoses.*

I am ashamed to tell you, but I will tell—
I had bristles sprouting on me.
I could not speak, but only grunting sounds
Came out instead of words.
I felt my mouth grow harder.
I had a snout instead of a nose,
And my face bent over to see the ground.
My neck swelled up with great muscles,
And the hand that lifted the cup to my lips
Made footprints on the ground.

Seals that landed on the Faroe Islands in the North Atlantic were thought, as late as the end of the last century,
to appear in human form once a year. An article in the
journal of the Anthropological Institute, published in England in 1872, noted: "The seals which abound on the
rocky parts of the shore are regarded with profound ven-
eration, and on no account could a native be induced to
kill one, as they are said to be the souls of their departed
friends."

"That Starling Was My Husband, George"

Early English and Scottish ballads rhapsodize about the
souls of men and women migrating into various animals, birds, or plants, and Breton folklore speaks of the
spirits of fishermen and sailors materializing in the bodies of white seagulls. Seagulls themselves are remarkably
eloquent on the subject of reincarnation as Richard

Bach illustrates in his ever-popular novel *Jonathan Livingston Seagull.* Sullivan the gull is talking:

> Do you have any idea how many lives we must have gone through before we even got the first idea that there is more to life than eating, or fighting, or power in the Flock? A thousand lives, Jon, ten thousand! And then another hundred lives until we began to learn that there is such a thing as perfection, and another hundred again to get the idea that our purpose for living is to find that perfection and show it forth. The same rule holds for us now, of course; we choose our next world through what we learn in this one.

Understandably, the concept of human beings reappearing with cloven hooves, sharp beaks, shaggy thighs, or any other animalistic appurtenance has always been a favourite butt of merriment, even among those sympathetic to the idea of reincarnation. William Shakespeare seized upon the theme in *Twelfth Night*, causing Malvolio to poke fun at the Pythagorean idea "that the soul of our grandam might haply inhabit a bird."

Scoffers come and go, yet the belief lingers on. Today there are millions of people from widely divergent cultures who remain convinced that humans can and do reincarnate as lesser beings. Residents of Japan far from the sprawling urban centres still hear in the plaintive singing of the pine insect the voice of the loved one who has been reborn among the bushes of the fields. On the Micronesian island of Yap, souls of the recent dead are said to come back as small, shining cockchafers. In March, 1975, villagers in central Sri Lanka refused to help the island's archaeological department drive away hornets that swarmed around an ancient rock fortress during excavations. Their reasoning was simple: they believed the creatures to be reincarnations of the soldiers of King Kassapa I who had guarded the fortress in the fifth century.

Five years earlier, in Glasgow, Scotland, Mrs. Josephine Ralston had watched a starling swoop down to attend her daughter's wedding service. Later, she declared: "I have never been more certain of anything in my life. That starling was my husband, George." According to Britain's *Weekend* magazine, George Ralston, who had died two years earlier, had often told his wife: "I believe in reincarnation. If I come back to Earth it will be as a bird." The starling not only perched beside Mrs. Ralston for most of the service but also fluttered to join the bride and groom at the altar and later followed the wedding party into the vestry for the signing of the register. As the congregation dispersed, the bird flew to a tree outside the church, chirped loudly, and flew away.

Thousands of miles away on the "Roof of the World," a fly falling into a cup of tea is seen as a catastrophe by Tibetans, according to Heinrich Harrer. The fly "must at all costs be saved from drowning," he writes in *Seven Years in Tibet*, "as it may be the reincarnation of one's dead grandmother. If at a picnic an ant crawls up one's clothes, it is gently picked up and set down." During Harrer's stay, a national decree was issued forbidding the general construction of buildings because worms and insects might easily be killed as work progressed!

Then there's the tragic story of fifteen-year-old Steven Shea who, in the spring of 1976, plunged fifty feet from a multi-storey car park in his home town of Letchworth, England. In his diary police found the clue to his bizarre death—a passage from Richard Adams' *Watership Down*, the best selling novel about life in a rabbit warren, and a note which read: "I'm going to kill myself and become a rabbit." Yet Steven's obsession for transmigration into an animal body as splashed across British newspapers under the headline, "Tragedy of the Rabbit Fantasy Boy" is not so extraordinary when placed in farthest historical perspective.

No Eastern religion developed a wider world view around the idea of reincarnation than that of the Jains of India who teach that everyone passes through literally millions of earth, water, plant, fire, wind, insect, animal, and human incarnations. The water incarnations alone—each of which could last from less than 1 second to 7,000 years—range across seas, lakes, rivers, rains, dew, hoarfrost, snow, hail, ice, clouds, and fog! Believing that every jot of matter accommodates living spirits trapped by their own misdirected will in the cruel round of rebirth, the Jains adopted the philosophy of *ahimsa*, or noninjury, towards all living things. Their exaggerated regard for life is maintained to this very day and devout Jains are expected to follow *ahimsa* to its minutest detail, with no concessions; for example, they may not kill any grubs found in vegetables.

Western tourists in India are puzzled by the tedious progress of white-garbed Jain monks who, wearing masks to prevent murderous inhalations, are careful to whisk away all possible insects from their path. The most pious Jains decline to travel by car because of the havoc wreaked on insect life and they arrange, when ascending mountains designated as shrines, to be carried aloft in sedan chairs by Hindu bearers whose regard for life doesn't extend to the meticulous preservation of the gnat, grub, and beetle populations.

Vegetarianism rests on the principle that living creatures infused with divine spirit should not be consumed by human beings. Imagine, then, the plight of Burmese fishermen whose very livelihood runs contrary to their nation's religious tradition. In the social scale, only an undertaker has more difficulty in marrying off a daughter than a fisherman whose misdeeds are destined to bring him back to earth in one of the lower, probably aquatic, realms. Because necessity long ago demanded that they rationalize their lot, the fisher folk, rather than killing fish and incurring punishment in the next life, merely place their catch on the riverbank to dry. Should the fish be unfortunate enough to expire during the course of this operation, so be it. The fishermen, at least, can't be blamed! Government officials ducked responsibility in the same way when Burma was under military rule in the late 1950s. When soldiers attempting to clear stray dogs from the capital city of Rangoon were ordered to place poisoned meat along the major streets by night, pure meat was prudently mixed with the tainted variety. In this way, the dogs were granted the opportunity to exercise free choice and their killers were acquitted of any violation of Buddhist law.

Shamans of the Cherokee Indians devised an equally ingenious way to pardon the tribe's hunters for killing animals for food. After assigning to every animal a definite lifeterm which could not be curtailed by violent means, the shamans ruled that, should any animal die prematurely, the death is only temporary. The body would be resurrected immediately from spilled blood drops to renew its existence until the close of the predestined period.

As recently as 1870, maids at the vicarage of St. Cleer, Cornwall, refused to kill spiders because they believed their late master, Parson Jupp, had been reborn as one.

Tigerish Appetites Among the Tupinambi

Deep-rooted in the lore of African and South American tribes is the belief that one's enemies can reincarnate in the bodies of wild beasts. In Latin America, the most feared form adopted by reborn adversaries is the South American tiger or jaguar. Sixteenth-century Peruvian historian Garcilasso De La Vega wrote of jaguar-worshipping tribes whose members would offer themselves unresistingly on encountering the beast. Speaking as if they were these jaguars reborn, cannibals have been known to explain their fondness for human flesh in terms of tigerish appetites. Explorer Hans Staden, held as a slave among the Tupinambi of the Brazilian coast many years ago, described a grim visit to his Indian master:

He had before him a great basket of human flesh, and was busy gnawing a bone. He put it to my mouth and asked if I did not wish to eat. I said to him: "There is hardly a wild animal that will eat its kind; how then shall I eat human flesh?" Then he, resuming his meal, said: "I am a tiger, and I find it good."

The Zulus accepted that their dead pass, according to rank, into various kinds of serpents and lizards. The Betsileo of Madagascar—who tied nobles' corpses to the central pillar of the family hut and allowed them to putrefy—believed that serpents called *fanany* were formed in a pot placed beneath the dead body. The soul-bearing infant *fanany* was carried to the tomb after the human remains had been buried and, several months later, a full-grown python emerged to be treated like royalty. The souls of ordinary members of the Betsileo were assumed to pass into crocodiles while any undesirables in the tribe languished as eels. A common practice among the Bagesu and Wanyamwesi tribes of East Africa was to throw out their dead to be devoured by hyenas. Consequently, the cry of a hyena in the evening was always fraught with meaning—it was the voice of the last person who had died in the neighbourhood.

Native belief has not always required human souls to migrate into animal bodies. In many parts of the world, animals are thought to reincarnate as their own kind just as regularly. In fact, when food is at a premium, the pressure is on for human beings to do all they can to hasten this process. To this day, fish bones are thrust into the pole walls and palm-leaf thatch of homes belonging to members of the Warao tribe of Venezuela. This architectural contribution is made out of respect and anticipation, for it is believed that from the old bones new fish will be born. To ensure their salmon supplies remain plentiful, the Kwakiutl Indians of British Columbia take great care to throw the bones and offal of gutted fish back into the sea so that the reincarnating salmon soul is able to reanimate them. Setting fire to the bones, they strongly believe, would eliminate the possibility of rebirth. The Hurons and Ottawa Indians never burned their fish bones for the same reason, fearing they would antagonize the fish souls and drive away from their nets the embodied fish that remained.

The Eskimos of the Bering Strait, believing that seals, walrus and whales remain attached to their bladders after death, practised a ritual to speed up the rebirth of game so essential to their survival. Hunters carefully removed and preserved the bladders of all the sea beasts they killed, presenting them at a solemn annual festival.

Hungarian artist Desider Mockry-Meszaros painted prehistoric scenes which he claimed to remember from remote incarnations. In the *New York Times* of February 9, 1930, he said: "The memory of the mammoth I used to fear then has come back to me crystal clear. I knew the face of the Earth when it was barely cooled off from the volcanic age. And memories of a still earlier incarnation as a dweller in the underworld of another planet supply me with subjects for my brush and pencil."

After being honoured with dances and offerings of food, the bladders were taken outside and thrust through the ice into the frigid water. By returning the bladders to the sea, the tribesmen imagined that the souls of animals, flattered by such gracious treatment, would return willingly in new bodies for a fresh round of spearing and harpooning.

Haeckel's Law

Instincts of activity and migration point to animals, birds, and fish repeating patterns learned over many lives. After four generations of being removed from nesting materials African weaver birds, for example, are still capable of constructing nests that only their species can create. And freshwater eels, salmon, and steelhead trout migrate to the identical rivers which served as home to their forebears, being drawn through rivers and oceans, one can suppose, by long-inculcated awareness of chemicals, temperature, velocity, and direction. But it is Haeckel's Law that most implies reincarnation from the standpoint of biological science. Named after a German scientist of the past century, this law states: "In the ontogeny, the phylogeny is recapitulated." This is to say that during the earliest formative stage of any individual life there are a series of body changes which reflect the evolutionary history of the species. Each stage in the development of the human embryo is an awe-inspiring recapitulation of forms corresponding to unicellular protozoan life, jellyfish, worms, gill-bearing reptiles, and apes! Most biologists attribute this progressive development to programming within the genetic material. But in so doing they deny the spiritual component which surely resides at the very heart of the chemical process.

It is said that the soul's experience in recent lives is reflected in human beings and beasts alike. Paying allegiance to this principle, Himalayan yogi Sri Swami Sivananda (1887-1963) has stated emphatically that pampered pets reveal themselves to be humans who have taken a tumble on the evolutionary staircase. He wrote:

> Some dogs get royal treatment in the palaces of kings and aristocratic people. They move in cars, eat good food, and sleep on cushions. These are all degenerated human beings.

Swami Sivananda and those of similar persuasion are in the minority, however. Most professors of the soul hold that unremitting upward momentum is inherent to spiritual and physical evolution. This would indicate that animals endowed with special qualities of affection, loyalty, and intelligence have almost attained the human level whereas people with brutish natures have joined the family of humans fresh from bestial existence. Sybil Leek, the British-born witch who died in Florida in 1982, had this to say about savages, criminals and loutish personalities in general:

> When we meet people who "behave like animals," we can perhaps understand them better if we view

them as recently evolved egos who have just made it to the human kingdom. They are like children in a kindergarten who cannot be expected to understand, much less follow, all the rules that man in his evolution has learned.

Rebirth, as a means of dispelling ignorance and provoking understanding, is the key to the continuity of this learning. To be born once is to open one's books; to be born many times is to undertake a course of instruction. Only through repeated births can there be growth and consolidation, the fulfilment of promise, the granting of spiritual significance to otherwise meaningless innovation. The greater the number of incarnations, the better the individual's chances of understanding the plan behind the process. And as surely as birth follows death, human respect for life in all its forms

---

For years, Rosemary Brown, author of *Unfinished Symphonies*, wrote down music dictated to her by the spirits of dead composers from Bach to Debussy. When Franz Liszt was asked why she, having no musical knowledge, should have been chosen for the task, he replied that her services had been volunteered "in an earlier life." He also did his best to explain the process of reincarnation: "What happens is rather like the putting out of a fresh shoot on a tree or a plant. On Earth, you think of yourselves as complete beings. But actually only part of you has manifested through the physical body and brain. The rest is still in spirit, but is linked and one with you."

advances with the developing awareness of our furthest beginnings.

The Climb to Superconsciousness

But where is all this evolution leading? From minerals to plants to animals to humans . . . to what? Just as a rock is brushed by swaying foliage yet cannot divine its sensibility, so we are blindly rubbing shoulders with our future. That future lies in the development of superconsciousness, a state beyond the pull of bodily reincarnation. It's conceivable that the denizens of this New Tomorrow of the mind will look upon humans in much the same way—though, one would hope, with greater compassion—that humans regard animals. Presumably, on some other plane of supersensible reality, Tomorrow is already here with the human race, even now, impaled like a butterfly specimen under its successor's gaze. That gaze would take in the interminable recurrence of the same old mistakes leading to the same old suffering. And yet, like the animal kingdom, the human race cannot be expected to evolve, of itself, into a state of perfection. Progressive stages of development satisfy that requirement. The human race can be compared to a class in school that will never improve in overall performance because those who learn their lessons move up to be replaced by others from a lower grade. The graduates, according to the discarnate Frederic Myers, a former Cambridge University classics professor who, after his death in 1901, communicated his experiences to mediums in different parts of the world, gradually evolve through the higher planes, passing beyond matter and form to dwell "not only outside of time but outside of the universe" and to become one with God.

As farfetched as such celestial peregrinations might appear, they are surely no more impossible than the human procession from the mineral kingdom. Evolution will not be constrained by our narrow-minded image of ourselves. Wrote Sri Aurobindo, India's late master yogi: "The soul is not bound by the formula of mental humanity; it did not begin with that and will not end with it; it had a prehuman past, it has a superhuman future."

"We wake and find ourselves on a stair. There are other stairs below us which we seem to have ascended; there are stairs above us, many a one, which go upward and out of sight."

— Ralph Waldo Emerson

I I

FEARLESS FIGHTERS
AND THE SUICIDE
FALLACY

"He is not slain when the body is slain."

– Bhagavad-Gita (2:20)

"Suicide thwarts the plan of the entity which sends out the personality. . . . Fortunately the entity is far beyond the reach of man's destructive tendencies. . . ."

– Manly P. Hall

B ECAUSE HE KNOWS NO FEAR, the warrior who believes in reincarnation is the most indomitable of fighting men. So visceral is his acceptance of rebirth that he can wade into the most frightful carnage confident of emerging spiritually unscathed. No matter how threatening or disadvantageous the battle situation, his inner composure will not falter. For the man who goes to war *knowing* he will return to earth is, in a sense, already dead inside. Resigned to the unthinkable, he has surpassed a purely intellectual understanding of reincarnation; he has plunged into the very process itself.

History teems with fearless fighters who have literally laughed at death. Buddhist tradition holds that reincarnation originally belonged to the warrior caste who guarded the doctrine from misappropriation by the masses. The Celts, the Druids, the Essenes, the ancient Germans and Scandinavians, many North American Indian tribes, and, more recently, the Japanese in World War II, were all emboldened by the reincarnation connection. Each step towards death brought the next life a little closer, a life that could only be enriched by the valour, suffering, and sacrifice of the present moment.

All who saw these campaigners in action and lived to tell the tale marvelled at their fortitude. Struggling against the Romans during the first century A.D., the Essenes, a monastic order living in Palestine, impressed the Jewish historian Flavius Josephus with their capacity to be "above pain, by the generosity of their mind." He wrote in *The History of the Jewish War*:

> They smiled in their very pains and laughed to scorn those who inflicted torments upon them, and resigned up their souls with great alacrity, as expecting to receive them again.

While others fight for life, warriors who embrace reincarnation fight for their lives. The twin exhortations of destiny and just cause override the karmic inadvisability of taking human life to inspire poised, purposeful fanaticism. It was this fanaticism that unnerved Roman legionnaires, in Britain under Suetonius Paulinus in A.D. 61, who were charged with subduing the rebellious Celts and Druids. Sounding as though he is relating nightmare images, the Roman historian Tacitus described the ghoulish reception that awaited the advancing Roman army on the sacred Isle of Mona, now called Anglesey:

> On the shore stood the opposing army with its dense array of armed warriors while between the ranks dashed women in black attire like the Furies, with hair dishevelled waving brands. All round, the Druids lifting up their hands to heaven and pouring forth dreadful imprecations scared our soldiers by the unfamiliar sight . . .

In ancient Celtic mythology, the corpses of slain warriors were thrown into a cauldron of rebirth from which they arose refreshed and ready for renewed fighting. They were, however, unable to speak, which might well have been a symbolic way of communicating that the ordinary soldier, remembering nothing of his previous incarnation, was incapable of voicing his experiences. While Julius Caesar, the great Roman general and statesman, noted that the Celts were "in a great degree excited to valour" by the fearlessness that stems from belief in reincarnation, the Roman poet Lucan was clearly envious that the Druids were unmoved by the greatest human fear of all, the fear of death. "Hence their warrior's heart hurls them against the steel," he writes in the *Pharsalia*, "hence their ready welcome of death, and the thought that it were a coward's part to grudge a life sure of its return."

It's no accident that the dialogue of the Bhagavad-Gita, the great Hindu scripture suffused with rebirth teaching, is conducted on the battlefield. For the message of reincarnation is never more immediate or more pressing than when human life is at stake. As opposing armies mass on the field of Kuruksetra, Lord Krishna advises his friend and devotee, Arjuna, that there is no birth and death for the soul which "can never be cut into pieces by any weapon." Urging dauntlessness in the cause of religious principles, Krishna instructs his disciple:

"Death of a Thousand Cuts" was a punishment employed in eleventh century China to prevent the reincarnation of the most pernicious criminals. Crimes of treason, murder of a close relative or of three or more people belonging to the same family, and the mutilation of a living person in the cause of witchcraft all merited this excruciating penalty in which an adept swordsman sliced the body of the offender 999 times. In accordance with the belief that reincarnating spirits must assume their previous corporeal forms, *ling ch'ih* or "death by slicing" aimed to literally shred the convict's chances of rebirth. "The offender is tied to a cross and, by a series of painful but not in themselves mortal cuts, his body is sliced beyond recognition," wrote Ernest Alabaster in *Notes and Commentaries on Chinese Criminal Law*. Torture, however, was reduced almost to a minimum, the death blow generally being dealt with the third slash.

> Only the material body of the indestructible, im-
> measurable and eternal living entity is subject to de-
> struction; therefore, fight, O descendant of Bharata.
>   (Bhagavad-Gita, 2:18)

Many North American Indian warriors were in-
stilled with similar conviction of their perpetuity. To die
honourably in combat was to ensure a happier rebirth,
Indian lore being laden with accounts of slaughtered
braves who have returned to life. In 1873 the French
anthropologist Alphonse Pinart explained the "extraordinary fierceness" of the Tlingit Indians of British Columbia in recording that, rather than fearing death, they
sought it out "fortified by the expectation of soon returning to this world and in a better position."

Hoaxed by Mythology

Ironically, the very creed which made the Indians so im-
placable in local battles sapped their resistance at the
most critical junctures of history—when they were
under attack, in various parts of the Americas, from
European adventurers. Ancient legends prevalent the
breadth of the continent had told for centuries of the return of the "dawn heroes" said to be of fair complexion,
mighty in war, and destined to recover their power, glory,
and lands of old. Initially, therefore, the pale-skinned
invaders of the New World, instead of encountering uni-
fied opposition, were received with bemused wonderment which sometimes erupted spontaneously into

joyous welcome. No wonder the Aztec and Incan em-
pires toppled so precipitously to the imperialist ambitions of a few heavily armoured Spanish ruffians! On the
eastern seaboard of the United States, the Maryland Indians fell victim to the same mythological hoax. They convinced themselves that the white men landing on their
shores were the reborn representatives of a long-lost generation bent on reclaiming territory that once was theirs.

Reincarnation in the proud Japanese fighting tradition is a cry of defiance swelled by the most fervent
longing to serve the fatherland forever. Rebirth to the
warrior of Japan is *Shichisho Hokoku* or *Serve the Nation
for Seven Lives*, a slogan which adorned the headbands of
kamikaze pilots in the final stage of the World War II.
This rallying shout of determination and derring-do—
more an ardent desire for rebirth than a deep-seated
conviction of its reality—dates back to the fourteenth
century and the noble failure of the samurai Kusunoki
Masashige, faithful servant of the Emperor Godaigo.
Masashige had masterminded victory after victory
against superior forces, culminating in the Battle of
Minato River in 1336 when his troops were hopelessly
outnumbered. Towards the end of the conflict, Masashige, bleeding from eleven wounds, limped from the
battlefield with his younger brother, Masasue, to a
nearby farmhouse to commit *hara-kiri* and thus avoid
capture. As they were about to disembowel themselves,
Masashige asked his brother what his last wish might be,
to which Masasue replied: "I should like to be reborn
seven times into this world of men so that I might
destroy the enemies of the Court." Delighted by this

answer, Masashige is said to have expressed the same wish before committing suicide.

So it was that the *kamikaze* pilots, faced with similar hopelessness in war, adopted identical yearnings in their suicidal missions against American warships in the Pacific. "You are already gods, without earthly desires. . . ," they were told by Vice-Admiral Takijiro Onishi, the man most responsible for initiating the suicide strategy. The pilots, most of whom were aged between twenty and twenty-five, volunteered readily for what was considered the privilege of *rippa na shi*, the "splendid death." Pleading to be dispatched into the skies and pouring out their thanks to senior officers when selected, they savoured in advance the exquisite moment of self-immolation as plane and pilot, diving at 570 m.p.h., slammed into the steel-hulled target, furiously ablaze. That was the dream. In reality, however, the single-seater *kamikaze* planes, their noses packed with high explosives, often missed the aircraft carriers' afterdecks and were swallowed up in the ocean. Yet, for the pilots, effectiveness was always subordinate to honour. Before flying to his death on October 28, 1944, Matsuo Isao of the Heroes' Special Attack Unit wrote:

> I shall be the Emperor's shield and die cleanly with my squadron leader and other friends. I wish that I could be reborn seven times, each time to smite the enemy.

By the war's end, some 5,000 Japanese had died in various *kamikaze* craft—planes, launches, and manned torpedoes. But they weren't the only fearless fighters from the Land of the Rising Sun clinging passionately to their ideals. In battle after battle in the Pacific War, Japanese soldiers avoided surrender by launching fierce, suicidal attacks. Perhaps the most fearsome scenes of all took place on the island of Saipan in July, 1944, when 3,000 Japanese, armed only with bayonets or sticks, charged into the concentrated machine-gun fire of the American marines. Wave after wave surged forward only to be mown down by the deadly hail of bullets. At intervals, new machine-gun emplacements had to be found because Japanese corpses were piled so high they were blocking the lines of fire.

Notwithstanding the end of hostilities and the emergence of Japan as a powerful industrialized nation, the "seven lives" spirit, though fading, was not allowed to perish. Yukio Mishima made sure of that. The country's foremost novelist of the modern age, Mishima railed publicly against the erosion of patriotism in Japan, and wrote fiction which often had a reincarnational theme. In his last work, a series of four novels called *The Sea of Fertility*, the protagonist reappears in successive books as the reincarnation of the hero who has gone before, his identification being three moles on the side of the chest that endure from lifetime to lifetime. Even as this work was being written, Mishima organized his own private army called the *Tatenokai*, or Shield society, with the aim of protecting the emperor from the threat of communism. On November 25, 1970, Mishima and four student members of the *Tatenokai* took an army general hostage at the military base at Ichigaya. There, wearing his *hachimaki* or headband emblazoned with the war cry *Serve the Nation for Seven Lives*, Mishima strode onto the balcony overlooking the parade ground to address a hastily convened gathering of soldiers on the subject of declining national values. Then he retired to commit *hara-kiri* before the captive general. Like Masashige and the suicide pilots who had preceded him, Mishima was in love with reincarnation, his will was strengthened by the idea, but it remained more of an impassioned hope than a belief. The last note this tragic Japanese hero left on his desk said it all: "Human life is limited, but I would like to live forever."

> Many of the so-called new religions of Japan include reincarnation among beliefs which have been laid down over the past 140 years. *Tenrikyo*—a religion that boasts more than two million adherents—teaches that man is reborn many times and that children inherit the consequences of their parents' previous lives.

The Revolving Door

Torn between indigenous Shintoism's honourable death and the reincarnational pulse of imported Buddhism, Mishima would have refrained from taking his life had he truly believed in rebirth. For all the courage that *hara-kiri* demands, reincarnationists warn of the karmic repercussions that flow from self-destruction. In countries where the population at large believes in reincarnation, suicide, being regarded as a petty injunction against cosmic law, is rarely attempted. For it is felt that the problems that precipitate such an act of desperation cannot be avoided; they will only regroup to launch another, perhaps more serious, attack in another existence.

The great Russian writer Leo Tolstoy remarked in his diary:

> How interesting it would be to write the story of the experiences in this life of a man who killed himself in his previous life; how he now stumbles against the very demands which had offered themselves before, until he arrives at the realization that he must fulfil those demands.

Perhaps it is the return of these onerous pressures, made weightier still by the burden of self-murder, that creates the tendency for suicide in one life to be succeeded by suicide in the life that follows. Dr. Ian Stevenson reports the bizarre case of Brazilian Paulo Lorenz who claimed to be the reincarnation of his dead sister, Emilia. Emilia killed herself by taking cyanide on October 12, 1921—fourteen months before Paulo's birth. For the first four or five years of his life, Paulo wore girls' clothes, played with girls and with dolls, and even shared his late sister's sewing skills. He also took on Emilia's self-destructive instincts. Paulo made several attempts to kill himself before committing suicide on September 5, 1966, by splashing inflammable liquid over his clothes and body and setting himself on fire. Stevenson noted in *Twenty Cases Suggestive of Reincarnation*: "In several other cases in which the related previous personality had committed suicide the subject has shown an inclination to contemplate and threaten suicide."

As much as the suicidal personality feels able to escape the world by getting rid of the body, reincarnation's revolving door ensures that all hope of dissolution is short-lived. Those who learn, under hypnosis, that they have killed themselves in past lives are quickly brought to the realization that suicide, far from being an answer to life's problems is, at best, a stalling tactic born of ignorance. In *Reincarnation as a Phenomenon of Metamorphosis*, Guenther Wachsmuth describes the suicidal act as the violent breaking of the lifeline "on the basis of a knowledge of a fraction." And he adds that, if the perpetrator could only realize the resulting intensification of difficulty which must enter the life to come, such interference would never be countenanced. Yet there are those for whom belief in reincarnation actually *encourages* the act of suicide. Mental health expert Dr. J. William Worden, assistant professor of psychology at the Harvard Medical School, cites several cases in which individuals have decided to take their own lives believing that a better life awaits them next time around! While it seems highly unlikely that self-destruction should be rewarded with contentment, psychics and clairvoyants generally agree that death brings no reprieve from suffering, no matter how weary of life those who kill themselves might be. The between-life experience is thought to be characterized by a strong sense of physical deprivation because the suicide's spiritual and physical selves are not ripe for separation. Thus begins a fruitless search by the grieving entity for the body so suddenly withdrawn.

The unabating popularity of suicide (31,142 successful suicides and some 775,000 failed attempts in the United States in 1994) and the proliferation of suicide manuals in the Western world over the past few years, demonstrate that both mystical insight and scientific evidence into the post-mortem state are being hugely disregarded as the act of suicide becomes more and more socially acceptable. The most blatant of the "how-to" guidebooks, a French publication titled *Suicide: Operating Instructions,* equates suicide with revolt against the established order—a more profound statement than the author intended—and even explains how to forge doctors' prescriptions for lethal drugs. An official of *Search,* a French suicide-rescue organization, condemned the manual with these words: "It's criminal. It goes against all our efforts. We're about rebirth. Their message is to flee from life."

How to stifle the self-destructive impulse? The only lasting antidote lies in the recognition that life, not oblivion, waits beyond the last heartbeat. As seductive as suicide might be to the deeply despairing, evolution will not be denied so presumptuously.

> "I cannot take my life, for the Will to accomplish the Object of Art would draw me back into life again until I realized that Object, and so I would only be re-entering this circle of tears and misery."
>
> – Richard Wagner, German composer

12

PLUTO:

PLANET OF REBIRTH

"Pluto kills or destroys but builds out of the elements of the destroyed—out of the old, something new . . ."
  – Fritz Brunhübner

"Pluto can call for a drastic showdown."
  – Alexander Ruperti

SUSPENDED in celestial deep freeze, the planet Pluto sweeps steadily across the outermost reaches of our solar system. Barely blessed with sunlight, this pale, mysterious orb is the most forbidding, most inaccessible planet known to humanity. Inhospitable is too kind an adjective for a world with little or no atmosphere, a craggy, cratered surface packed with ice and methane frost, and an average temperature of minus 346° Fahrenheit. Remote is too gentle a delineation for this refrigerated oath of the Almighty banished to eternal rotation in deep space. Even when at its closest to the sun, Pluto is well over *two billion miles* distant, registering but a faint and yellowish stellar image through the lenses of the most powerful telescopes.

Smaller than the earth, with a diameter of 1,860 miles, Pluto has completed its slow, cyclic swing towards the sun. At perihelion in September, 1989, the planet was 2,750 million miles from the solar furnace—hugely nearer, though hardly cheek by jowl, than its average distance of 3,667 million miles. Pluto reflects sunlight so feebly that it is only one-sixteen-hundredth as bright as the faintest star visible to the naked eye on a clear night. Even more occluded is the planet's moon, Charon, discovered in 1978.

Pluto itself was discovered as recently as 1930, at the depth of the Great Depression. Since then, astronomers have tended to preoccupy themselves with the riddle of the planet's origins while astrologers have considered this invisible glimmer in the night sky from a completely different perspective. They dwell on its significance for the race. Pluto, they say, is the harbinger of death and rebirth; Pluto is coming into its own; Pluto is casting a lengthening shadow upon the affairs of human beings. As ruler of death and rebirth, Pluto is recognized to be a particularly potent force during those rare ages when the planet is at large in Scorpio, its own sign of the zodiac and the sign of sex and death. The world has recently struggled through such an epoch. Pluto entered Scorpio on August 27, 1984, and remained there until November 10, 1995.

> Minerva, goddess of wisdom, rules the highest aspect of Pluto.

An Age Unprecedented

Astrologers the world over branded the recent Pluto/ Scorpio age as being fraught with potential more magnificent and more terrifying than history has ever known. Geological upheaval, economic collapse, nuclear war, wondrous technological innovation, and the transformation of global consciousness were seen as distinct possibilities—the death of the old bringing on the birth of the new. For if Pluto has a cosmic mission it is to provoke the release of the enduring from the transitory and the outworn.

We survived the predictions of global conflict and massive earth changes but were rocked by the AIDS epidemic, diseases which mutated beyond the reach of drugs, and war and genocide in Bosnia and Rwanda— all distinctly Plutonian in character. The most sweeping change of all was invoked by the worldwide revolution in information technology. Widespread use of personal computers combined with the introduction of the Internet and electronic mail ushered in the dawn of planetary consciousness. The Pluto/Scorpio age saw the emergence of one world, electrically if not spiritually.

However, astrologer Caroline Keenan—who examines the current Pluto/Sagittarius transit at the close of this chapter—cautions that all events set in motion during the recent Pluto/Scorpio age have not necessarily come to light. "Scorpio, a fixed sign, tends to retreat into its own obsessions and works from within," she says. "It sets the 'Great Game' and assigns clues for us to follow, whether we are intrepid or foolish."

Profound global change—physical, social, and spiritual—is Plutonian by nature and change at its most extreme is indicated every time Pluto is granted greatest freedom by Scorpio. This moody, passionate transit happens only once every 248.4 years—the time Pluto takes to complete its orbit around the sun—and lasts, on average for twelve years. Just how extraordinary are these eras? Life being the testing ground for astrological assertion, past Pluto/Scorpio ages were traced by computer and cross-referenced with the course of history over the past 2,000 years. Intriguingly, this computer search of correlation revealed that some of the world's most revolutionary events transpired during Pluto/Scorpio periods, events that often precipitated a form of planetary rebirth. The findings can be summarized as follows:

Pluto/Scorpio
Period   Events

A.D. 10–22   • Life and crucifixion of Christ. Traditionally, Jesus Christ is said to have died in A.D. 33, but the research of German historian Robert Eisler and Toronto astrologer William Koenig pinpoint A.D. 21 as the year of the crucifixion. Ancient records tell of Jesus' death taking place in the seventh year of Roman Emperor Tiberius, who acceded to the throne in A.D. 14. According to Koenig, the appearance of Halley's comet in 12 B.C. was the fabled star of Bethlehem heralding the Saviour's birth.

504–515 • Rise of the Frankish empire under Clovis. Uniting many of Europe's barbarians under one ruler, the empire ranged, by A.D. 800, from the Atlantic to the Danube.

997–1008 •Widespread conversion of the Russian people to Christianity in the reign of Vladimir the Saint.

• China forcefully reunified under the Sung dynasty—the dawn of three centuries of economic prosperity.

• Vikings land on the coast of North America.

1244–1255 • Expansion of the Mongol empire across Asia and Europe.

• Heretics hunted and burned at the stake in the first furious years of the Inquisition.

• Women's power and influence curtailed. Society succumbs to enduring ecclesiastical intimidation.

1490–1502 • The height of the Renaissance meaning, literally, "rebirth"; new learning, science, art, and literature.

• The Great Age of Discovery—Christopher Columbus lands in the New World; Vasco da Gama sails to India around the Cape of Good Hope.

• Negro slavery introduced to the West Indies.

1737–1748   • The birth of the Industrial Revolution. Having its beginnings in the English textile industry, the new mechanization transformed civilization. Work and leisure would never be the same again.
• Massive earthquake kills 300,000 in Calcutta, India.

Pluto in Sagittarius

Pluto swept into Sagittarius in November, 1995, and will stay there until November, 2008, promising more radical global transformation. Jupiter, lord of the winds and champion of expansion and excess, rules Sagittarius. On the other hand, Saturn, ruler of contraction and discrimination, holds sway over the ascending sign of Capricorn. This presents an image of great contradiction: generosity yet parsimony, burning yet reaping. Such a configuration suggests upset and division precipitated by physical cataclysm and political realignment (see global chart on page 207).

It must be emphasized that this interpretation is based on mainstream tropical astrology, the system that has gained the acceptance of western civilization. Long out of fashion in the west, sidereal astrology (in which Pluto entered Scorpio in January, 1993, and will remain there until January, 2011) is now enjoying a renaissance. Its proponents argue that theirs is a more spiritual astrology which incorporates greater understanding of karma and rebirth. The systems diverge because tropical astrology symbolizes the relationship between earthly seasons and the planets while sidereal astrology directly reflects the heavens' fixed constellations with the planets in their real astronomical positions. Tropical astrology gives the position of a planet by sign; sidereal astrology gives the position by constellation. The sidereal system, universal in origin, bears traces of the ancient Vedas, the Egyptians, Babylonians, Aztecs, and Mayans. All these astrological systems are capable of examining past lives and contemplating the progress of the soul in the *bardo*. Yet reincarnational links can be traced with tropical astrology, too. Like its sidereal counterpart, tropical astrology observes the Nodes of the Moon—the point where the Moon's orbit intersects the ecliptic—as the major significator of karmic past and future.

Astrological computation—the appraisal of universal energy interacting in the physical world—is the framework of accountancy through which rebirth proceeds. Just as worlds are affected, altered, and reborn by the interplay of cosmological unfoldment, so individuals are embodied in birth after birth according to the same principles. Astrology measures where we stand in the eternal order, each horoscope reflecting ancient causes. Clarice Toyne explains neatly in *Heirs to Eternity*:

> A soul is born at a certain time (as time is accounted in this our solar system) because of what he is. He is not as he is because of the star under which he was born. He is conceived and born at a certain astrological moment because the energies of his soul

tune-in with the cosmic flow of star-forces at that particular time.

The same tuning-in applies, on a much grander scale, to the current positioning of Pluto, Sagittarius, and the planet Earth. A specific pattern of energy is created by each predictable arrangement of the heavens. And this force field affects all consciousness on and within the globe—including that of rocks and minerals.

> The ancients believed in successive reincarnations of the Earth. According to the Stoics, the world was periodically rejuvenated after being consumed by conflagrations. "This is due," wrote Philo, "to the forces of ever-active fire which exists in things and in the course of long cycles of time resolves everything into itself and out of it is constructed a reborn world."

God of the Underworld

The name Pluto, from the Greek *Plouton*, signifies fertility and is thought to be rooted in the Sumerian *Borotun*, meaning "deliverer of the womb." In ancient Greek mythology, Pluto exemplifies power and will as the unscrupulous god of the underworld. In his gloomy domain deep below ground, he receives and regenerates the souls of the dead. For Pluto ("the rich one," in Latin) is the gatekeeper of immortality and his subterranean passages are running over with the collective past of the human race. Enthroned beside his consort, Persephone, he is always invisible, a quality symbolized by his hood, made from the scalp of a dog. In keeping with this guise, Pluto's influence is veiled and usually operates subliminally for long periods before revealing itself in drastic change. Even the planet's recent discovery after untold cycles of manipulation is illustrative of the Plutonian character.

Pluto represents the unconscious—individual and collective—and governs forces buried deep in the psyches of human beings and nations. Along with many of her contemporaries, American astrologer Isabel M. Hickey maintains that the planet's obscure energy is at work behind the restlessness, chaos, and confusion of the modern world. She felt that Pluto's transit through Scorpio would ensure the elimination of "ancient wrongs and evils" by touching off "a purging such as the world has never known." Although Edgar Cayce didn't express himself quite so apocalyptically, he did predict that Plutonian forces would culminate in worldwide geological upheaval by the year 1998. And he did remark (reading 1100–27) before World War II:

> Within the next hundred to two hundred years there may be a great deal of influence (of Pluto) upon the ascendancy of man; for it's closest of those to the activities of the Earth, to be sure, and is a developing influence, not one already established.

Pluto rules places of horror and destruction, earthquakes and volcanoes, caves, catastrophes, wars, epidemics, and floods. There's the obvious link with Plutonium, the synthetic radioactive element notorious for its major role in the construction of nuclear warheads. But the planet is also very much concerned with the fecundity that springs from death. In the words of astrologer Stephen Arroyo: "One of the paradoxical aspects of Pluto's nature is that its symbolism incorporates both the old life forms which are ready to be eliminated *and* the very power that will shatter those forms and effect . . . psychological-emotional surgery." Volcanic ash, for example, may suggest destruction, but it also produces the most fertile soil. Cave clay and mineral springs are found in the depths of the Earth but their properties can give new life to the sick. Archaeological discoveries, the raising of submerged treasures, cemeteries, pyramids, and temples are all Plutonian. And Pluto governs interest in reincarnation, development of spiritual insight, and the pineal gland, our degenerated organ of clairvoyance. Fritz Brunhübner, who wrote the first, classic work on Pluto in 1934, spoke of the planet being responsible for reanimation and refinement of the pineal gland which would help to lead humanity "out of the mechanization and mechanical technology of our times into an epoch of revivification, of resurrection, of magic and creative power."

Like his contemporary, Edgar Cayce, Brunhübner was "thoroughly convinced" that massive Earth movements would raise the lost continent of Atlantis from the ocean floor. Rebirth of the untraceable would go hand in hand with the death of the obsolete. The influence of Pluto, he wrote, "will be transplanted to the whole international, political, and economic life . . . the new spirit knocks on the door with hammer blows and dictatorially demands the reorganization and changeover."

Global Rebirth

As unwelcome as change by coercion might be, the action of Pluto, like death itself, is essential for the rebirth that evolution demands. To be reborn, first you must die! Pluto's task is to press for evolutionary perfection, to push the individual and the race through hoops of renewal in life as in death. Ideally, humanity will pursue and bring about its own rebirth by uniting in caring, understanding, and tolerance of individual differences. But, as Alexander Ruperti points out in *Cycles of Becoming*, if humans are incapable of such enlightened behaviour, then the world's population may be compelled to unite in death . . .

> Through the fire of man-made or planetary cataclysms, nuclear war, or telluric upheaval, Pluto will teach people to know and feel (Scorpio) that we are all individually concerned with everything that happens to human beings everywhere on the globe.

If Pluto must invoke annihilation, it is also the turning point, the catalyst of fresh beginnings. In penetrating to the core of experience, in painfully tearing away the ephemeral from that which lasts, Pluto, the gatekeeper, is obliged to offer new horizons. Dane Rudhyar, California's grand old man of astrology, wrote that Pluto "guards the path that leads through unconscious death or conscious Crucifixion to some type of celestial reintegration." Which is all very well until we are reminded that, in this madcap nuclear age, the path over which Pluto stands sentinel is the warpath. But if humanity is flirting with a showdown of the darkest Plutonian forces, maybe that's because, in some dim cranny of the collective unconscious, the race knows there is nothing to lose from wholesale destruction. Even the Apocalypse can take on positive overtones when seen as a flashpoint of rebirth. For exactly how the reincarnation of global consciousness is achieved matters little. From the grandest spiritual perspective, whether it is realized in the fullness of vitality or in mass extermination, the requirement is the same: *to be reborn, first you must die*!

> "Behold now the hope and desire to go back to our own country, and to return to our former state, how like it is to the moth with the light! . . . This longing is the quintessence and spirit of the elements, which, finding itself imprisoned within the life of the human body, desires continually to return to its source. And I would have you to know that this very same longing is that quintessence inherent in nature, and that man is a type of the world."
>
> – Leonardo da Vinci

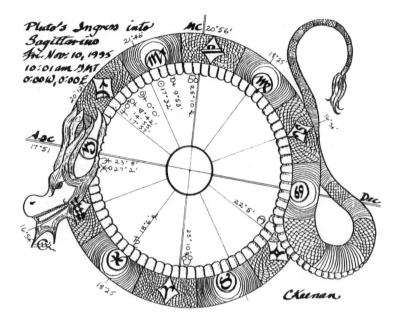

Pluto's Ingress into
Sagittarius
Fri. Nov. 10, 1995
10:01 am GMT
0:00 W, 0:00 E

PLUTO/SAGITTARIUS TRANSIT: NOV. 10, 1995 TO NOV. 27, 2008

Global Chart Drawn and Analyzed
by Astrologer Caroline Keenan

As I look at this chart the phrase that comes to mind is: "joyous survival." Despite—or, perhaps, because of—the dire consequences of Pluto in Scorpio, the consciousness of our troubled planet has been raised. We have survived genocide and the putrefaction of plagues to rise from the ashes into a developing new consciousness. Still bearing a great burden of karmic debt, we have suffered losses and gained wisdom. We may not feel richer from a material perspective, but we seem to have profited in the way of humanity as this chart—despite the great difficulties yet to come—*is* full of hope and joy. Hope and joy, in this instance, is an admonition of sorts. In order to feel joy one needs to *be* joyous. The joyousness of this chart is not an emotion that follows good fortune but a state of mind, a way of being.

One very important aspect of the planet Pluto is the phoenix that rises from the ashes. This Pluto/Sagittarius transit can be considered the era of the Phoenix, the transformation, the age that leads us to the next level. The fire and mutability at work indicate a shift in faith and focus—possibly even a shift in our polar axis—as our solar system gradually slips into a photon belt that will change the complexion of physical light seen in our world. This change is indicative of enlightenment.

Pluto, a symbol of reincarnation in the language of astrology, is one member of a karmic trilogy. Its partners are always the Nodes of the Moon, representing the path, the future (north) and the past (south), and the Twelfth House, the dustbin of the universe and the repository of our chronic ills.

In this chart, all the planets tenant the oriental sky, as well as being imprisoned there by the Nodes of the Moon. The Moon is the only exception, appearing in the occidental sky which grants a modicum of free choice. The following planets all tenant Sagittarius (universal fire) in the Eleventh House of hope: Pluto (metamorphosis, subterranean forces, corruption, renewal, elimination, power); Venus (aesthetics, values, women, influence, charm, co-operation); Mars (assertiveness, violence, action, men, elegance, the cutting edge) and Jupiter (the power of command, society and its belief structures, conviction, unlimited growth). Opposing these planets is The Moon which represents great masses of people and, in this instance, translates the shifting air sign of Gemini into emotional or reactive responses from the population. This leaves far too much room for panic.

Midpoint between The Moon and the Sagittarian group, the planet Saturn is lodged in Pisces. Saturn is commander of structures and universal law and represents the bare bones of existence. Removing all that is unnecessary and setting limits and boundaries, Saturn always seems to start a new phase by shaking us down to our inner limits. The great mutability of this configuration allows for much confusion and dilemma while indicating there are many who would turn outlaw. "Sagittarius is the original cowboy," declared California astrologer Richard Ideman. "He walks out of the saloon and rides off in all directions."

There is another major point of strife. The ascendant—rising in the movable, universal earth sign of Capricorn—is conjunct Neptune and Uranus. This is in conflict with the Nodes of the Moon which, bisecting the chart in Libra/Aries, have entrapped all but The Moon. The ascendant represents activity and Neptune is the psi factor or collective unconscious that gathers all in a single action, ruling the waters, gases, synthetics, beliefs, and all mind-altering substances. This creates confusion, illusion, and reflected images, combining with Uranus as it realigns our electrical fields to create ingenuity, revolution, innovation, and explosions. All this interaction indicates the following during the thirteen-year Pluto/Sagittarius passage:

Changing Weather Patterns: The increased unpredictability of storms and rain, much speculated upon by the media and scientists, must accelerate during this transit. The great planet Jupiter, lord of fire, wind and excess, graces his own sign, Sagittarius, lending his capricious capacity for sweeping change.

Volcanic Activity and Geophysical Upheaval: Expect an increase in both intensity and frequency. It is, indeed, time for the long-awaited "Big One." Consequently, this is not a good time to move to the seashore. Those intending to survive are advised to acquire a tectonic map, possibly from the local department of mines or resources, and move away from indicated fault lines. Volcanic activity will produce a great deal of ash and debris, an attempt by our planet to refertilize and reinvent herself. Utter destruction is not indicated—just a paring down to the bare bones of the planetary body.

Problems with Food Production and Distribution: Under such precarious conditions, food will be an essential concern—especially in large urban areas and other places dependent upon importation of foodstuffs. The ash that will fall on the world, accompanied by a great deal of rain, will replenish us. But replenishment will take time. People should stock their homes with essential supplies: dried, canned, and preserved food.

Energy Crisis: With so much emphasis on changing weather and tectonic activity, disruption of essential services is likely to follow. Transportation powered by electricity, gas, oil, and other fuels is at risk. Many industrial processes may be curtailed. This, in turn, will provoke fresh assessment of our wasteful consumption of natural resources.

Government: Both the United States and Canada have Moon in Gemini in their founding charts which suggests an element of twinning, or of being split in two. Much global redivision is indicated either politically or as a result of physical cataclysm. Political instability has already been evident as the patched-together countries in the world have tried to retreat into their component parts. Unwieldy federal controls may no longer function and may disintegrate.

Technology: Another giant leap forward seems likely. We teach ourselves how our brains function through the use of technology and, in so doing, expand our abilities.

Elimination: Although no planets tenant the Twelfth House, Jupiter and all its activities govern the action in this chart. Jupiter is the planet of excess and everything that involves Jupiter is always accomplished massively. Apparently, we have all gathered to witness, and be a part of, some great transforming energy surge. All that has been spoiled will have to be eliminated. And while many will lose their lives, most of us will remain to see the New Order come into existence.

Summing Up: The positioning of Pluto, The Nodes of the Moon, and the conditions of the Twelfth House suggest that we stand ready for the dawning of a New Order. Those of us who choose to live will open our awareness to the reality that we—every rock, tree, bird, animal, and human being on this planet—are a single, sentient entity. We must ride forth with an open mind to meet the future fearlessly and with confidence.

We will survive!

13

THE PERSONAL INVESTIGATION OF PAST LIVES

". . . Explore the River of the Soul; whence or in what order you have come . . ."

– Zoroaster

"Every incarnation that we remember must increase our comprehension of ourselves as we are."

– Aleister Crowley

H UMAN MINDS are like anchors that have lain too long on the ocean floor: to be fully appreciated, they must be lifted from the muddy deception of their working environment and scoured of clinging deposits. Just as an anchor is habitually coated with seaweed and barnacles, so the mind is beset by swarms of thought and emotion that mask its true nature. These layers of mental obscuration must be removed before the personal investigator of past lives gives the slightest consideration to actually probing for memories of earlier incarnations. Through deep meditation, attention must be withdrawn from all compelling distractions, internal as well as external, and turned over to contemplation of the eternal backdrop. Then, and only then, can the mind—calm, unencumbered, and receptive—be plumbed for its treasure trove of recollection.

It's not easy. The emotions of each new birth, compounded by the cares, worries, and distractions of the present moment, screen the self from mind-images of former lives. That which is coarser and nearer will always blot out the finer and more remote. To surpass the consciousness of everyday living, to discard temporarily the normal way of perceiving and coping with the world, goes against all societal conditioning and requires the utmost persistence. Much like the search for gold, the trail that leads to the awakening of past-life memory usually zigzags over exacting terrain which must be negotiated tirelessly if the priceless vein, hitherto existing only at the suggestion of a stranger, is to be found and excavated. Needed all at once are the ability to relax, the power of concentration, the will to proceed, and the patience to wait for results.

The technique—and there are many variations on a basic theme—is carried out without a guide or helpmate and without the aid of hypnosis. Indispensable, however, are quiet surroundings and a strong desire to cross repeatedly the chasms that separate birth from death. Yet more is required of the individual than mere desire for knowledge of past lives. Would-be explorers must have firmly decided they are willing to undertake—and ready to handle—this always unpredictable quest. Colin Bennett, the author of *Practical Time Travel,* a handbook published in 1937 to encourage the welling up of reincarnational experience, cautions the personal investigator: "Cutting adrift, however temporarily, from the particular position in time and space which we call the present moment sounds exciting and is exciting, but is no more suitable for the spiritually unstable than is crossing the Atlantic in a fishing boat the right kind of adventure for the physically timorous." British reincarnation researcher J. H. Brennan adds: "If your doctor has warned you to avoid excitement do not turn to exploring your past lives as a soothing sedentary occupation." Assuming, however, that the adventurer feels equipped for the journey, there's nothing left to do but set out . . .

> "Is it possible by a system of selective thinking to reach only those past incarnations which are sufficiently free from cruelty and grossness to place no serious burden upon the brain of a highly-strung person whose nervous system is attuned to the comparative refinement of modern civilized life? Can we, to put it bluntly, bowdlerize our time-travel experience? I know of no way to do so by any act of deliberation."
>
> – Colin Bennett

Tracking Backwards

Many names are given to the retrieval of past-life information. They range from the tantalizing "Magical

Memory" of Aleister Crowley, the English mystic with the satanic reputation, to the long-winded *pubbeni-vasanussatinana* of Buddhism. Gautama Buddha himself, although he was said to have recalled 550 of his own past lives, didn't explain (at least, not for the record) just how he remembered his previous existences except to say that anyone who wished to do likewise "must be perfect in the precepts, bring his emotions to a state of quiescence, practice the trances diligently, attain to illumination, and dwell in solitude." Buddha laid great stress on determination to succeed because "if the mind be fixed on the acquirement of any object, that object will be attained." A devotee, he said, should say to himself:

> Let me call to mind many previous states of existence, as, one birth, two births . . . twenty births . . . one hundred births, one thousand births, one hundred thousand births . . . saying: I lived in such a place, had such a name . . . Then I passed from that existence, and was reborn in such a place. There also I had such a name, was of such a family, of such a caste, had such possessions, experienced such joys and sorrows, and such a length of life. Then I passed from that existence and was reborn in this existence. Thus let me call to mind many former states of existence, and let me precisely define them.

Buddhaghosha, a sage whose name means the Voice of Buddha, gave more explicit instructions as to how past lives could be retrieved. In a passage from the *Vishuddhi Marga* or *Path of Purity* he advised fellow

Buddhists to meditate deeply on events which have just taken place, and then to recall them in reverse succession. Absorbed in after-breakfast meditation, when he has returned from collecting alms, the devotee should

> . . . consider the event which last took place, namely his sitting down; next the spreading of the mat; the entering of the room; the putting away of bowl and robe; his eating; his leaving the village; his going the rounds of the village for alms; his entering the village. . . . Thus must he consider all that he did for a whole day and night, going backwards over it in reverse order.

Once a full day's remembrance has been achieved without any gaps or obscure episodes, says Buddhaghosha, the devotee should push back his memory—still in reverse order—to the day before, and the day before that, ten days before, a month, a year, ten years, twenty years, and so on. Any broken links in the chain of memory must be repaired by plunging back into the trance of association. When memory has been revived uninterruptedly as far back as conception, the supreme challenge is to harness sufficient intensity of concentration to penetrate even further to a name and form at the moment of death in the previous life. Buddhaghosha is sympathetic to the extreme arduousness of this test, recognizing that "this point of time is like thick darkness and difficult to be made out by the mind of any person still deluded." Nevertheless, he urges a nondespairing outlook, calling upon the student to repeatedly fix his mind on the void which "in no long time" will yield the desired knowledge. Once the previous existence has been retrieved, other existences will be easier to call to mind, says Buddhaghosha. In his book *A Hermit in the Himalayas*, Paul Brunton writes that the learned monk who instructed him in Buddhism had practised these meditations for twenty years and could testify to their effectiveness. But the monk also admitted that few Buddhists were able to pursue the method with success as the concentration and effort required were so fearfully difficult and prolonged.

> "There is . . . a system of Yoga whereby the yogi is taught to enter the dream-state at will, in order to explore scientifically its characteristics as compared with the waking state, and then to return to the waking state without breaking the stream of normal consciousness. Thus is realized the illusory nature of both states. The practice also enables its master to die and to be reborn without loss of memory—death being the entry into a dream-state and birth the awakening."
>
> – W. Y. Evans-Wentz

The Vehicle of Yoga

Yoga has been defined as "the cessation of agitation of the consciousness" and is, accordingly, a perfect vehicle for the generation of past-life memory. Ironically, Hindu belief in reincarnation is one reason why many natives of India shun yogic practices. Firmly assured of future lives, they consciously postpone personal striving for perfection to another lifetime! But that neither negates nor alters the aim of yoga (stemming from the Sanskrit word *yuj* meaning union) which is to awaken cosmic consciousness at the earliest opportunity and so to leap clear of the dreaded wheel of rebirth. Remembering past lives is part of the overall process. The indeterminably ancient sutras of Patanjali, the earliest yogic texts, point out that all experience of previous births remains in *chitta*, that is, in the subconscious mind. This experience can be recovered at will by the advanced spiritual aspirant through *samyama*, or the rapt absorption of thought waves. Patanjali wrote: "Concentrate on the impressions of the past; know past lives."

Rudolf Steiner said the same thing in a different way when he replied "The entrance to the path is opened by right meditation" in answer to those curious to know why people do not normally remember past lives. More explicitly, Steiner recommended that those wishing to recover memories of pre-existence enlist the help of an imaginary detachable double every time something seems to happen by chance. Suppose a tile falls from a roof and injures a person's shoulders. Rather than blame this injury on bad luck, the person should visualize an imaginary man or woman who climbs onto the roof in question, loosens a tile and quickly returns to ground level so that the dislodged tile may fall on his/her shoulders. Steiner said that this exercise of seeing ourselves deliberately bringing about events that may appear to happen by accident "can ultimately promote in every human being a kind of certainty of having existed in an earlier life—certainty through having engendered a feeling of inner impressions which he knows were most definitely not received in this life."

For Aleister Crowley, a frequent dam in the river of past-life memory was the suppression of painful episodes, primarily death experiences, by the subconscious. "One instinctively flinches from remembering one's last, as one does from imagining one's next, death," he wrote. But if the "tricks of the trade" were practised diligently, even "Freudian forgetfulness" could be conquered so as to liberate the full flood of Magical Memory. Crowley's backward-looking past-life exercises bear more than a passing resemblance to the Buddhist technique expounded some 2,500 years earlier. First of all, he urged would-be adepts to learn to write backwards with either hand, to walk backwards, to speak backwards ("Eh ma I" instead of "I am He") and to read backwards. He then invoked the Buddhaghosha method of recalling events in reverse order. A regression of five minutes must be perfected before extending the backward run to a day and, eventually, a lifetime. (Says Crowley: "The extension from a day to the course of his whole life will not prove so difficult as the perfecting of the five minutes.") Practice, which in time becomes almost mechanical, should be carried out at least four times a day. Only when the mind has been allowed to return one hundred times to the hour of birth should it be encouraged to run back even further—and that's when the Magical Memory, with any luck, starts to unfold. Crowley cautions all to cross-check with historical and geographical fact the contents of these apparently prein-carnate recollections "always reflecting upon the fallibil-ity even of such safeguards." But there's another test for the real thing. He writes in *Magick in Theory and Practice*:

> Genuine recollections almost invariably explain oneself to oneself. Suppose, for example, that you feel an instinctive aversion to some particular kind of wine. Try as you will, you can find no reason for your idiosyncracy. Suppose, then, that when you explore some previous incarnation, you remember that you died by a poison administered in a wine of that character, your aversion is explained by the proverb: "A burnt child dreads the fire."

And there are other intimations of authenticity. Crowley again:

> There is a sense which assures us intuitively when we are running on a scent breast high. There is an *oddness* about the memory which is somehow an-noying. It gives a feeling of shame and guiltiness. There is a tendency to blush. One feels like a school-boy caught red-handed in the act of writing poetry. There is the same sort of feeling as one has when one finds a faded photograph or a lock of hair twenty years old among the rubbish in some forgotten cab-inet. This feeling is independent of the question whether the thing remembered was in itself a source of pleasure or of pain. Can it be that we resent the

idea of our "previous condition of servitude"? We want to forget the past, however good reason we may have to be proud of it. It is well known that many men are embarrassed in the presence of a monkey.

When the personal investigator does not experience this self-consciousness—expressed more forcefully by Colin Bennett as self-disgust—the accuracy of the memory is more open to question than usual. Distrust, as well as rigorous historical enquiry, should be directed towards any glamorous past life that emerges. And distrust should turn to outright scepticism if results indicate the investigator is the reincarnation of a famous person. As conceivable as a past life of historical renown might be, it is much more likely to be the product of overblown fantasy, self-deception being an ever-present danger in every occult area of inquiry. The groundbreaking work of responsible reincarnation researchers can only be undermined by the myriad claims of those convinced they once were Napoleon, Julius Caesar, Henry VIII, Cleopatra, Joan of Arc, and others. Enough is enough.

> "I well understand why God might shut men off from accessible knowledge of the past beyond their past. Genealogical elitism is aggravating enough. Imagine how hard it would be to live with someone, say, who had been Abraham Lincoln once. And could remember everything."
> – D. Keith Mano

Gazing into the Past

Mercifully, the act of sustained mental retrogression is not the only way to contact past lives without undergoing hypnosis. There's a technique for visualizing a clock face in order to "think away" the dial and bring on a trance state that carries the investigator back through time and space. Not so difficult as back-pedalling the memory to past lives, the following exercise still makes huge demands:

> To begin, select a clock face which can be watched quietly and without interruption. Note the size of the face and every single detail that it encloses—the outline of the numerals, the shape of the hands, the manufacturer's name, the layout and ornamentation. Concentrate on assimilating a complete picture of the clock face and, after five minutes, close your eyes and try to recall precisely what you have been looking at.
>
> Only when the dial has been reproduced in the mind's eye with perfect clarity should the dismantling process begin. First, imagine the minute hand has been removed so that the dial is complete in every detail but for its single-handedness. Next, "think away" the hour hand; then remove the ornamentation and the maker's name. Acutely aware that time itself is being thought into nonexistence, you similarly despatch the numerals. You are now confronted with a blank clock face which must be seen to become smaller and smaller until it disappears

completely. All the while, you are thinking: "Time is flowing backwards." Now all that remains is the clock's support. When this has been imagined into extinction the last link with time has been removed and the resulting trance state carries you back into another life . . .

As uncomplicated as this method may sound, immediate success is highly improbable. A few weeks of diligent practice can bring results to the wilful and the persevering, but there are those who proceed with this exercise in vain.

By gazing intently into a crystal ball or goldfish bowl filled with water, a road of living memory can be thought into existence, a road leading from the self into the deepest heart of the crystal. Tibetans employ this method with black crystalline stones found in mountain streams while, in India, natives use a small bowl or saucer—or even cupped hands—filled with ink. Once a strong psychic link has been established between the investigator and the object of concentration, time slowly recedes, rolling backwards through the present life before leaping into past incarnations. The procedure has an inbuilt speed of its own and will not be hurried. Initially, no more than twenty minutes or half an hour should be spent on this exercise, to be repeated not more than once a day until results become decisive. Writes Colin Bennett: "The earliest superphysical phenomenon is often a clouding of the crystal's surface with thin blue haze which may extend above the sphere and hover over it like a patch of mist. Once this appearance is seen it is only a matter of patience before the cloud in front of the crystal's face parts or disperses giving place to a picture."

Alternatively, an archetypal symbol can be used as the object of concentration—a symbol such as an eye, circle, sun, cross, triangle, or, perhaps, one of the numbers from one to ten. Acting as a mind-sensitizer, the chosen symbol (visualization can be aided by a drawing) will become a channel for the drawing of energy from the deep unconscious and the inner eye will be swept by flashes of scenes from past lives. Each passing fragment constitutes a potential clue and the investigator is advised to jot down each one in the hope that a pattern will emerge of one or more former lives.

The annotation and analysis of dreams can also awaken deep memory. The individual's dream records tend to hover around a few central thoughts and incidents—pointers to deeply felt experiences of the past which have contributed greatly to the character and personality of the present. To dream is to travel beyond time, and to travel beyond time is to swirl through a maelstrom of hints and impressions that may reveal who we are, where we've been, and where we're going. Making sense of this fourth-dimensional bombardment is another matter altogether. Colin Bennett recommends that prolonged study of personal dream records be followed by lying back, closing the eyes, relaxing all muscles, and allowing the mind to become as blank as possible. "Out of the resulting state of semi-consciousness," he says, "the sought-for truth appears as though it were an incident acted upon a stage, or seen in a moving picture."

The worldwide Rosicrucian Order, with 250,000 members in more than 180 countries, has preserved and developed more than eighty different types of exercises for the restoration of past-life memory. The underlying motive of these mental workouts is that of the Rosicrucian movement itself—to awaken cosmic consciousness in the individual. Taking various approaches to meditation and guided visualization, the exercises are directed at answering the question: How can I be more effective, more creative, and more whole today? Rosicrucians stress that the value of the reincarnational experience is determined by its usefulness during this lifetime. "The most important point to remember," notes the *Rosicrucian Digest* of October, 1979, "is that at the individual level, reincarnation becomes not a question of proof or faith but of personal *experiences* that give meaning and dimension to our present life."

Seers and occultists have long talked about the Akashic Records as the indelible impressions left upon the etheric substance of the universe by everything that has ever happened. In a lecture given in 1931, Edgar Cayce described a typical out-of-body journey which gave him access to this warehouse in the sky. "I entered this temple and found in it a very large room, very much like a library," he said. "Here were the books of people's lives, for each person's activities were a matter of actual record, it seemed. And I merely had to pull down the record of the individual for whom I was seeking information." Far from being the sole preserve of great mystics, these Akashic Records—which Cayce said were "to the mental world as the cinema is to the physical world"—are open for inspection by anyone who is able to travel to the astral plane. J. H. Brennan says that by an act of imagination it is possible for the individual to create an astral shell capable of interacting with the Akashic Records. He suggests flexing the imagination with a walk towards Cayce's library, visualizing the scene for no more than ten minutes daily for the first two weeks and thereafter—at least until complete identification is achieved—for no longer than fifteen minutes. The investigator's patience will be sorely tried as he is asked to do the following:

(a) For the first week, after relaxing the mind with closed eyes, visualize walking down a corridor towards a door. Clarify and add to the picture each day until the corridor takes on absolute familiarity.

(b) No earlier than a week later—when the corridor is as vivid as it can possibly be—picture opening the door and entering a massive library. Spend at least two weeks, preferably longer, building up minute detail of this library. Note the multitude of sections, the billions of volumes on the shelves, the vast space involved. For in this collection is recorded every detail on every person who has ever lived.

(c) Attempt no short cuts—they will only ruin the project. Every possible detail must be assimilated before the vision is complete. When this happens, keep building and re-examining the picture for another week. Then walk to the section of the library which houses your life history and

> search the shelves for the volume that bears your
> name. Withdraw the book and read your rein-
> carnational history. Before acceptance, cross-
> check all the resulting information—some of
> it visualized, some arising in picture-image
> form—with known facts.

Akashic exploration may not always be so straightforward. Occultist Alice Bailey warned that fleeting
glimpses of the Akashic film don't necessarily pertain to
the viewer as much as the viewer would like to think
they do. "This is not the case," she wrote, "any more
than the people and activities seen out of any window in
a big city reveal to the onlooker his own relatives, friends
and pursuits." Certainly, only the most vigorous visualization can bring results. And even these results are suspect until proven sound.

The mystic Isaac Luria (1534–1572) was said to recognize the souls of all he met. Writes Ernst Müller in *History
of Jewish Mysticism*: "Looking at the forehead of a man
he could tell at a glance from what particular source his
soul was derived and the process of transmigration
through which it had passed and what its present mission was on earth. . . . He was able to tell men their past
as well as predict their future, and to prescribe for them
the rules of conduct calculated to make amends for their
shortcomings in a previous existence." Luria, who spent
thirteen years as a hermit in a hut on the banks of the
Nile, died of a plague.

The Christos Experience

Retaining visualization as the primary technique, it *is* possible—some would say preferable—to explore past lives with the help of others. The Christos Experience, in which a person's ankles and "third eye" area are massaged simultaneously to induce lucid, conscious "dreaming," has carried its subjects into the wildest terrain for the most exotic experiences. Writer Gerry Glaskin, who has championed the technique which he found in an obscure West Australian magazine in 1971, confessed to being "shattered" by his first Christos voyage. He wrote in *A Door to Eternity*:

> Prior to this experience . . . I had not even considered, let alone been convinced of, the possibility of previous lives or reincarnation. My religious upbringing had denied it completely. But now, nevertheless, I could clearly see "myself" with dark skin, long thin limbs, and a body well over six feet tall, with long and very different features to myself—a man, moreover, in this thirties, instead of almost fifty as I was then. "I" was dressed in a garment and headband that I could only conjecture to be Egyptian . . .

In another Christos journey, Glaskin saw himself as a primitive being on the run from other savages. One woman experimenter described being in the body of an albatross gliding over cold southern oceans. And, as if to show the method can conjure up future visions too, a man who had described a small village surrounded by mountains later returned from his honeymoon in Norway to reveal that he had visited the exact scene encountered during his Christos experience! Here's an abbreviated description of the technique:

(a) The subject, who must be relaxed, is to lie, shoeless, on the floor with a cushion under his head. One helper massages the subject's ankles for two to three minutes to aid relaxation. The other—usually the Christos "guide"—massages the "third eye" position, that is, the lower centre of the forehead. This massaging is done vigorously with the edge of the curved hand and should continue until the subject's head is buzzing.

(b) Ask the subject—who is now encouraged to talk so that he will later feel at ease in describing the experience—to visualize himself growing 2 inches longer through the bottoms of his feet. Once the subject has stretched, ask him to return his feet to their normal position. The process is repeated, but this time the subject is asked to grow longer through his head. Return to the feet, asking the subject to visualize a 12-inch stretch. Repeat the process through the head—and return. Back to the feet for a 24-inch stretch. This time the subject must *hold* the stretch while extending the same distance through the head. Once extended 4 feet, he should feel himself expanding, like a balloon.

(c) Ask the subject to use his expanded consciousness to describe fully his own front door and its
surroundings—including what he is standing
on and what is above him when he looks up.
Next, ask him to imagine he is standing on top
of his roof and to describe the scene below. Now
tell him to rise about 500 yards and to keep describing all he sees. He should turn slowly, in a
complete circle, relating all. Ask him what time
it is and elicit a description of the weather conditions. Get him to change the scene from day
to night and back to day again and ask him to
compare both scenes. Next—to give him an as-
surance of safety—ask who is changing daylight
to darkness. It is very important that he realizes
he has control over whatever he sees.

(d) Now for the experience which could yield a past
life. Tell the subject to keep the picture in bright
sunlight so that he can see where he lands. Ask
him for a description of his feet (bare or with
shoes?), the ground he is standing on, the people and events around him, his clothes, his features, etc. Keep pressing for more and more
details. Watch the eyelids for rapid-eye and eye-
muscle movements—the faster the flicker, the
more successful are the subject's visions. Follow
up his answers with pertinent questions. Let the
visit take its course until the subject wishes to
return to the present. He is not in a trance and
should, if asked, be able to identify local sounds
while experiencing the events of a different time

frame. Although the full procedure is likely to take an hour or more, the subject will probably think he has been travelling for only a quarter of the time.

Visualization is given another twist by Bryan Jameison's "montage time-lap" method in which imaginary light switches, placed strategically on the body, are turned off one by one before a make-believe elevator carries the subject to the threshold of a past-life experience. The average, first-time subject takes only eight minutes to reach an altered state of consciousness. "Doing a time-lap regression is amazingly easy," writes Jameison. "It doesn't involve the use of drugs, a deep hypnotic trance, arduous meditation, hocus-pocus or any mysterious rite . . . It's as easy as playing tic-tac-toe." Devised for subject and guide, the method goes like this:

(a) Choose a very dimly lit room without any distractions. Ask the subject to lie down and take five deep breaths with eyes closed.

(b) Instruct the subject to visualize common wall light switches at the key body points and to turn them off in the following order: right foot, right knee, right hip, left foot, left knee, left hip, back of right hand, right elbow, right shoulder, back of left hand, left elbow, left shoulder, top of the head, mid-forehead, throat, base of the spine, back of the neck.

(c) Once the subject has visualized an elevator, ask him to approach it, push the call button and, on its arrival, to step inside and face the front. Guided by his superconscious, he should then select a floor most conducive to the reliving of a past life and describe what he sees when the elevator stops and the doors open. (SPECIAL NOTE: If the subject sees a life scene on leaving the elevator, ask him to check whether he's in a former body. If clouds are seen instead of a hallway, ask him to move into the clouds and go back in time to the first important earth life. Should this happen, disregard the next step.)

(d) If the subject sees a hallway or tunnel, ask him to move to the end of the passage, describing his progress. Then ask him to locate and move through a door leading from the passageway and to report what he sees on the other side. If he's confronted with a scene from a past life, check to see whether he's in a body. This being so, he should breathe deeply and relax in his new surroundings.

(e) Question the subject as to identity, age, race, and ability to use his senses. Ask him to go back in time to the age of fifteen and move him slowly through that life, hitting as many major events as possible. Allow him to experience death and to review the life as a whole. Inquire about the possibility of people prominent in that life having bearing on the present existence. (NOTE: Should the subject start to relive a particularly exciting or traumatic episode, he will begin breathing heavily. If this happens, ask

him to leave the body temporarily or move him
forward to a more peaceful period.)

(f) Invite the subject to return to the first Earth life
relevant to that of today and repeat the life-
death cycle. Bring him forward in stages of
twenty-five, fifty, or one hundred years, granting the opportunity of experiencing as many
lives as possible. The subject can return to the
present moment whenever he wishes—simply
ask him to take a deep breath and open his eyes.
To reduce the risk of headache, ensure that he
remains still for a few minutes at the close of the
regression.

As overwhelming as intellectual conviction might
be, nothing convinces quite like the emotional jolt
of personal experience. That's why the investigation of
past lives is worth pursuing: the plausible stands to be
transformed into the tangible, unifying the head with
the heart. The finest results, however, cannot be won
through mere technique. A new way of being is called
for in which the horizons of perception are rolled back
in all directions. In *The Memory of Past Births*, Charles
Johnston, a retired member of the Bengal Civil Service,
wrote in 1899 "it is only in proportion as we inherit our
immortality, and consciously rise above the barriers of
time, that we can possibly inherit the memory of our
past." A past, moreover, that can help dissolve some of
the perplexity of the present, for everything that we are
has its roots in bygone incarnations. Unconsciously, we
are the aggregate of all our lives. In striving to make the

unconscious conscious, in demanding to *know*, lies the thrill and the reward of the personal investigation of past-life memory. At times, the evidence may be hard to come by and even harder to interpret. But, in the words of Aleister Crowley: "Anything which throws light upon the Universe, anything which reveals us to ourselves, should be welcome in this world of riddles."

> "By living according to the dictates of the soul, the brain may at last be made porous to the soul's recollection, and then our past lives will be an open book to us."
>
> – Pamphlet on reincarnation and karma published in 1923 by the Theosophy Company.

Symbols of Rebirth

THE MOON. Primitive philosophers, taking their cue from the waxing and waning of the moon, postulated that mankind was fated with similarly endless cycles of death and rebirth. When the new moon appeared, elders among the San Juan Capistrano Indians of California would gather to recite: "As the moon dieth and cometh to life again, so we also having to die will again live." And the natives of the Congo clapped their hands and cried out: "So may I renew my life as thou art renewed."

THE LOTUS. Eastern symbol of spiritual rebirth.

THE SUN. Rising each day from the womb of Mother Earth, the sun was hailed by primitive man as lord, master and shining exemplar of the process of reincarnation.

THE WHEEL. An unadorned version of the wheel of life that, as a well-tried metaphor of the Eastern religions, turns man through revolution upon revolution of birth and death.

THE PHOENIX. The most ancient and cross-cultural symbol of rebirth is the phoenix, a mythical bird of gorgeous plumage which lived in the desert for five hundred years. Immolating itself on a funeral pyre, the phoenix rose anew from its own ashes to live another cycle. From India to Persia, from Ireland to Egypt, the phoenix appears in myth and legend. To the Japanese, the fabled bird is *Kirin*; to the Turks, *Kerkes*.

THE PEACOCK. In the East, the peacock represents rebirth in the imagery of Hinduism, Buddhism and Islam.

14

FROM THE DALAI LAMA TO THE POPULATION CONUNDRUM

"Were an Asiatic to ask me for a definition of Europe, I should be forced to answer him: It is that part of the world which is haunted by the incredible delusion that man was created out of nothing, and that his present birth is his first entrance into life."

    – Arthur Schopenhauer

"Thinking the soul is unbodily among bodies, firm among fleeting things, the wise man casts off all grief."

    – *Katha Upanishad*

THE NATURE of the case for reincarnation is multi-faceted and multidimensional, often quixotic yet essentially changeless. Here are some further perspectives on rebirth seen from a variety of windows.

Reincarnation Personified

The fourteenth Dalai Lama, self-exiled ruler of 6,000,000 Tibetans, is the most famous personification of rebirth in the world today. Each Dalai Lama (a Mongolian expression meaning "greatest teacher") is understood to be not only his predecessor reborn but also the reincarnation of the entire line of Tibetan god-kings traceable to the year 1391. Whenever a Dalai Lama dies, an exhaustive search is mounted for the infant reincarnation of the dead leader who, as the embodiment of *Chenrizeg*, the Buddhist god of grace, is considered to rush back to earth in order to help the human race. Far from being a masquerade orchestrated by Tibetan king-makers to placate a public with metaphysical inclinations, the search incorporates stringent recognition tests not unlike those employed by Western reincarnation researchers. While lesser candidates are easily disqualified by these trials, eye-witnesses have testified to the remarkable responses they elicit from the real Dalai Lama.

The present Dalai Lama, whose personal name is Tenzin Gyatso, was born on June 6, 1935. He was found after search groups had fanned out eastwards from Lhasa, the Tibetan capital, in response to mystical hints that the new ruler was to be found in the direction of the rising sun. First of all, the head of the late Dalai Lama (who sat in state after his death in 1933) was found mysteriously turned to the East from the traditional southerly position. When the state oracle was consulted about this development, the monk seer, deep in trance, flung a white scarf in an easterly direction. Praying incessantly for further guidance, the Tibetan regent went on a pilgrimage to the lake of Chos Khorgyal, as all who peer into its depths are said to be able to see something of the future. The regent's gaze was met by a vision of a three-storeyed temple with a turquoise roof standing close to a house with carved gables and blue eaves. Details of the vision were written down and kept secret by the search parties which, in 1937, set out to look for the infant king in much the same fashion as the wise men of the East had ventured in search of the baby Jesus. Tibetans at large, knowing the recovery of their monarch was vital to the national interest, were eager for news of the mission's progress. To be without the Dalai Lama was to be an orphan nation.

One search group, disheartened after months of arduous and fruitless wandering on horseback, had penetrated deep into Chinese territory. In their panniers were objects that had belonged to the thirteenth Dalai Lama. Although several boys had been questioned along the way regarding these objects, none had come close enough in their answers to meet divine requirements. But as they entered the village of Takster in the Chinese province of Chinghai, the searchers' spirits revived dramatically at the sight of a three-storeyed temple standing not far from a family dwelling. The scene was just as the vision had described. Excitedly, the leader of the party exchanged clothes with a servant, a customary ploy during these all-important searches so that the royal inquiry could proceed in humble places without attracting unwanted attention. Entering the kitchen of the "house of the blue-coloured eaves," the leader was greeted by a two-year-old who demanded the rosary draped around his neck. The rosary had belonged to the thirteenth Dalai Lama and the disguised leader promised to hand it over if the boy could tell him who he was. The child replied "*Seraga*" which, in the local dialect, means "a lama of Lhasa's Sera monastery." The boy proceeded to name correctly each member of the search party. And, from an assortment of articles gathered to mislead, he identified, without the least self-consciousness, more rosaries, a drum, and a walking stick that had belonged to the previous Dalai Lama. Furthermore, the boy's body was found to bear all the marks of a true incarnation of *Chenrizeg*— large, noticeable ears and moles placed on his trunk in precise accordance with tradition. The boy's parents turned out to be pure Tibetan, even though they lived in an area that had been annexed by China for twenty-seven years. Satisfied they had located the reborn Dalai Lama, the party arranged for the future ruler of Tibet to be escorted back to Lhasa. The journey, however, could not be undertaken before the searchers agreed to pay the blackmailing provincial governor 300,000 Chinese yuan (roughly $300,000) for their precious charge.

When the Chinese invaded Tibet in 1959, the Dalai Lama fled to India with many other Tibetans. He is still based there today, with headquarters at Dharamsala in the Himalayas, but spends much time visiting other Buddhist countries as well as Western nations. In his memoirs *My Land and My People*, the Dalai Lama summed up his understanding of the rebirth principle:

The immediate source of a body is that of its parents. But physical matter cannot produce mind, nor mind matter. The immediate source of a mind must, therefore, be a mind which existed before the conception took place; the mind must have a continuity from a previous mind. This we hold to prove the existence of a past life.

Although the Dalai Lama has only the haziest of recollections of being discovered by the royal search party back in 1937, he does remember recognizing people and places known in Lhasa by his predecessor. And he chooses to interpret the continued oppression of Tibet by its Chinese conquerors in terms of national karma engendered in another age. "The aggression must have come because we did something bad," the Dalai Lama told the *New York Times* in November, 1967.

Though he lacked conscious knowledge of architecture, Swedish psychiatrist Dr. Axel Munthe (1857–1949) rebuilt the temple of the Roman Emperor Tiberius on the Isle of Capri. Many believed that he was Tiberius reborn. English author Clare Sheridan wrote of Dr. Munthe: "He had the qualities and faults of Tiberius; his tyranny and kindliness . . . He might have been, and I believed he was, a reincarnation of the Imperator, drawn back to the scene of his past and doomed in this life to pay back an overburdened karma."

Coming Back Alike

Successive incarnations, it is contended, can bear great physical resemblance to one another. Joseph Myers, a parapsychologist and consulting engineer of Lexington, North Carolina, declares: "One's personal appearance shouldn't alter from one life to the next any more than a man's appearance will be altered by age during one lifetime." Myers is convinced he was Edward Bellamy, the nineteenth-century writer of utopian novels. He even claims to remember writing these works and says he recalls most vividly the author's agonizing death from tuberculosis. Photographs of the two men show there *is* a strong likeness between Myers and Bellamy.

Encouraging the flow of reincarnational memory and psychic intuition by prolonged daily meditation, Myers has since claimed that Walt Disney was Charles Dickens reborn, that Mario Lanza was Caruso, that George Bernard Shaw was Voltaire, that Danny Kaye has sprung from Hans Christian Andersen. As similar as illustrations of these and other celebrated pairings are seen to be, Myers' like-begets-like hypothesis is by no means incontestable. Its fascination is that it brings a new dimension to the widely accepted assertion that predominant traits are carried over from life to life.

English mystic Clarice Toyne makes the same case as Myers in her book *Heirs to Eternity*. Besides binding G. K. Chesterton to Samuel Johnson and Sir Winston Churchill to Thomas Wentworth, she, too, pairs off Shaw and Voltaire, Kaye and Andersen, pointing out that the linking of names comes to her, spoken clearly, while she's preoccupied with chores or while walking her dogs. On researching the lives and likenesses of the suggested subjects she would "thrill to find the same bone formation of the head, the same physiognomy, the same subtlety of countenance." Clarice Toyne here explains the uncanny resemblance of apparently consecutive incarnations:

> Always there is a comparable overall energy-charge which *is* the inner being, which enters and sustains the new form. The ladder of natural evolution is gradual and slight in its changes, not sudden and startling in differences of form and mental calibre. So, a returning soul has features similar to his or her last lineaments even when there is a change of race.

In 1946, long before Clarice Toyne and Joseph Myers had voiced their claims for reincarnational look-alikes, Harold W. Percival maintained in his 1,000-page metaphysical treatise *Thinking and Destiny* that photographs taken of the average individual at corresponding periods in two or more lives would show little change. The features furnished by heredity—no matter who the parents may be—are the same for a string of lives, Percival believed.

Reincarnation researchers have sometimes attested to physical likeness shared between their subjects and claimed previous personalities. The case of Sinha Oliviero, daughter of a prosperous Brazilian rancher, is typical in that people knowing both Sinha and Marta Lorens, who professed to remember living as Sinha, were impressed by similarities in their appearance and handwriting. Sinha died of tuberculosis at the age of twenty-eight in October, 1917, having promised her friend Ida Lorens, the wife of the local schoolteacher, that she would return as her daughter. Ten months later, Marta Lorens was born and—at the age of two-and-a-half years—began to speak volubly about Sinha's life.

Sentenced to death by a Houston, Texas, jury on May 13, 1982, killer Herman Clark said he was not afraid to die because of his belief in reincarnation. Thirty-six-year-old Clark murdered Joseph McClain during a burglary which prosecutors said was planned with intent to commit rape. Three women and a ten-year-old girl testified that Clark had sexually abused or raped them. Prosecutor Ira Jones expressed the wish that Clark would return to earth as a little girl, the better to understand his crimes.

Life Readings of the Sleeping Prophet

Edgar Cayce, the greatest American clairvoyant of the twentieth century, didn't believe a word he was saying. The date was August 10, 1923, and Cayce, deep in a self-imposed hypnotic trance, was asserting—contrary to his conscious belief—that people are reborn in different bodies. Listening subsequently to a transcript of his words, Cayce was shocked and confounded. For reincarnation was alien and repulsive to the sensibilities of this devout Presbyterian who taught a Sunday school class and read the Bible daily.

Arthur Lammers, the well-to-do printer who had paid Cayce's expenses from Selma, Alabama, so that he could question him on reincarnation, was as delighted as the famous seer of Virginia Beach was dismayed and disillusioned. The answers given by the "sleeping prophet," as Cayce was known, were all Lammers needed to confirm his already well-developed fascination with rebirth, the occult, and Eastern religions. Although initially fearful that his subconscious faculties had been commandeered by the devil, Cayce gradually came to accept reincarnation, realizing that it did not impugn the teachings of Jesus Christ. In time, he saw Jesus as an advanced adept who had materialized in twenty-nine previous incarnations.

While using his trance powers principally for healing, Edgar Cayce gave 2,500 "life" readings over the next twenty-one years. Drawing on the Akashic Records and the individual's unconscious mind, he described personal histories spanning many incarnations. The readings pointed strongly to the recurrent grouping of souls on Earth and detected "karmic patterns," often tracing present infirmity to deeds—or lack of deeds—in past lives. Cayce believed each soul has subconscious access to characteristics and skills accumulated in previous lives while also being subject to the influence of lives ruled by negative emotions such as hate and fear. The sleeping prophet was bluntness itself. He once told a deaf person: "Then do not close your ears again to those who plead for aid." And a sufferer of tuberculosis of the spine was greeted with: "The entity thwarted others and is meeting it now in himself." Again and again, in readings given for children suffering from all kinds of afflictions, Cayce would say: "This is karma, for both the parent and the child." The conventional conception of heredity was denied outright. When someone asked: "From which side of my family do I inherit most?" Cayce retorted: "You have inherited most from yourself, not from your family! The family is only a river through which the soul flows."

According to Cayce, the rapacious Conquistadors who stormed across Latin America in the sixteenth century suffered for their slaughter and plunder by reincarnating collectively in Spain in modern times. The cruelty they had unleashed against the Aztecs and the Incas they vented against themselves retributively during the Spanish Civil War. Similarly, those who participated in the destruction of Atlantis are now said to be on Earth in large numbers. Cayce declared:

> Granting that reincarnation is a fact, and that souls once occupied such an environ as Atlantis, and that these are now entering the Earth's sphere—if they made such alterations in the Earth's affairs in their day as to bring destruction on themselves—can there be any wonder that they might make such like changes in the affairs of peoples and individuals today?

Few of the life readings—almost half of which trace a person's reincarnational history back to Atlantis—give data that can be verified and many, suspiciously, are linked with the lives of famous people. Jesus Christ (a number of children had been "blessed by Him"), Nero, Reubens, and Captain Kidd, as well as a courtyard full of priestesses and regal personages, figure in the readings which show very little change of sex in successive incarnations. For all this, some readings were nothing short of astounding. In *Many Mansions*, Gina Cerminara tells how one of Cayce's visitors was informed he had been Barnett Seay, a Southern soldier in the Civil War, in his former life. He was told further that he had lived in Henrico County, Virginia, and that records pertaining to this former personality still existed. Eagerly, the man set off for Henrico County to be redirected to the Virginia State Historical Library where many old registries had been relocated. Pursuing the scent to the library's archives, he found a record of Barnett A. Seay who had enlisted in General Lee's army as a colour-bearer in 1862, at the age of twenty-one.

Cayce himself was said to have been last born in 1742 as John Bainbridge, an adventurer who ranged from Florida to the Canadian border involving himself in skirmishes with Indian tribes. But he also recalled other incarnations—including one as a priest named Ra-Ta who lived in ancient Egypt. He's on record as predicting that he will return to Earth in 1998, possibly as "a liberator of the world."

> "That as lived today is as tomorrow today for today is tomorrow, tomorrow is today."
>
> – Edgar Cayce

Xenoglossy

People who speak spontaneously in an unknown, perhaps extinct, foreign language are compelling witnesses
for the reincarnation hypothesis. This rare, involuntary
talent is known as xenoglossy—a term coined by the
Nobel prize winning French physiologist and psychical
researcher Dr. Charles Richet—and stems from the
Greek *xeno*, meaning strange or foreign, and *glossa*, meaning tongue. Never lacking in dramatic impact, xenoglossy
suggests the outpouring of subconscious memory.

In a case reported in the *Journal of the American Society for Psychical Research* (July, 1980), Dr. Ian Stevenson
and Dr. Satwant Pasricha argue that Uttara Huddar, a
single woman living in west central India who suddenly
changed personality and started speaking nineteenth-
century Bengali, was most probably giving vent to
memories of a former life. Uttara, whose native tongue
is Marathi, was thirty-two years of age when, in 1974,
she became Sharada, a shy, married woman with a taste
for Bengali clothes, food, and devotional songs. Uttara
and her family had to communicate with gestures until
speakers of Bengali could be located.

While Sharada was poorly educated and subservient,
as might be expected of a housewife of West Bengal in
the early 1800s, Uttara is outgoing and highly educated,
having obtained a master's degree in English and public
administration. Uttara couldn't remember what took
place during her times as Sharada, who was utterly lost
in the modern world, being a stranger to cars, trains,
and modern appliances as well as Uttara's locality and

family to whom she referred in Bengali as "these people." Furthermore, Sharada, whose appearances lasted for days or weeks at a time, seemed unaware of anything that followed a snake bite on the toe which appeared to have ended her life at the age of twenty-two. Sharada's linguistic style (her ability to carry out conversations in Bengali is defined as "responsive xenoglossy") was devoid of all modern terms which have crept into the language since the industrial revolution. The researchers established that there was very little chance that Uttara could have inherited or acquired through normal channels her sudden, fluent knowledge of Bengali. And they found genealogical records bearing the names of a family corresponding to information given by Sharada. An 1827 property agreement between relatives named by Sharada was brought to light.

Although possession by a discarnate entity cannot be ruled out, much of the evidence points to the persistence of past-life memory. Uttara had a phobia about snakes as a child and her mother suffered nightmares, when pregnant with Uttara, of being bitten on the toe by a snake. In summing up the case, Stevenson and Pasricha declare: "We cannot say how Uttara obtained these memories of a previous life; but the feature of responsive xenoglossy tells strongly against the interpretation that she acquired them by extrasensory perception. We are, therefore, entitled to conjecture, at least provisionally, that Sharada was a previous incarnation of the person now identified as Uttara."

Back in November, 1930, the *New York Evening Post* reported that a four-year-old girl living in Warsaw was able to speak Gaelic even though her parents conversed only in Polish. More recently, the popularity of hypnotic regression has encouraged a greater incidence of xenoglossy. Normally English-speaking Californians have surprised themselves by talking in all kinds of languages, including jungle dialects, while lying on Dr. Morris Netherton's couch. Most extraordinary of all was the case of a blond, blue-eyed eleven-year-old boy who was taped for eleven minutes as he spoke in a Chinese dialect. The tape was taken to an elderly Chinese professor at the Department of Oriental Studies, University of California, who confirmed, much to his amazement, that the boy was reciting a text from a forbidden religion of ancient China. "With some people," says Netherton, "there is no language at all. All I get are grunts and groans and I get them to translate." Thorwald Dethlefsen reports that, while conducting a regression in German, he can usually extract certain answers in the "original language." But some hypnotherapists would rather avoid altogether xenoglossy's confusing exoticism. Dr. Edith Fiore writes that ". . . just to be on the safe side, before regressing subjects I suggest that they will respond to me in English."

One of the finest and most carefully studied examples of xenoglossy was uncovered by Dr. Joel Whitton of Toronto whose anonymous subject—a psychologist with a "responsible position in the assessment and treatment of children with learning and behavioural disorders"—remembered under hypnosis two ancient languages that, presumably, he had spoken during previous incarnations. The first language was Norsk, the precursor of modern Icelandic. In deep trance, he remembered a life as a raiding warrior in a small Viking army about the year A.D. 1000 and heard the voice of Thor, his assumed previous personality, respond to questions about his ship and life at sea. He then wrote down a phonetic rendering of these responses which were later examined independently by specialists fluent in Icelandic and Norwegian. Several words and phrases were identified, most of them relating to the sea and ships.

The psychologist also described living as a young man in Mesopotamia (part of Persia) in A.D. 625 and proceeded to write in the language of the day. (This, strictly speaking, is xenography rather than xenoglossy). Samples of his spidery, childlike script were verified

A reincarnation formula of recognition was adopted by the Druses of Syria, Lebanon, and Jordan during the early Middle Ages. A Druse catechism dating back to 1012 shows how a fellow Druse can be distinguished from others. When asked: "Man, do they grow the *thlilij* (myrobalan tree) in your country?" the true Druse answers: "Yes, it is planted in the hearts of the believers." Next, he is presented with two earthen water bottles, one full and the other empty. If he pours the water from the full bottle into that which is empty he symbolically acknowledges rebirth and is clearly a Druse. Modern-day Druses are thought to be the descendants of mystics from various nations who took refuge in the mountains of Syria when the Christian church turned vengeful against nonconformists.

by Dr. Idrahim Pourhadi of the Near East Section of Washington's Library of Congress as being *Sassanid Pahlavi*—a form of writing that has not been used since A.D. 651 and bears no relation to present-day Iranian.

An Ailment Relieved

As Canada's only university professor lecturing on the empirical evidence for reincarnation, Ian Currie adopted a purely academic approach to his subject—but he had reckoned without past-life reprisals! After writing *You Cannot Die*, a best-selling documentation of immortality, Currie developed a personal ailment which left him in nagging discomfort at the height of the book's American promotion during the summer of 1979. For the next three years, doctors could do nothing for him, attributing the physical symptom to psychological causes. And this, in turn, set Currie wondering about the hidden influence of past lives. So he approached Toronto's Dr. Joel Whitton, psychiatrist, neurophysiologist and past-life therapist, in the hope of ridding himself of the troublesome symptom.

Regular weekly hypnotherapy sessions with Whitton enabled Currie to tap seven past-life personalities ranging from a builder in ancient Egypt to a seventeenth-century nun in the Low Countries before making contact, early in 1983, with what he describes as the "key life"—a priest/astronomer living in Central America over 1,000 years ago. The priest, says Currie, did not live up to his vow of celibacy and this led him, eventually, to stab a rival lover to death. Since examining this past life through the veil of a light hypnotic trance, Currie has experienced a gradual diminishing of the symptom as well as a growing awareness of reasons for certain depressive, authoritarian, and ascetic personality characteristics. "The past-life images," says Currie, a former sceptic who came to believe in reincarnation after assessing the wealth of documented evidence, "carry a strong sense of emotional and intellectual conviction."

Currie feels that his interest in occult matters can be traced to this Central American existence where he failed to wield his power and influence responsibly. "I blew it," he confesses. "Now I am trying to advance knowledge of life after death in a more positive way." In four of the lives contacted in his past-life inventory, Currie's former wife, Margaret, figured prominently, though not necessarily as marriage partner. Other relatives and friends have also made appearances.

The regressions convinced Currie, who died in 1992, that his waning ailment was rooted in guilt repressed for centuries. He has also been assured of the long arm of karmic retribution. For after witnessing his knife murder in Central America all those years ago, he saw himself tortured, mutilated, and dispatched by a knife blade under similar circumstances while living as an Indian in the American southwest before the Spanish conquest.

A national survey by the University of Chicago's opinion research centre indicates that 61 out of every 100 Americans have experienced *déjà vu*.

Déjà Vu

It happens seldom but it happens to almost all of us: an intestinal shock of recognition when encountering, ostensibly for the first time, a particular scene or individual. *Déjà vu* ("already seen") belies the presumed originality of all life experience and suggests the arousal of subconscious memories from other lives.

General George "Blood and Guts" Patton, America's irascible hero of World War II, was convinced he had lived before and backed up his claim with a wartime *déjà vu* experience at the French town of Langres. Patton was assuming his first command and a French liaison officer offered to show him around the town's fine Roman ruins. "You don't have to," Patton retorted. "I know this place. I know it well." Although the general had never been there before, he directed his driver around the ruins, pointing out the old amphitheatre, the drill ground, the forum, and the temples of Mars and Apollo. Besides laying claim to having fought with Caesar's legions in a previous existence, Patton maintained he had reincarnated many times as a warrior. This conviction is forcibly expressed in a verse from his poem *Through a Glass Darkly*, written in 1944, the year before his death:

> So as through a glass and darkly
> The age-long strife I see
> Where I fought in many guises
> Many names—but always me!

Reflecting common experience, literary archives are replete with *déjà vu* episodes. For example, the poet Shelley, when walking with friends in a part of England he had never before visited, told a companion: "over that hill there is a windmill." As they reached the top of the hill and were granted a view of the windmill he had described, Shelley fainted with emotion. The Scottish novelist Sir Walter Scott noted in his diary on February 17, 1828: "I cannot, I am sure, tell if it is worth marking down, that yesterday, at dinner time, I was strongly haunted by what I would call the sense of pre-existence, *viz.*, a confused idea that nothing that passed was said for the first time . . ." The first verse of Dante Gabriel Rossetti's poem *Sudden Light* strongly evokes the archetypal *déjà vu* experience:

> I have been here before
> But when or how I cannot tell;
> I know the grass beyond the door
> The sweet keen smell,
> The sighing sound, the lights around the shore.

As modern music superseded literature as the favourite form of sentimental expression, reincarnational references

---

In 1956, three female members of a Liberace fan club paid thirty-four guineas at Sotheby's, the celebrated London auctioneers, for a letter written by composer Franz Liszt to the Emperor of France. Why? Because Liberace claimed to be a reincarnation of Liszt.

to *déjà vu* rode the airwaves. Crosby, Stills, Nash and Young built sweet, repetitive harmony around the idea in a 1970 album titled *Déjà Vu*. And, ten years later, Dionne Warwick enjoyed a smash hit with a song of the same name.

Past-Life Artistry

For past-life artist Isolde Bauer the incarnations are in the eyes. Staring into a person's eyes—be they alive or gazing from a photograph—she enters a trance with the aid of yoga breathing. Then she concentrates on the images the trance produces; images of her subject's previous existences. Gradually, the mind pictures, faces from the past, are translated to paper or canvas with her left hand. This, in itself, is extraordinary because Isolde is normally right-handed.

German-born Isolde, who now lives in Las Vegas, Nevada, was originally a portrait painter who counted politicians and business people among her clientele. But in 1974 an out-of-body vision experienced while undergoing major surgery radically altered her way of working. "I felt as if a veil had been lifted from my eyes," she said. "Everything was bright and sharp. Colours were incredibly beautiful. When I looked at people, I could see the psychic energy of their auras. I began having flashes of past-life images flickering across the faces of those around me. When I told my friends what I was seeing, they kept asking me to describe their past lives. I decided that I would paint what I was seeing."

Isolde's paintings are composed of faces from other lives built around the present likeness. A past-life reading accompanies each portrait which is executed in monochromatic black or brown charcoal, oils, pastels, acrylics—whatever medium the subject prefers. Usually Isolde works from photographs in the quiet surroundings of her home. "The eyes are the key," she insists. "When I get the eyes done the way I want them, the past-life images begin to reveal themselves. The modern day face changes for a split-second. In many ways it is an automatic process—I merely get things started and then the painting constructs itself." Isolde maintains that most of her subjects—who include such metaphysical heavyweights as Dick Sutphen, Hans Holzer, and Peter Hurkos—are gripped with a sense of familiarity on seeing their past-life grouping.

The ability to see faces in split-second transformation is not confined to Isolde Bauer and her past-life artistry. Clinical psychologist Ronald Wong Jue of Fullerton, California, tends to see people in past-life images while working to relieve psychosomatic illness. "I focus on the energy of my clients and the images come," says Dr. Jue. "It's an inner movie in my mind. Sometimes, when my clients share the image, they go into a regression. It's an intuitive approach."

British hypnotherapist Jo Kirby recounted the awakening of her clairvoyant powers one day in June, 1980. She was travelling on the London subway and her head was reeling from the sudden transformation in the people seated nearby. A pretty girl in a short dress became a tramp with a chin of grey stubble. A plump, middle-aged housewife was changed into a much younger woman in a nun's habit. And a young man, dressed casually in T-shirt and jeans, appeared as a last-century naval officer dressed in a uniform with brass buttons. "It was like a fancy dress party," Jo Kirby recalled. "And it ended up driving me mad. After a lot of meditation I eventually found a way of shutting off the images."

> According to Marcia Moore and Mark Douglas in *Reincarnation: Key to Immortality*, souls "are now cycling in and out of incarnation at such a great rate that their rapid transit is causing a veritable traffic jam of entities commuting between the planes. As a result, we have confusion and congestion at Earth's heir port of incoming souls."

The Population Conundrum

Critics of rebirth like nothing better than to point at the fast-rising world population and exclaim: "If reincarnation is a fact, where do all these 'new' people come from?" Certainly, the global population doubled from A.D. 25 to 1500, doubled again by 1800, and has more than quadrupled since then. But the sceptics fail to take into account the length of the between-life or *bardo* state which, the evidence from hypnosis suggests, has been steadily diminishing as world change has accelerated. This alone could create the rise in population. It might well be that when there was little change from generation to generation entities chose longer breaks between incarnations, whereas today's rapid advances act as a magnet for souls ever hungry for new experiences.

Dr. Edith Fiore's hypnotherapy casebook tells her that anyone under forty years of age has probably lived before during this century, while many people are experiencing their third or fourth life since 1900. Dr. Helen Wambach, whose subjects reported increasingly shorter periods out of incarnation as they made pointed references to impending global destruction, said of the current burgeoning population: "In my own mind, I liken it to the cast of a musical gathering onstage for the finale." One of Dr. Wambach's studies, involving 1,100 people who were invited to locate at random three incarnations from ten time periods scattered across 4,000 years, reproduced the estimated upward population curve of the Earth. The hypnotized subjects apparently demonstrated that increasingly faster reincarnations have boosted population figures over the last few centuries. Leading Theosophist Dr. Annie Besant noted in 1893 that the answer to the vexing population growth question lies in the number of unbodily egos always being "enormously greater" than those incarnate. She wrote:

> The globe is as a small hall in a large town, drawing the audiences that enter it from the total population. It may be at one time half empty, at another crowded, without any change in the total population of the town.

Not to be left out of the debate are the supposed additions to and subtractions from the human race—entities graduating to human bodies from the animal kingdom and the rebirth of highly evolved humans on a higher plane. Joe Keeton is quick to point out that as the human population rises, the animal population goes down. "Where have all those pieces of life force gone?" he asks. "Is that where we get such human beings as concentration camp guards?"

Dr. Ian Stevenson notes that plausible estimates of the total number of people who have lived on earth range from 69 billion to 96 billion. This would leave each member of the human race—currently estimated at 6 billion people—with approximately 11 to 16 past lives.

> "If we could see ourselves and other objects as they really are, we should see ourselves in a world of spiritual natures, our community with which neither began at our birth nor will end with the death of the body."
>
> – Immanuel Kant

15

COMING BACK
ALIVE

"It is rebirth that gives the birth of an incomplete being in a body its promise of completeness and its spiritual significance."

– Sri Aurobindo

"How come one person is born a genius and another a boob; one is born beautiful and another ugly; one is born healthy and another crippled? The concept of rebirth on earth, perhaps after an interval occupied by the individual in distilling out of memories of a life just ended such wisdom as his reflective powers enabled him to extract, would enable us to believe there is justice in the universe."

– C. J. Ducasse

RECENT RESEARCH and case studies confirm and promote the growing acceptance of reincarnation in the last years of the twentieth century.

Matchless Scientific Evidence
from the Global Expert

Canadian-born Dr. Ian Stevenson, for twenty-five years the world's leading investigator of reincarnation, in 1997 published an exhaustive study of birthmarks and birth defects which bear dramatic correlation with remembered wounds and injuries from remembered previous lives. *Reincarnation and Biology* is an illustrated, two-volume study of well over 2,000 pages. Citing worldwide case histories drawn from three decades of intensive research, the book documents the apparent trans-dimensional significance of physical manifestations ranging from the tiniest blemishes to serious bodily defects. "I am now able to show," states the careful scientist, "that a wide variety of deaths in different countries may figure in birth defects related to previous lives."

While Dr. Stevenson—who in 1995 was awarded the American Society for Psychical Research's first Myers Memorial Gold Medal "for outstanding work in the field of psychical research"—characteristically refrains from asserting that rebirth is the reason for the close physical correspondence reaching from one life to the next, the clear inference is both hard to miss and difficult to refute. As he has steadfastly proposed since publishing his first paper on reincarnation in 1960, Dr. Stevenson argues that his painstakingly-documented case histories are no more than *suggestive* of reincarnation. But this latest work adds a persuasive physical component to a research program that earlier relied exclusively on memory.

The case studies in *Reincarnation and Biology* focus on the strong resemblance of individuals' physical abnormalities to marks made by remembered accidents and injuries in previous lifetimes. Here are some examples:

The Case of the Returning Cattle Thief: Thailand

Shortly after his birth, Thiang San Kla was seen to bear six birth defects and birthmarks, the most prominent being located on the back of his head. His uncle Phoh—a notorious cattle thief—had been killed by a knife wound to the back of his head about a year before Thiang's birth. The fatal blow was struck by a member of a posse of more than 30 villagers at Ban Ar Vud who believed Phoh was about to steal their cattle.

Dreams of Phoh—Thiang's father's older brother—had been reported by Thiang's parents in the months leading up to the birth of their child. They had both experienced Phoh requesting to be reborn as their child. Because of these dreams, Thiang's parents were ready to accept that their son was indeed the reincarnation of Phoh. The child confirmed this acceptance as soon as he could speak by making verifiable statements and identifying several people. This, in turn, convinced members of his family that they were witnessing a genuine instance of rebirth.

When Thiang was visited by a policeman who had investigated Phoh's cattle stealing and his murder, the boy addressed him by name and also named correctly those who were involved in the killing. In particular,

Thiang expressed a desire for revenge against a man
called Chang, the actual killer. One of Thiang's birth defects comprised a partly detached nail on his right big
toe, the tissue beneath the nail being darkly pigmented.
For some years before his murder, Phoh had suffered
from a chronic infection of the same toe.

The Case of the "Tax Collector": India

Lekh Pal Jatav was born in 1971 in a village in Mainpuri
District, Uttar Pradesh, with a severe deformity of his
right hand. Every finger as well as a large portion of his
thumb was missing. As soon as this defect was observed,
someone jokingly suggested that the baby, in his past
life, must have been a tax collector whose writing hand
was severed by an irate taxpayer. Tax collector in Hindi
translates as *lekh pal*—the very name the boy was given.

When Lekh Pal was old enough to speak, he talked
about living before, telling his older sister that his hand
had been cut by a fodder chopping machine. Investigation indicated that he might be the reincarnation of
Hukum Singh, a child who had lived in a village in the
same district but who was unknown to Lekh Pal's family.
When he was three and a half, Hukum Singh placed his
hand in a fodder chopping machine. While his fingers and
thumb were immediately severed, the wound soon healed
and the right-handed boy began to use his left hand. Some
ten months after the accident, Hukum Singh had died of
a completely unrelated illness in either September, 1970 or
1971. The date is uncertain because the records are incom-

plete, meaning, nevertheless, that his death took place either one year or immediately before the birth of Lekh Pal.

The Case of the Boy Who Was Shot Like a Rabbit: Turkey

A severe defect of the right ear prominently marked Semih Tutusmus at his birth in 1958 in Turkey's Hatay province. When he was less than two years of age, the boy began talking about being murdered in his previous life by a man named Isa Dirbekli. He claimed to have been shot in the right ear. He also gave his name in that life—Selim Fesli—and went on to name his wife and six children. At the age of four, Semih walked about two kilometres to the home in which he said he had lived in his earlier incarnation, introducing himself to the family. Further, happy visits ensued, but the boy's mood was entirely different whenever he spotted Isa Dirbekli. Suddenly flaring with anger, Semih would react by hurling stones at the man.

By the time he was twelve, Semih was threatening to kill Dirbekli in revenge for what he considered to be a deliberate act of murder. Dirbekli, however, claimed that he had been out shooting birds when he took aim at Selim—who was asleep on the ground—thinking he was a rabbit. He then realized his mistake and fled the scene rather than face the wrath of Selim's sons. While Selim died in hospital six days after the shooting, Dirbekli was eventually arrested and imprisoned for two years. Semih's anger at Dirbekli subsided as he grew into manhood. As his memories gradually faded, plastic surgery provided an excellent replacement for his right ear and long hair helped to conceal the birth defect.

The Case of the Burning Vehicle: Burma

When she came into the world in 1974, Ma Khin Hsann Oo was covered extensively with large, hyper-pigmented birthmarks. Neither her parents, a cultivator and his wife, nor anyone else in the family questioned the cause of the markings until Ma Khin, at eighteen months of age, began talking about a previous life. By the time she was three years old, she said she had lived before as Ahmar Yee and that she had died from burns when a vehicle had overturned and caught fire. "Shik-koe's car overturned," she would say, while remaining silent on the circumstances of the accident.

Her family—who lived in Ywathit village in the Tatkon Township of Upper Burma—concluded that the little girl was talking about the life of a local woman, Ma Ahmar Yee, who had died of burns when a truck in which she and many others had been riding tipped over and burst into flame. The truck was owned by an Indian Moslem called Shik-koe and the accident cost ten lives. Dr. Stevenson writes that two other children besides Ma Khin Hsann Oo appear to remember being killed in the conflagration.

> Dr. Ian Stevenson likens reincarnational memory to the effect of carbon paper: when the top copy (the body) is destroyed, the image remains.

A Successful Quest for Past-Life Offspring

As a child, Jenny Cockell was haunted by dreams in which she was a woman named Mary. She saw herself lying in a large, white-walled room with tall, multi-paned windows. Alone and near death, all she could think about were the eight children she was leaving behind. Little Jenny would wake up in tears, sobbing quietly in anger because it was too soon to leave the children. But, fearing her father would punish her, she was afraid to call for comfort and kept the disturbing images to herself. Only in passing did she mention to her mother the dreams and waking memories which, she believed, had their origins in a previous lifetime.

Growing up in England with the mixed emotions of a child and an adult made great demands on Jenny. Although highly intelligent (she is a member of Mensa), she disliked the predictability of school and did not do well academically. The passing years, rather than dimming her memories, brought Jenny more and more "mind snapshots," as she called these inklings from her troubled past. Most of all, she remembered the children and could describe their looks, habits, and characteristics. She was sure she had lived in Ireland and recalled a village cottage in some detail, particularly the kitchen where Mary spent most of her time. As a child, Jenny had drawn maps showing the cottage and its location in relation to other local landmarks. As an adult, she tried to piece the jigsaw puzzle together and felt compelled to search for the children she once knew.

In *Yesterday's Children*—the strange but true story of a quest that was ultimately successful—Jenny Cockell tells how she placed newspaper advertisements, made telephone calls to strangers, and scoured a small area of Ireland for clues to another existence that nagged at her consciousness. Jenny had always known that the period she was remembering extended, roughly, from 1898 to the 1930s. She spoke openly about her memories to relatives and close friends, to her husband when married, to her son and daughter when she started her own family, and to anyone else willing to listen to her story or help with her search.

Eventually, Jenny made contact with Northampton hypnotist Jim Alexander who agreed to help her attempt to recover, with the aid of trance, any past-life memories. At their initial session on January 6, 1988, Jenny described, under hypnosis, a cobbled street in Malahide lined with market stalls. Then she slipped into Mary's last moments, a scene that had recurred in her dreams. Jenny emerged from trance weeping uncontrollably.

The first session led to a series of tape recorded regressions aimed at retrieving graphic details about Mary's life and the identity of her children. Deeper images were recovered and, in 1989, Jenny set out for Malahide to conduct on-the-spot research. There she found that Mary Hand had married John Sutton, a soldier, a taciturn man, in Jenny's memories, who was seldom at home. Six children had been christened at St. Sylvester's Catholic Church, Malahide: Jeffrey (1923), Philomena (1925), Christopher (1926), Francis (1928), Bridget (1929), and Elizabeth (1932). After Mary's death in Rotunda Hospital, Dublin, a month after Elizabeth was born, her children had been despatched to orphanages.

Jenny was convinced, however, that this list of her children was not complete and persisted with her research. After a letter seeking information was published in a Dublin newspaper, Jenny heard from one of Mary's grandchildren, the daughter of Jeffrey, who confirmed there had been eight children. Jenny then spoke to Jeffrey, the second son, by telephone and, later, to Sonny, the eldest son.

By 1993, Jenny had made contact with all eight children except Bridget who, it was confirmed, had died in Australia. The most remarkable recounting in *Yesterday's Children* is the meeting on September 23, 1990, between Jenny Cockell and "her" long-lost son, Sonny, who had since moved to Leeds, England. The quiet, gentle man—old enough to be Jenny's father—asked how she could explain her memories of his mother. "I said that, for me," Jenny responded, "it had to be reincarnation, but this was not the only way of looking at it. I didn't expect everyone to see it in a similar way. He thought about this, and seemed happy to leave it at that."

When Jenny revealed that she had waited, as Mary, on a wooden jetty for someone to arrive in a boat, Sonny reacted excitedly. "As a boy," he said, "I used to caddy on the island for the golfers, and at dusk my mother would wait for me on the jetty so that we could walk home together." Sonny also confirmed Jenny's memory that she had responded to her children's call when they had found an animal trapped in a snare. Meeting Sonny shed light on other aspects of Mary's life, particularly her fear and reluctance to remember husband John Sutton. Sonny explained that Sutton was often violent towards her, especially after he had been drinking. Sometimes, Sonny—the only child not to be sent to an orphanage when Mary died—would intervene to prevent his mother from being beaten. Asked how much Jenny resembled Mary, the elderly man immediately responded: "I can see my mother in her eyes."

In 1992, as a direct result of Jenny's research and contact with the family, Sonny went to Ireland to meet his youngest sister, Betty, for the first time in sixty years. He was also reunited with other family members. At Sonny's house in Leeds, Jenny was able to meet Phyllis, a woman over sixty years of age, who had been missing from the list of Mary's children. At that time, she was handed what is thought to be the only surviving photograph of Mary Sutton who was pictured with Phyllis when she was just two years old.

Jenny Cockell concludes *Yesterday's Children* with these words: "Now, at the age of 39, I have found most of [my] children and know what happened. If none had been willing to listen to me I could not have found anything out. By his acceptance, Sonny has given me what I have searched for. The sense of responsibility and guilt has fallen away, and I feel a sense of peace that I have never really known before."

After writing *Yesterday's Children*, Jenny Cockell joined her "other" family members in Malahide for a grand reunion which was filmed as a television documentary. Said Jenny: "They all wanted to go back and look at the cottage ruins. This was the first time I had met all of them together and the first time everybody had been together since 1932." Hypnotist Jim Alexander told *Rein-*

carnation International that he could not say the case study of Jenny Cockell was proof of reincarnation without a shadow of doubt "because there is probably another explanation." But he added, "I consider in a court of law it would be enough to convict."

> "Death and birth are the vesper and matin bells that summon mankind to sleep and to rise refreshed for new advancement."
>
> – Thomas Carlyle

"I Was Shot Down During WWII*"*

Another verifiable case study from England also began with disturbing childhood images. These images, however, were not drawn from dreams but, instead, were precipitated by a Christmas present. As a young boy, Martin Heald was given the Christmas gift of a field telephone set. Pressing a green button on the telephone in reply to his father's demonstration, he was drawn to a second, red button which bore the full alphabet, followed by lots of unusual dots and dashes.

Writes Heald: "My father quickly explained that this was Morse code and started to tap out "sos" on the telephone. The bedroom began to fade almost immediately and, within a matter of seconds, I was floating high above the clouds, staring into a darkened night sky. Directly below my elevated vantage point I could see an aircraft being pursued by a much smaller and faster aircraft.

After the second attack, the larger aircraft exploded with a deafening roar, sending a jolt of panic and terror through my already trembling body. I was just about to scream out for help when the terrible scene vanished as quickly as it had appeared. I tried to explain to my father what had happened, only to be laughed at and reminded about my fantasy and daydreaming exploits."

This experience of Heald's was just the beginning of a long series of inexplicable events during his childhood years—all seemingly linked with World War II and what the boy could only describe as inklings of the spiritual world. But he tried to live a normal life and, following five rather uneventful years at secondary school, he responded to an advertisement for the Royal Air Force seen on television. Heald applied for the trade of electrician, took the necessary tests and medicals at the local RAF careers information office, and was invited back for an interview.

After congratulating Heald on his test results, the careers officer informed him there was at least a year's waiting list for the job. Then he offered him an alternative trade as a special telegraphist which involved working with computers, sophisticated communications equipment, and Morse code. Several weeks later, Heald attempted the Morse code aptitude tests and felt a strange *déjà vu*, reminding him of his youthful experience with the field telephones. When he returned to the careers information office for his final interview, Heald was warmly received by the officer who was intensely curious about his knowledge of Morse code.

"Congratulations!" he was told.

"What do you mean?" asked Heald, perplexed.

"Well, you are the first person in the history of these particular tests to attain the full 100 per cent score."

At the time, Heald attributed his performance to a fluke and, four years later, he left the RAF for a new marriage and a civilian life. It wasn't long, however, before his marriage broke down irretrievably and he ended up in shared accommodation. Yet this move heralded the beginning of a two-year period of strange happenings, most notably a series of premonitory dreams about air crashes, nearly all of which came true. During this time, Heald met a young nurse called Jennifer in whom he felt able to confide his fascination with otherworldly matters. He shared some of his dreams with her, especially those concerning air crashes which were increasing both in number and clarity. In 1992, Jennifer decided to move to Holland when she was offered a one-year contract as a child minder. The post included accommodation and the use of a car.

Heald decided to follow her there and, seeking a fresh start, gave away all his books and artifacts involving the paranormal. "After all," he writes, "what had it brought me? One failed marriage, plus a host of minor problems, including the portentous dreams." Heald was able to find a factory job and an apartment in Hoorn, a former fishing port in the north-west of the country. But he couldn't rid himself of the troubling air crash dreams. One particularly lurid premonition involved an airliner that crashed shortly after take-off in Macedonia. Heald was so conscious during this dream that he made mental notes of his surroundings, the flight control tower in the distance, the hilly terrain, the weather, and the aircraft itself which seemed strangely shaped. On waking he sketched the dream as best he could and, the following evening, showed Jennifer the drawing. The next day he purchased a copy of *The Dutch Telegraph* to scan the careers page and under the headline AIRCRAFT ACCIDENT IN MACEDONIA came upon a report of the very crash he had foreseen. All the details Heald had sketched, including the aircraft's strange shape, were contained in the report. Yet the photograph of the crash scene was strangest of all. It seemed to have been taken from the same position occupied by Heald in the dream.

Soon afterwards, Heald's landlady handed him a business card bearing the name of a so-called "aura reader," Saskia de Bruin. She felt that the reader might be able to shed some light on his unusual predicament, particularly the recurring dreams. Although sceptical, Heald acted on his landlady's advice to find his distrust quickly evaporate as Saskia de Bruin accurately and unhesitatingly described his childhood years in some detail. de Bruin told Heald he had moved to Holland to pick up the pieces of his previous life. She went on to give a fascinating description of his last life in England, telling him that he had joined the Royal Air Force during World War II and had been shot down somewhere over Holland while proceeding to a bombing mission over Germany. de Bruin then urged Heald to visit a regression therapist in order to relive some of the scenes and integrate the experience into his present circumstances. This would curtail the horrifying premonitions, she explained.

One fine summer evening in 1994, Heald arrived in Enkhuizen, the home town of regressionist Josee Van Asten, whom he had picked at random from the pages of a telephone book. Van Asten told Heald that he would be extremely lucky if memories of his previous life would surface during the initial session. Yet lucky he was. Ushered into trance, Heald saw pictures of brilliant clarity that confirmed he had lived as an airman in England more than half a century earlier. The images were laden with emotional conviction.

The next day, Heald transcribed a tape recording of the session, noting his former name of Richard Seymour, his father's vocation—vicar of a church—and the year of the crash, 1942. His body, he said in response to a question of Van Asten's, had been destroyed when his aircraft exploded. Richard Seymour, Heald learned, was a radio operator which explained—in this lifetime—his boyhood "vision" with the radio telephone set, his willingness to join the Royal Air Force, and his facility with Morse code.

Some weeks later, Heald contacted historical societies in England in hope of substantiating what he had learned under hypnosis. But the long search appeared fruitless late in 1994 when no corroborative information was forthcoming. There was, however, one consolation: Heald's recurring dreams about air crashes had ceased. By May, 1995, Heald was no longer pressing for an evidential conclusion to his past-life recall. But his enthusiasm was re-ignited when the imminent fiftieth anniversary of the end of WWII was played and re-played on every European television station. Once more, he felt gripped by an uncanny sense of *déjà vu* and by a range of emotions that were not his own.

During one particularly heart-wrenching day, Heald was visited by a former work colleague who suggested a walk to the local library. As his friend went to collect a magazine from the desk, Heald was sitting patiently in the rest area when his gaze fell upon a magazine advertising World War II as a collector's area of interest. One of the articles inside concerned a collector of information about Allied crashes over Holland from 1939–1945. The collector's address was provided. So Heald wrote to him providing the information he had gleaned from hypnosis. A reply promptly arrived explaining that, although the information Heald had provided was limited, a copy of his letter had been sent to a colleague who specialized in English casualties. Two weeks later, Heald received the very confirmation he had been seeking. A crash report (see below) confirmed every last detail of his life as Sgt. Richard Seymour.

CRASH REPORT
SEYMOUR, Sgt. RICHARD HENRY CREED

1166511. RAF (V.R.) 158 Sqdn. 20th. July, 1942. Son of
the Revd. Archibald Thomas Seymour and
Mary Seymour, of Swallowfield Vicarage, Berk-
shire. Panel 93
Date of crash: 20th. July, 1942
Time of crash: 02.52
Aircraft: Halifax Mk II

Codes: WII62 NP-D
Squadron: 158
Base: East Moor Yorkshire
Crashed near/in: North Sea 30 kms. N of the island of Terschelling, Netherlands
Crash due to: Night Fighter Oberleutnant Egmont, Prinz ZUR LIPPE WEISSENFELD II./NJG2
Killed: Sgt. Arthur Ernest WATKINS, Obs, 21, 1331702, RAF (VR), Grave 7.C.6
Sgt Patrick Joseph DILLION, Pilot, 1378506, RAF (VR), Grave 7.C.II
Sgt. William Henry ROGERS, Fe, 520277, RAF, Grave 7.C.12
Sgt. Herbert Edward GODFEREY, Ag (Midupper-gunner), 23, 4405482, RNZAF, Grave 7.E.14
Missing: Sgt. Robert FORGIE, Ag (Reargunner), 653037, RAF, Runnymede Panel 83
Sgt. Douglas Arthur REDLER, Ab, 25, 1169796, RAF (VR) Runnymede Panel 92
Sgt. Richard Henry Creed SEYMOUR, Wop/Ag, 21, II66511, RAF (VR) Runnymede Panel 93
Cemetery: Sage War Cemetery Oldenburg (Germany) Burials were initially in the Lutheran Cemetery at Borkum.
Take Off Remarks: 23:56
Target: Naval Yards at Vegesack.

(Details collected by Mr. J. G. J. de Haan, Kronen-land 1432, 6605 RW WIJCHEN, The Netherlands)

Complete abstention from corporal punishment in Inuit families derives from the commonly held belief that the parent-child relationship may well have been reversed in the past and could be again in the future. Seen in karmic perspective, the expression "This hurts me more than it hurts you,"—so often used by Western parents when caning their offspring—takes on deeper meaning than consciously intended.

A Tribe Returned

The idea that people reincarnate in groups from one lifetime to the next has become a realistic prospect for American past-life regressionist Janet Cunningham. In her work as a therapist, she has found herself unwittingly at the heart of strikingly similar testimony from many patients who said they had lived as North American Indians who were massacred by white soldiers. The evidence suggests that those who reported being killed while living as members of the Oglala tribe in the Dakotas have reincarnated in the twentieth century in order to resolve deeply felt emotions from these earlier existences. They have returned to be healed and, in some cases, to become healers themselves.

In her book *A Tribe Returned*, Cunningham tells how, in order to work through their guilt, some of the soldiers responsible for the massacre are now married to members of the tribe. And the therapist reveals that she was one of the leading characters in this remarkable drama—Falling Star, the daughter of the tribe's leader, Silver Eagle. Both were slaughtered. If readers react with scepticism to such a storyline, the author is entirely sympathetic. Throughout the narrative—which contains vivid and sometimes grisly recall of the events leading up to the massacre—Cunningham expresses her own doubts and incredulity. She even resisted being regressed herself for as long as possible, perhaps for fear of influencing others or because she was not yet ready to face the anticipated horrors of that lifetime. While collecting her material, she was unaware of documented evidence on other group reincarnations and was later relieved to find that her discovery was not the first of its kind.

The writing of the book was difficult indeed. "The programming of my culture and society said this story was not possible," Cunningham declares. Later, she asks: "Is it true? Did the tribe exist?" While the "memories" were strong, convincing, and led to floods of tears from the participants, the book offers no evidence that the massacre of the Oglala tribe actually occurred. "Could we have tapped into each other's unconscious minds and created a metaphor?" Cunningham asks. "Perhaps. Or—maybe—we are a tribe that has returned."

The soul of Abel passed into the body of Seth and then into that of Moses, according to the *Talmud*.

The Clock that Survived the Holocaust

Bruce Whittier, a Canadian goat farmer, knew nothing about the Jewish race. No Jews lived among the 1,600 people in the Nova Scotia town of Kingston where he grew up and there were no Jewish ancestors among his family which emigrated from England in the 1700s. Yet in April, 1991, Whittier inexplicably began to dream vividly that he was a Dutch Jew with a wife, a daughter, and a son who lived in Holland during World War II. The Germans were about to invade and, to escape them, the family had sought refuge in an old root cellar. Against one wall of the cellar stood a square table on which was placed an old clock. The family relied on the gentle chiming of the clock to chart the progress of each day. Whittier's dream ended with him crawling from the hideout to take his black and white dog for a walk very early in the morning. In the backyard, he was surprised by someone who accused him of a crime, shot the dog, and then turned to threaten him . . .

Whittier awoke from the dream greatly disturbed. Throughout the day, he fretted about the frightening images, asking himself relentlessly what their significance might be. For the next two nights, the dream recurred. On the third night another dream indicated that the clock was now situated close to his home in Canada. The dream even gave specific directions to locate the clock: travel on Route 1 to a new antique shop where the timepiece will be found.

For several weeks, Whittier delayed making the journey in search of the clock. While he waited, his dream images continued, providing more details. He saw himself at Auschwitz concentration camp where dust and ashes covered everything. He looked on as he and his wife were summoned to the edge of a large trench dug as a mass grave. Then they were both shot dead.

Whittier's response to these dreams was acutely emotional, but he was at a loss to understand why. Not only was he not Jewish, but he was also just 29 years old—much too young to remember a war that had taken place long before his birth. Eventually, he set out to look for the antique store which had appeared in his dreams. Exactly as indicated, he found a new antique shop—called *In Tyme*—on Route 1. Inside the store, Whittier saw many lovely antiques, but no clock. Then, as he was about to leave, the storekeeper emerged from a back room. As he closed the door behind him, the very clock from Whittier's dream was revealed. "I was not only stunned," writes Whittier in *From Ashes to Healing*, a collection of true mystical stories collected by Rabbi Yonassan Gershom, "I was in shock. That clock was mine, or at least it had been in another life."

Whittier was not about to tell a complete stranger that he had dreamed about owning his clock in another incarnation and yet he yearned to know more about its history. The shopkeeper explained that he had just returned from a buying trip to Europe. He had purchased many pieces in Holland where the authorities had opened some old warehouses crammed with possessions confiscated by the Nazis from Dutch Jews during World War II. The clock had been among the collection.

As much as Whittier wanted to hold the clock in his hands, the object of his desire was much too expensive to justify such behaviour. Feeling that he had no plausible excuse to handle the clock, he left the shop without doing so. But its image nagged him for weeks afterwards. And as Whittier brooded about "his" long-lost possession, he recalled other incidents in his life that resonated with the prospect of having lived before as a Dutch Jew. When he was nine or ten, he experienced rising panic as his parents were watching a war movie. The name of the film is forgotten, but he clearly remembers being sent to his room and not being allowed to watch television that evening. Later, as a young teenager on a shopping expedition, be bought two Jewish skullcaps—one made of brown velvet; the other of multicoloured silk. Each day, after school, he would wear one of the caps while studying because it made him feel as though he "belonged."

In August, 1995, after talking with Hasidic storyteller Rabbi Gershom, he decided to undergo hypnotic regression in an attempt to understand his disturbing dreams and uncanny fascination with Judaism. Ushered into trance by local hypnotist George McAdoo, he saw himself as a Dutch Jew named Stefan Horwitz who was married to a woman named Helene. They had two children. He also visualized the clock, a family heirloom that had belonged to his grandmother in that lifetime. Hypnosis enlarged on his dreams and showed him gruesome details of life at Auschwitz. Extreme privation dominated the images which culminated in his being pushed towards a mass grave, feeling a shot "like a hot knife going through me" and then falling onto a heap of bodies.

Mercifully, Whittier's death was succeeded by a magnificent vision of floating in white light. When McAdoo asked why he had chosen such a traumatic incarnation, Whittier replied: "I was *sent* there. To obtain a higher level of peace. To gain strength and knowledge, to grow, to be able to teach and to guide others." After experiencing the ultimate peace and joy of what can only be the *bardo* or between-life state, Whittier was able to release the pain and fear of his Holocaust memories. And while his longing for the clock—the price of which far exceeded the family budget—persisted, that longing was not in vain. As Rabbi Gershom told Bruce Whittier's story across the North American continent, people came forward to make donations to a "Ransom the Clock Fund" so that the antique timepiece could be returned to its rightful owner. In May, 1996, the clock was finally redeemed from its long exile and brought to the Whittier home where it now occupies a place of honour.

Lord Dowding, the air chief marshal who directed the Battle of Britain, believed that those who dispensed torture and death during the Inquisition were reborn to suffer in World War II concentration camps. "I have some reason to believe," Dowding declared mid-way through his speech on reincarnation at a London meeting of the Theosophical Society in November, 1945, "that those who sowed the seeds of abominable cruelty at the time of the Inquisition reaped their own harvest at Belsen and Buchenwald."

Six-Year Probe Targets Children
with Past-Life Memories

Children who remember having lived before are more
mature, have greater verbal skills, and better memory
than other youngsters, reports Professor Erlendur Haraldsson in *The Journal of Nervous and Mental Disease*
(1995). These children also performed much better
in school and were more socially active than a control
group. The results of the study—conducted in Sri
Lanka—were not obtained without difficulty. One of
the problems facing Prof. Haraldsson was that most
children claiming past-life memories are aged between
two and five years old and there are few objective psychological tests of personality for children so young. Accordingly, he moved to an older group, all of whom had
claimed memories of past lives when they were younger
even though most had stopped talking about them. The
tests were carried out on twenty three subjects—eight
boys and fifteen girls between seven and thirteen years
of age.

Prof. Haraldsson concluded at the end of his six-year
study that children claiming past-life memories

- are generally more mature than their peers
- demonstrate much greater knowledge of words
  and understanding of language
- remember recent events more clearly
- perform better in school, are better behaved, and
  work harder
- are *not* more suggestible than other children

Teachers who cooperated in the study felt that the children with past-life memories generally got along better with other children, skipped school much less frequently, were more highly motivated and less disobedient, and were less explosive and unpredictable than others. However, the children's parents reported a higher degree of behavioural problems than was registered with the control group. They spoke of their offspring as being more argumentative, more stubborn, more talkative, more likely to get hurt, too concerned with neatness or cleanliness, less likely to "show off" or clown around, more nervous, highly-strung or tense, and more inclined to perfectionism.

Writes Prof. Haraldsson: "The repeated and sometimes clamorous statements that the subjects make about the claimed previous life often embroil them in unpleasant ways with other members of their family. For example, some of the children deny that their parents are their parents and demand to be taken to their 'real parents' who, they may say, loved them more. A small number of the subjects actually try to leave home to find the previous family by themselves. Some children may grumble about the humble circumstances of their family and boast of having had better food, clothing, servants etc. in the previous life. Parents in cultures having belief in reincarnation [such as Sri Lanka] do not often suppress a child's statements because they think he or she is fantasizing; but, in a substantial number of cases, they become vexed with the child because of the content of what the child is saying and because of his or her unusual related behaviour."

Prof. Haraldsson insists that his data does not support the view that children who remember past lives are suffering from social isolation. Their modest-to-normal suggestibility test scores, along with low scores for confabulations, "seem to indicate that previous-life memories may be internally-generated, at least initially, and may not be influenced by other people."

Napoleon believed fervently in reincarnation. He would cry out to his marshals: "I am Charlemagne! Do you know who I am? I am Charlemagne!"

Searching for Past-Life Treasure

At four years of age, American Jim Bethe started talking about his memories of being a British soldier who fought in the Napoleonic Wars. Yet this childhood recall involved no ordinary infantryman. For as long as he can remember, the boy who grew up to be a Prescott, Arizona, numismatist acquiring one of the largest collections of Napoleonic medals in the United States has carried "certain knowledge" of having buried a treasure chest of jewels during that military incarnation.

Past-life regressions conducted with hypnotist Frank Baronowski in Phoenix during 1988–89 only confirmed Bethe's inner certainty. Corroborating and enlarging upon his intimations, the sessions revealed that his past-life personality was Jonathan Seman, a cartographer with the King's Army who lived from 1769 to 1834 and who was married to a woman named Mary Merton. While stationed in India during the last years of the eighteenth century, Seman acquired a small casket of stolen jewels which he had brought back home and hid below ground in the Welsh Gower Peninsula.

Following the advice of clairvoyants as well as information gleaned from his own regressions, Bethe set out in 1994 to see whether he could unearth the buried treasure. A film crew from the British TV show *Schofield's Quest* was on hand to record the drama as dowser Elizabeth Sullivan helped direct diggers to a precise location on a wet and windy winter's day. After prolonged excavation the search ran abruptly into a solid "floor" of concrete, disappointing everybody. Filming and digging were suspended until another inclement day when the excavators managed to break through the concrete floor. Deeper underground, a much older wall and brick arch were uncovered which inspired considerable excitement among the treasure hunters.

Bethe immediately recalled a hypnotic session in which he had spoken unequivocally about the jewels being hidden in such a spot. "I take it to Wales where I have a hiding place," he had told British hypnotist Tom Barlow. "I cross the pasture to the incline near the woods. There is a barnyard there, buildings."

"Is there just one chest there?" inquired Barlow.

"No," Bethe replied. "I have my casket of jewels and I have grandfather's iron box that he gave me when he passed. There are three boxes of treasure here." Then he gave more details about the elusive hoard. "It is in a place where few people came to walk. It is in the pigsty. I am opening one of the double doors and squeezing in and walking down into the cave."

Bethe had also mentioned that water surrounded the boxes of treasure, and the diggers soon found themselves mired in a large puddle. A second time, the treasure hunt had to be abandoned but—in a July, 1997, interview in Phoenix, Arizona—Jim Bethe, far from disheartened, spoke of launching a new expedition. Further occult investigation, he said, pointed to the treasure being located just 100 metres from the site of the last dig. Bethe was writing to media moguls Hugh Hefner and Steven Spielberg to plead for their support. "I can't do this on my own," he declared. "I need proper financial backing to fund and professionally document this search. And when we succeed," he added with a gleam in his eye, "we will prove the existence of reincarnation."

There is another riveting aspect of Bethe's claim to have lived before as Jonathan Seman. Strikingly reminiscent of Dr. Ian Stevenson's birthmark evidence cited at the beginning of this chapter, Bethe's large frame (he is six feet three inches tall and weighs 245 lbs.) bears the following impressions of his supposed previous incarnation:

He has a birthmark on his back corresponding to a stab wound with a curved dagger allegedly suffered by Seman in 1799 during the Siege of Seringapatam at Mysore, India.

Jonathan Seman apparently lost his left eye in 1809 when he was shot by a man named Edward King. In this life, Bethe has a cataract in his left eye.

From birth, Bethe has endured extraordinarily rough and calloused hands and feet that are often painful. No amount of moisturizing cream can soothe this affliction of sore, cracked skin. Bethe has since learned that Seman's hands and feet were thrust into a fire—an excruciating method of torture designed to yield the location of his buried treasure.

The number of lives of the Buddha has been estimated from as few as 400 to as many plants as there are in the universe. Some 550 narratives of his births in various animal and human forms appear in the *Jatakas* or birth stories. Virtue doesn't always predominate. In one existence he killed his step-brother out of greed for an inheritance and, in another, had been an ill-mannered boy who knocked the begging bowl from an old man's hand. In Central Java, in a valley surrounded by active volcanoes, a huge, pyramidal shrine called *Boro Budur* is ornamented with carvings depicting Buddha's lives. In one remote incarnation he is shown as a turtle bearing shipwrecked sailors to shore.

Postscript: Princess Diana (1961–1997)

Diana, Princess of Wales, whose tragic death in a Paris car wreck shook the world in 1997, believed in reincarnation. *The Daily Telegraph* reported that, following Diana's fatal accident, prayers were offered all day at the Hindu Temple in Neasden, North London. Followers should have been celebrating the temple's second anniversary but, instead, they sang *bhajans* and *kirtans* (devotional songs) for the *atma* or soul of the Princess.

The Telegraph added: "Gulu Lalvani, the Asian businessman who found himself the centre of attention after taking Diana to a nightclub earlier this year, reflected Hindu belief when he said last night: "She believed in reincarnation. She'll be back." Princess Diana is said to have told friends that she believed she had been a nun in a previous life.

> "We all return; it is this certainty that gives meaning to life and it does not make the slightest difference whether or not in a later incarnation we remember the former life. What counts is not the individual and his comfort, but the great aspiration to the perfect and the pure which goes on in each incarnation."
>
> – Gustav Mahler (1860–1911)

BRINGING IT ALL
BACK HOME

"A person whose life's vision is limited to this one fleeting incarnation is like the plough horse which views its life work as a single furrow, never able to appreciate how one furrow blends with the many others."

    – Bryan Jameison

"It is not enough to know about reincarnation; we must live it."

    – Guenther Wachsmuth

THE NARROW PROSPECT is detonated, the walls come tumbling down, and, suddenly, everything makes sense. It's like being relieved of the misapprehension that one day is not an entire lifetime after all; that human existence is much vaster, much grander, and invested with far greater meaning than one could possibly have imagined.

In extending one life to many lives, reincarnation grants significance to each existence, just as a lifetime of personal development counts on each day's vital contribution.

Hope accompanies this broader vision. Not naive, idealistic hope, but hope founded on a blending of faith and reason. Reincarnation tells us that even the most tragic, sordid deaths are just more births in the making, and that nothing can ever happen on the myriad journeys of unfoldment except opportunities to learn and grow. So it is that lives on Earth, shaped by karmic propensities, become charged with meaning. Each thought, word, and deed is rich with purpose as it bears the cause of effect to come. And this brings home the truth that we are thoroughly responsible and accountable for who we are and what we do; that we can't blame circumstance, or external forces of any kind, for our lot in life. We make our beds, as the saying goes, and we must lie in them.

Although the lives of well-heeled criminals and poverty-stricken saints suggest a dearth of justice in the world, justice becomes apparent in the wider context granted by a succession of existences. Only through many lives can joy and misery and the glaring inequalities of life be justified. Words such as "coincidence," "accident," and "unfairness" lose their currency as the individual accepts that he or she has generated every action and reaction along the way. Reincarnation means that each of us is partaking in an ultimately joyous progression of self-realization spanning an incalculable number of embodiments. A sense of incompletion instills a craving for experience which keeps bringing us back until our potential is fulfilled in perfection. Destinies shaped individually merge and interact with the collective destinies of families, groups of like-minded people, nations, and the world at large. This is how we grow.

Thought for affluent Westerners: Are we born into the materialistic succour of the West because evolution has not yet made us resilient enough to endure the common suffering of the East? Or are we being rewarded for past virtues?

As Natural as Breathing

There's nothing extraordinary about reincarnation. It's as natural as breathing and just as compatible with the unceasing ebb and flow of the universe. Unfortunately, our protracted alienation from primordial rhythms and our brainwashing by materialism's false assumptions cause rebirth to be seen by many as a quaint indulgence, a corollary of wishful thinking held by the eccentric and the simple-minded.

Yet consider the transformation of earthly existence were reincarnation accepted into the soulstream of the global population as a guide by which to live. Acutely aware of reaping harvests of past deeds while simultaneously sowing the seeds of future lives, most people would behave very differently. Life on the planet would be overhauled—and hugely for the better. Wars, crime, racism, nationalism, and sexual chauvinism would be radically diminished. For who can harm, or harbour prejudice against the kind of person one has been or will be, especially if retribution can follow in another life? The nagging fear of death would be eliminated and

replaced with acceptance of the opportunity for transformation. Doctors who strive to prolong life with the
aid of every available artificial means would see themselves as sad clowns flaunting their ignorance of cosmic
renewal. Few would be so rash as to attempt either suicide or abortion, and genetic engineering would be
recognized by all as meddlesome and dangerous. Care
would be taken not to encourage the extinction of
animal and plant species lest rungs be removed from
the evolutionary ladder. And those who consign their
corpses to graves of ice in hope of subsequent technological resuscitation would acknowledge they are wast-
ing their money in trying to preserve the old body when
they stand to inherit a new one free of charge!

Acceptance of reincarnation demands a complete
overturning of prevailing attitudes inculcated by a civilization that has long overidentified with the body. This
overidentification is locked into our very language. We
say, for example, "I am hungry," when we mean to say,
as some Indians *do* say, "My body is hungry." Annie
Besant comments in *Reincarnation*:

> If we were in the habit of identifying ourselves in
> thought, not with the habitation we live in but with
> the Human Self that dwells therein, life would be-
> come a greater and serener thing. We should brush
> off troubles as we brush the dust from our gar-
> ments, and we should realize that the measure of all
> things happening to us is not the pain or pleasure
> they bring to our bodies, but the progress or retar-
> dation they bring to the Man within us; and since

> all things are matters of experience and lessons may
> be learned from each, we should take the sting out
> of griefs by searching in each for the wisdom en-
> wrapped in it as the petals are folded within the
> bud.

Similarly, the urgency and anxiety springing from the race against time evaporate once we realize we have all the time and all the lives we need. Eternity is our heritage and reincarnation, requiring worldly time for its expression, gives time freely. To steep oneself in infinity brings nothing but exhilaration. Nobody is pretending that psychic surrender to adverse conditions and the seeming ravages of time is easy to accomplish as we cope with the daily vicissitudes of the material world. But a certain serenity should ensue if Goethe's "continual law of Die and Be Again" can be absorbed into our being. For the value and the power of reincarnation cannot be discovered by examining the theory like a fossil under glass or by toying intellectually with its precepts. It must be lived. And this entails a rebirth of the way we think and feel; the metamorphosis that follows from truly believing we are immortal beings forging our souls through a multitude of lifetimes on the global anvil.

For all the evidence of past lives and future lives and for all the speculation about worlds being reborn across aeons of time, reincarnation addresses itself most pointedly to the present moment. While other lives and other ages take care of themselves, the present is all we have and always the only available life is this one. Nothing ever matters but the *now* with its marvellous incorporation of all reincarnational history. For even as we are today what we established yesterday, we will surely be tomorrow what we establish today. Therein lies the challenge of reincarnation—a challenge that prompted this advice from the great German philosopher Friedrich Nietzsche:

Live so that thou mayest desire to live again—that is thy duty—for in any case thou wilt live again!

> "The laws of reincarnation and karma make possible the constant progress of all living things. Not only does man grow, but the sticks, stones and stars grow with him. All are unfolding together; all life is growing up in space and toward space."
>
> – Manly P. Hall

> "He who has reached the goal, is fearless, is without craving, is passionless, has cut the thorns of life; this is his final body."
>
> – The Dhammapada (24:351)

BIBLIOGRAPHY

Books

Aquarian Gospel of Jesus the Christ, The, (Transcribed from the Akashic Records), Marina Del Rey, Cal.: DeVorss & Co., 1981.

Arroyo, Stephen, *Astrology, Karma and Transformation.* Davis, California: CRCS Publications, 1978.

Aurobindo, Sri, *The Problem of Rebirth.* Pondicherry, India. Sri Aurobindo Ashram Trust, 1973.

Bache, Christopher, PH.D., *Lifecycles: Reincarnation and the Web of Life.* New York: Paragon House, 1990.

Bailey, Alice A. *Esoteric Astrology.* New York: Lucis Publishing Company, 1979.

_____, *The Light of the Soul.* New York: Lucis Publishing Company.

Banerjee, H. N., *Americans Who Have Been Reincarnated.* New York: Macmillan, 1980.

Banerjee, H. N. and Oursler, Will, *Lives Unlimited.* New York: Doubleday, 1974.

Barlow, Fred, *Mental Prodigies.* London: Hutchinson's, 1952.

Bennett, Colin, *Practical Time Travel.* London: Rider, 1937.

Bernstein, Morey, *The Search for Bridey Murphy.* New York: Pocket Books, 1978.

Besant, Annie, *Reincarnation*. Madras, India: The Theosophical Publishing House, 1975.

Besterman, Theodore, *Collected Papers on the Paranormal*. New York: Garrett, 1968.

Blavatsky, H. P., *The Secret Doctrine*. Los Angeles: The Theosophy Company.

Bowman, Carol, *Children's Past Lives: How Past-Life Memories Affect Your Child*. Element Books, 1997.

Brandon, S. G. F., *Religion in Ancient History*. New York: Charles Scribner's & Sons, 1969.

Brennan, J. H., *Reincarnation: Five Keys to Past Lives*. Wellingborough, Northants: The Aquarian Press, 1981.

Brunhübner, Fritz, (translated by Julie Baum) *Pluto*. Washington: American Federation of Astrologers, 1949.

Campbell, Joseph, *The Masks of God: Oriental Mythology*. New York: Viking Press, 1962.

_____, *The Masks of God: Primitive Mythology*. New York: Viking Press, 1959.

Cannon, Dr. Alexander, *The Power Within*. London: Rider and Company, 1950.

_____, *Powers That Be*. London: Francis Mott Company, 1934.

Capra, Fritjof, *The Tao of Physics*. New York: Bantam Books, 1980.

Carr, Donald E., *The Eternal Return*. New York: Doubleday, 1968.

Catholic Encyclopaedia, The. New York: Robert Appleton Company, 1911.

Cavendish, Richard, ed., *Man, Myth and Magic* (Vols. 12, 17). London: Marshall Cavendish Corporation, 1970.

Cerminara, Gina, *Many Mansions*. New York: William Sloane, 1956.

Chuang Tzu, *The Musings of a Chinese Mystic*. London: John Murray, 1955.

Christie-Murray, David, *Reincarnation: Ancient Beliefs and Modern Evidence.* Newton Abbot, Devon: David and Charles, 1981.

Cockell, Jenny, *Yesterday's Children.* London: Piatkus, 1993.

Cohen, Daniel, *The Mysteries of Reincarnation.* New York: Dodd Mead, 1975.

Crowley, Aleister, *Magick.* New York: Weiser, 1979.

Cunningham, Janet, *A Tribe Returned.* Crest Park, California: Deep Forest Press, 1995.

Dethlefsen, Thorwald, *Voices from Other Lives.* New York: M. Evans and Co., 1977.

Easton, Stewart C., *Man and World in the Light of Anthroposophy.* New York: The Anthroposophic Press, 1975.

Eberhard, Wolfram, *Chinese Festivals.* New York: H. Schuman, 1952.

Eliade, Mircea, *Rites and Symbols of Initiation.* New York: Harper Torchbooks, 1958.

Evans-Wentz, W. Y., *The Fairy Faith in Celtic Countries.* London: Oxford University Press, 1911.

_____, ed., *The Tibetan Book of the Dead.* London: Oxford University Press, 1960.

_____, ed., *Tibet's Great Yogi Milarepa.* London: Oxford University Press, 1974.

Ferguson, John, *An Illustrated Encyclopaedia of Mysticism.* London: Thames and Hudson, 1976.

Fiore, Dr. Edith, *You Have Been Here Before.* New York: Coward, McCann and Geoghegan, 1978.

Ford, Arthur, (as told to Jerome Ellison) *The Life Beyond Death.* New York: Berkley Medallion Books, 1972.

Frazer, Sir James George, *The Belief in Immortality.* (Vol. 2), London: Dawsons of Pall Mall, 1968.

_____, *Folk-Lore in the Old Testament.* London: Macmillan, 1918.

_____, *The Golden Bough,* London: Macmillan, 1963.

Fremantle, Francesca and Trungpa, Chogyam, *The Tibetan Book of the Dead.* Boulder, Colorado: Shambala Publications, 1975.

Furst, Peter J., *Stones, Bones and Skin: Ritual and Shamanic Art.* Toronto: The Society for Art Publications, 1977.

Gallup, Dr. George, Jr., *Adventures in Immortality.* New York: McGraw-Hill, 1982.

Gaskell, G. A., *Dictionary of All Scriptures and Myths.* New York: Julian Press, 1977.

Gershom, Rabbi Yonassan, *From Ashes to Healing.* Virginia Beach, Virginia: A.R.E. Press, 1996.

Glaskin, G. M., *A Door to Eternity.* London: Wildwood House, 1979.

_____, *Windows of the Mind.* New York: Delacorte Press, 1974.

Goldberg, Dr. Bruce, *Past Lives, Future Lives.* North Hollywood, Cal.: Newcastle Publishing, 1982.

Grant, Joan, *Far Memory.* New York: Harper and Row, 1956.

Gray, Louis Herbert, ed., *The Mythology of All Races.* Boston: Marshall Jones, 1918.

Gribbin, John, *White Holes.* New York: Delacorte Press, 1977.

Gris, Henry and Dick, William, *The New Soviet Psychic Discoveries.* Englewood Cliffs, N.J.: Prentice Hall, 1978.

Grof, Stanislav, *Varieties of Transpersonal Experiences: Observations from LSD Psychotherapy.* Chicago: Nelson-Hall, 1975.

Grof, Stanislav and Grof, Christina, *Beyond Death.* New York: Thames and Hudson, 1980.

Guirdham, Arthur, *The Psyche in Medicine.* Jersey: Neville Spearman, 1978.

Gunaratna, V.F., *Rebirth Explained.* Kandy, Sri Lanka: Buddhist Publication Society, 1971.

Hall, Manly P., *Reincarnation, The Cycle of Necessity.* Los Angeles: The Philosophical Research Society, 1978.

Harrer, Heinrich, *Seven Years in Tibet.* London: Pan Books, 1956.

Hastings, James, ed., *Encyclopaedia of Religion and Ethics.* Edinburgh: T. and T. Clark, 1934.

Head, Joseph and Cranston, S. L., eds., *Reincarnation: The Phoenix Fire Mystery.* New York: Crown Publishers, 1977.

Hickey, Isabel M., *Pluto or Minerva: The Choice is Yours.* Watertown, Mass.: Fellowship House Bookshop, 1977.

Holzer, Hans, *Patterns of Destiny.* Los Angeles: Nash Publishing, 1974.

Howe, Quincy, Jr., *Reincarnations for the Christian.* Philadelphia: The Westminster Press, 1974.

Humphreys, Christmas, *Karma and Rebirth.* London: John Murray, 1943.

Jameison, Bryan, *Explore Your Past Lives.* Van Nuys, Cal.: Astro-Analytics Publications, 1976.

Jast, L. Stanley, *What it all Means.* London: T. Werner Laurie, 1941.

Johnston, Charles, *The Memory of Past Births.* New York: Metaphysical Publishing, 1899.

Judge, William Q., *The Ocean of Theosophy.* Los Angeles: Theosophy Company, [n.d.].

Kelsey, Denys and Grant, Joan, *Many Lifetimes.* New York: Doubleday, 1967.

Langley, Noel, *Edgar Cayce on Reincarnation.* London: Howard Baker, 1969.

Laws of Manu, The. Delhi, India: Motilal Banarsidass, 1967.

Leek, Sybil, *Reincarnation: The Second Chance.* New York: Stein and Day, 1974.

Lenz, Frederic, *Lifetimes.* New York: The Bobbs-Merrill Company, 1979.

Lowell, Laurel, *Pluto.* St. Paul, Minn.: Llewellyn Publications, 1973.

Lucas, Winafred Blake, PH.D., *Regression Therapy: A Handbook for Professionals (Vols. 1 & 2).* Crest Park, California: Deep Forest Press, 1993.

Mabie, Hamilton Wright, *In the Forest of Arden.* New York: Dodd, Mead & Co., 1891.

McDermott, Robert A., ed., *The Essential Aurobindo*. New York: Schocken Books, 1973.

Moody, Dr. Raymond A., Jr., *Life After Life*. New York: Bantam Books, 1981.

Moore, Marcia and Douglas, Mark, *Reincarnation: Key to Immortality*. York Cliffs, Maine: Arcane Publications, 1968.

Moore, Marcia and Alltounian, Howard Sunny, *Journeys into the Bright World*. Rockport, Mass.: Para Research, 1978.

Morris, Ivan, *The Nobility of Failure*. New York: Holt, Rinehart and Winston, 1975.

Moss, Peter with Keeton, Joe, *Encounters with the Past*. New York: Penguin, 1981.

Müller, Ernst, *History of Jewish Mysticism*. Oxford: Phaidon Press, 1946.

Müller, Max, ed., *The Sacred Books of the East*, London: Oxford University Press, 1880–1890.

Netherton, Morris and Schiffrin, Nancy, *Past Lives Therapy*. New York: William Morrow, 1978.

Newton, Michael, PH.D., *Journey of Souls: Case Studies of Life Between Lives*. St. Paul, Minnesota: Llewellyn Publications, 1995.

Ouspensky, P. D., *A New Model of the Universe*. New York: Vintage Books, 1971.

Parameswara, P., *Soul, Karma and Re-brith*. Bangalore: P. Parameswara, 1973.

Parrinder, Geoffrey, *The Indestructible Soul*. New York: Harper and Row, 1973.

Patanjali, Bhagwan Shree, *Aphorisms of Yoga*. London: Faber and Faber, 1973.

Perry, W. J., *The Origins of Magic and Religion*. Port Washington, N.Y.: Kennikat Press, 1923.

Prabhupada, His Divine Grace A. C. Bhaktivedanta Swami, *Bhagavad-Gita As It Is*. New York: The Bhaktivedanta Book Trust, 1976.

Prophet, Elizabeth Clare, *Reincarnation: The Missing Link in Christianity*. Corwin Springs, Montana: Summit University Press, 1997.

Pryse, James M., *Reincarnation in the New Testament*. New York: Elliott B. Page, 1900.

Ram Dass, *Grist For the Mill*. Santa Cruz: Unity Press, 1977.

———, *The Only Dance There Is*. New York: Anchor Press, 1974.

Reyna, Dr. Ruth, *Reincarnation and Science*. New Delhi: Sterling Publishers, 1973.

Ring, Kenneth, *Life At Death*. New York: Coward, McCann and Geoghegan, 1980.

Roberts, Jane, *The Nature of Personal Reality*. Englewood Cliffs, N.J.: Prentice-Hall, 1974.

———, *The Seth Material*. New York: Bantam Books, 1981.

Rudhyar, Dane, *An Astrological Triptych*. New York: Asi Publishers, 1968.

Ruperti, Alexander, *Cycles of Becoming*. Davis, California: CRCS Publications, 1978.

Russell, Jeffrey B., *A History of Witchcraft*. New York: Thames and Hudson, 1980.

Schecter, Jerrold, *The New Face of Buddha*. New York: Coward-McCann, 1967.

Seward, Jack, *Hara-Kiri: Japanese Ritual Suicide*. Tokyo: Charles E. Tuttle Co., 1968.

Shepard, Leslie, ed., *Encyclopaedia of Occultism and Parapsychology*. Detroit: Gale Research Co.

Sivananda, Swami, *What Becomes of the Soul after Death*. Himalayas, India: Divine Life Society, 1972.

Smart, Ninian, *The Long Search*. Boston: Little, Brown and Co., 1980.

Sogyal Rinpoche, *The Tibetan Book of Living and Dying*. San Francisco: HarperSanFrancisco, 1992.

Spencer, Sir Baldwin, *Native Tribes of the Northern Territory of Australia.* London, 1914.

Steiner, Rudolf, *An Outline of Occult Science.* Spring Valley, N.Y.: Anthroposophic Press.

Stemman, Roy, *Reincarnation: True Stories of Past Lives.* London: Piatkus, 1997.

Stevenson, Dr. Ian, *Cases of the Reincarnation Type,* (Vols. 1-3). Charlottesville: University Press of Virginia, 1974.

_____, *Reincarnation and Biology: A Contribution to the Etiology of Birthmarks and Birth Defects.* Praegar Publishers, 1997.

_____, *Twenty Cases Suggestive of Reincarnation.* Charlottesville: University Press of Virginia, 1974.

Stokes, Henry Scott, *The Life and Death of Yukio Mishima.* Tokyo: Charles E. Tuttle Co., 1975.

Sutphen, Dick, *Past Lives, Future Loves.* New York: Pocket Books, 1978.

Talbot, Michael, *Your Past Lives: A Reincarnation Handbook.* New York: Harmony Books, 1987

_____, *The Holographic Universe.* New York: HarperCollins, 1991.

Tatz, Mark and Kent, Jody, *Rebirth: The Tibetan Game of Liberation.* New York: Anchor Press, 1977.

TenDam, Hans, *Deep Healing: A Practical Outline of Past-life Therapy.* Tasso Publishing, 1997.

Toyne, Clarice, *Heirs to Eternity.* London: Neville Spearman, 1976.

Verny, Dr. Thomas, with Kelly, John, *The Secret Life of the Unborn Child.* Don Mills, Ont.: Collins Publishers, 1981.

Wachsmuth, Guenther, *Reincarnation as a Phenomenon of Metamorphosis.* New York: Anthroposophic Press, 1937.

Walker, Benjamin, *Hindu World.* London: George Allen and Unwin, 1968.

_____, *Masks of the Soul.* Wellingborough, Northants: The Aquarian Press, 1981.

Walker, E. D., *Reincarnation: A Study of Forgotten Truth*. New York: Theosophical Publishing Co., 1904.

Wambach, Helen, *Life Before Life*. New York: Bantam Books, 1979.

⸺, *Reliving Past Lives: The Evidence Under Hypnosis*. New York: Harper and Row, 1978.

Wangdu, Sonam, *The Discovery of the XIVth Dalai Lama*. Bangkok: Klett Thai Publications, 1975.

Weatherhead, Leslie D., *The Christian Agnostic*. London: Hodder and Stoughton, 1965.

Weisman, Alan, *We, Immortals*. New York: Pocket Books, 1979.

Whitton, Joel L., M.D., PH.D., and Fisher, Joe, *Life Between Life: A Scientific Exploration Into the Void Separating One Incarnation from the Next*. New York: Doubleday, 1986.

Wilber, Ken, *The Spectrum of Consciousness*. Wheaton, Illinois: The Theosophical Publishing House, 1977.

Wilson, Colin, *The Occult*. New York: Random House, 1971.

Wilson, Ian, *Mind Out of Time?* London: Victor Gollancz Ltd., 1981.

Zukav, Gary, *The Dancing Wu Li Masters: An Overview of the New Physics*. New York: Bantam Books, 1980.

Periodicals and Pamphlets

Arkansas Democrat Gazette, "Ex-teacher Says Love for Girl 1,000 Years Old," May 11, 1997.

Banerjee, H. N., "Murderer and Victim Meet," *Fate*, February, 1980.

Bannister, Paul, "Dead Man Lives Again in This Girl's Body," *National Enquirer*, October 6, 1981.

Bowen, Francis, "Christian Metempsychosis," *Princeton Review*, May, 1881.

Crehan, Father J. H., *Reincarnation,*Catholic Truth Society, London.

Crenshaw, James, "Xenoglossy—Proof of Reincarnation?" *Fate,* July, 1981.

Denton, Jon, "The Mysterious Memories of Jeremy," *The Sunday Oklahoman,* April 27, 1980.

Downer, Craig C., "Do Animals Reincarnate?" *Reincarnation Report,* October, 1982.

Duffy, David, "Tragedy of the Rabbit Fantasy Boy," *Sunday Mirror,* April 4, 1976.

Edvardsen, Annu, "Lilla Romy Moter Sin Mor Fran Sitt Tidigare Liv," *Allers,* Helsingborg, Sweden, April 19, 1981.

Gribbin, John, "Does the Universe Oscillate?" *Astronomy,* August, 1977.

Herron, Vanessa, "Of Kingfisher, Okla, and the Nine Lives of Ernie Shafenberg," *The Wall Street Journal,* August 31, 1981.

Journal of Nervous and Mental Disease, "Commentary on Dr. Ian Stevenson's 'The Evidence of Man's Survival After Death,'" Vol. 165, No. 3, September, 1977.

Koenig, William J., "Something to Think About," *The Compensator,* November, 1966.

Lewis, Emanuel, "Inhibition of Mourning by Pregnancy: Psychopathology and Management," *British Medical Journal,* July 7, 1979.

Meltzoff, Andrew N., and M. Keith Moore, "Imitation of Facial and Manual Gestures by Human Neonates," *Science,* October 7, 1977.

Psychic News, "Bird of Passage is Reincarnated Husband, Says Wife," August 22, 1970.

————, "Dowding Stands By Reincarnation," November 3, 1945.

The Rosicrucian Digest, "The Experience of Reincarnation," Parts 1, 2 and 3, October, November and December, 1979.

Reincarnation International, "I Was Shot Down During WWII," November, 1996.

————, "Children Who Remember Past Lives Are More Mature," July, 1997.

————, "Diana Believed in Rebirth," October, 1997.

————, "Incredible Physical Evidence for Reincarnation," October, 1997.

————, "Research Into Past-life Therapy," October, 1997.

Stemman, Roy, "A Question of Memory," *Reincarnation International,* January, 1994.

————, "Past-life Memories Inspire Hunt for Buried Treasure," *Reincarnation International,* March, 1995.

Stevenson, Dr. Ian, "The Explanatory Value of the Idea of Reincarnation," *Journal of Nervous and Mental Disease,* Vol. 164, 1977.

————, "Some Questions Related to Cases of the Reincarnation Type," *Journal of the American Society for Psychical Research,* Vol. 68, 1974.

————, "The Southeast Asian Interpretation of Gender Dysphoria: An Illustrative Case Report," *Journal of Nervous and Mental Disease,* Vol. 165, 1977.

Sunday People, The, "'Second Life' of a Gipsy," May 28, 1978.

Theosophy Company, The, *Reincarnation and Karma,* Los Angeles, 1923.

Time Magazine, "Going Gentle Into That Good Night," March 21, 1983.

Times, The, "The Controversial and the Problematical," December 20, 1980.

Touby, Frank, "Born Again," *Today Magazine,* October 4, 1980.

Viereck, George Sylvester, "Interview with Henry Ford," *San Francisco Examiner,* August 27, 1928.

Wambach, Helen, "Pleasures and Perils of Reincarnation Research," *Fate,* April, 1981.

Whitton, Joel L., "Hypnotic Time Regression and Reincarnation Memories," *New Horizons*, June, 1976.

_____, "Karma in Reincarnation," *The Rosicrucian Digest*, October, 1978.

_____, "Xenoglossia: A Subject with Two Possible Instances," *New Horizons*, September, 1978.

Tapes

Buckley, Dr. Paul, "Interview with Dr. Ian Stevenson," Toronto: Canadian Broadcasting Corporation, 1976.

"The Reincarnation Experiments," Sydney, Australia: Channel 7 and *The Sun*, March 22 and 23, 1983.

Kaplan, Dr. Pascal, "Reincarnation: Rediscovering A Lost Teaching." Lecture given at John F. Kennedy University, Orinda, California, 1980.

General Information

Reincarnation International Magazine
P.O. Box 10839, London, SW13 0ZG, England
Website: http://www.dircon.co.uk/reincarn/
e-mail: reincarn@dircon.co.uk

Credits

The Pluto transits of Scorpio were determined by Gord Hines of Zodiac House (P.O. Box 5803, Stn. 'A', Toronto, Ontario M5W 1P2) using the DR-70 Astrology Minicomputer by Digicomp Research Corp., Ithaca, N.Y., U.S.A.

The symbols of rebirth were drawn by Art Chappelle.

"The Clock That Survived The Holocaust" is by permission of The A.R.E. Press, Virginia Beach, United States.

INDEX

INDEX

OF QUOTATIONS